The Performance of Listening
in Postcolonial Francophone Culture

Contemporary French and Francophone Cultures, 52

Contemporary French and Francophone Cultures

Series Editor

CHARLES FORSDICK
University of Liverpool

Editorial Board

TOM CONLEY
Harvard University

JACQUELINE DUTTON
University of Melbourne

LYNN A. HIGGINS
Dartmouth College

MIREILLE ROSELLO
University of Amsterdam

DAVID WALKER
University of Sheffield

This series aims to provide a forum for new research on modern and contemporary French and francophone cultures and writing. The books published in *Contemporary French and Francophone Cultures* reflect a wide variety of critical practices and theoretical approaches, in harmony with the intellectual, cultural and social developments which have taken place over the past few decades. All manifestations of contemporary French and francophone culture and expression are considered, including literature, cinema, popular culture, theory. The volumes in the series will participate in the wider debate on key aspects of contemporary culture.

Recent titles in the series:

37 Ruth Bush, *Publishing Africa in French: Literary Institutions and Decolonization 1945–1967*

38 Nicki Hitchcott, *Rwanda Genocide Stories: Fiction After 1994*

39 Sara Kippur and Lia Brozgal, *Being Contemporary: French Literature, Culture and Politics Today*

40 Lucille Cairns, *Francophone Jewish Writers: Imagining Israel*

41 Leslie Kealhofer-Kemp, *Muslim Women in French Cinema: Voices of Maghrebi Migrants in France*

42 Katelyn E. Knox, *Race on Display in 20th- and 21st Century France*

43 Bruno Chaouat, *Is Theory Good for the Jews?: French Thought and the Challenge of the New Antisemitism*

44 Denis M. Provencher, *Queer Maghrebi French: Language, Temporalities, Transfiliations*

45 Nicholas Hewitt, *Montmartre: A Cultural History*

46 Oana Panaïté, *The Colonial Fortune in Contemporary Fiction in French*

47 Jason Herbeck, *Architextual Authenticity: Constructing Literature and Literary Identity in the French Caribbean*

48 Yasser Elhariry, *Pacifist Invasions: Arabic, Translation and the Postfrancophone Lyric*

49 Colin Davis, *Traces of War: Interpreting Ethics and Trauma in Twentieth-Century French Writing*

50 Alison J. Murray Levine, *Vivre Ici: Space, Place and Experience in Contemporary French Documentary*

51 Louise Hardwick, *Joseph Zobel: Négritude and the Novel*

JENNIFER SOLHEIM

The Performance of Listening
in
Postcolonial Francophone Culture

LIVERPOOL UNIVERSITY PRESS

First published 2017 by
Liverpool University Press
4 Cambridge Street
Liverpool
L69 7ZU

This paperback edition first published 2021

British Library Cataloguing-in-Publication data
A British Library CIP record is available

ISBN 978-1-78694-082-7 cased
ISBN 978-1-80085-577-9 paperback

Typeset by Carnegie Book Production, Lancaster

To my daughter, Audrey,
and my parents, Barbara and James Solheim

Dedicated to the memory of Paul Vieille (1922–2010):
founder of *Peuples Méditerranéens*,
feminist, humanitarian, friend

Contents

List of Illustrations   ix

Acknowledgments   xi

1   Introduction   1

Part I: The Performance of Listening in Literary Narratives

2   Cut Sound: The Literary Staging of Silence   23

3   Visual and Sonic Imagery in Postcolonial
     Francophone Culture   55

Part II: The Performance of Listening in Film and Theater

4   Citational Hooks: Music and Middle Eastern Gender
     Identities in Postcolonial Francophone Film and Theater   91

Part III: The Performance of Listening in Music

5   Covering French Universalism: Alter-Globalism in
     Kabyle Music in France   129

6   Beirut Calling: The Performance of Listening
     in Digital Discourses of Conflict   157

Bibliography   166

Index   173

Illustrations

1 Poster from La Grande Nouba   85
2 Mazen Kerbaj's 'Beirut: 19 July 06 2.10 AM'   159
3 Mazen Kerbaj's 'Recording Session: Mazen Kerbaj (Trumpet)
  vs. The State of Israel (Bombs)'   164

Acknowledgments

I would like to first acknowledge my contract position from 2014 to 2017 at the University of Illinois-Chicago, in the School of Liberal Arts and Sciences Freshman Experience Initiative. During these three years, I had a 2-2 teaching load and a yearly research stipend that made possible the revision and submission of this work for publication.

The research in this book and the lion's share of the writing took place while I was dissertating at the University of Michigan. Thank you to my generous and supportive dissertation committee: co-chairs David Caron and Jarrod Hayes, Peggy McCracken, and E.J. Westlake. My dissertation research would not have been possible without the support I received from several sources at the University of Michigan, including my residency at the Center for World Performance Studies (2007–08), grants from the International Institute, and several fellowships from the Rackham Graduate School, in particular the Predoctoral Fellowship (2010–11).

Mentors, friends, and colleagues provided important support for this project. My interest in French and Francophone cultures began in spring 1999, when I studied in Paris through the Illinois Program. The director of the program that year was Professor of French, Comparative Literature, and Women's Studies (now Emerita) Evelyne Accad. Evelyne opened her worlds to me: the quiet northwest corner of Paris where we lived, literature in French from North Africa and the Middle East, as well as the feminist community of *Les Filles de Tahar Haddad* in Tunis, where we traveled together later that semester. We have since performed together in the United States, France, and Lebanon. She also introduced me to her partner, sociologist Paul Vieille, who encouraged my work and brought me into his close circle of researchers near the end of his life, when I was writing the dissertation. Every time I chop garlic (which is almost every day), I think of standing in Evelyne's kitchen watching Paul prepare the salad while we talked about Cixous, Flaubert, *littérature-monde*, or the Peuples & Monde website, among so many other things.

While lecturing at Université de Paris-VII in 2008–09, I met Jane Weston Vauclair. With Katie Jones we founded the Paris French Studies Seminar, exchanged work and ideas, shored each other up, and ate and drank lots of marvelous things together. Through Jane, I met David Vauclair and Clara Laurent. My discussions with David and Clara about the veil debates in France helped move my thinking forward on their rhetoric, and how I wanted to address it in my work. Clara also introduced me to the work of film theorist Michel Chion. Since finishing the dissertation, I have stayed with Jane and David in Paris for research trips as well. Their hospitality and generosity—not to mention our mutual support and encouragement as contingent faculty-cum-independent scholars—is deeply appreciated.

I met Rosa Hocine in 2003, and she introduced me to the Kabyle community and l'Association de Culture Berbère in the 20th *arrondissement* of Paris, where I volunteered as a tutor during the subsequent periods of living in Paris. In the summer of 2005, she welcomed me into her home in Aubervilliers, which she shares with her mother and often with her niece, nephews, and several cousins as well, so that I could experience Kabyle life in the *banlieue* firsthand. I also stayed with Rosa during part of my first post-doctoral research trip back to Paris. Rosa, ma chère, tu m'as accueillie chez toi comme si j'étais de la tribu. Soirées heureuses, découvertes émerveillées à l'Association de Culture Berbère, musique d'Idir et de Djura, esprit chaleureux de la communauté, tout cela, que j'ai découvert grâce à toi, m'aura apporté cette connaissance concrète de la culture kabyle, si profitable à mon travail de thèse. Sans ton amitié si précieuse, ma vie sur Paname serait tout simplement inimaginable. A ta famille et à toi, mon âme-sœur, mille mercis!

Several other friends and colleagues—including tenured, tenure-track, and contingent faculty, as well as independent scholars and artists—have supported and encouraged my work through the postdoctoral years. My writing group with Julie Babcock and Danielle LaVaque-Manty has been a remarkable site of support and nourishment for critical and creative work alike. Mika LaVaque-Manty encouraged me to submit this work for publication sooner rather than later. Love and gratitude as well to Megan Biddinger, Landis Blair, Amelia Brunskill, Claudine Guertin-Ceric, Cynthia T. Hahn, Chad Lind, Jen Minarik, Afia

Ofori-Mensa, Yann Robert, Jessica Robbins-Ruszkowski, Josh Siegal, Urmila Venkatesh, and Shannon Winston.

To comic artist and jazz trumpeter Mazen Kerbaj, my gratitude for his generosity in offering nonexclusive rights to use the picture 'BOUM' for the cover of the book, as well as permission to reprint 'Beirut: 19 July 06 2.10 AM' and 'Recording Session: Mazen Kerbaj (Trumpet) vs. The State of Israel (Bombs).' The poster from La Grande Nouba is used with permission from La Cité de la Musique and photographer Valerie Belin.

For my daughter, Audrey, who was bumping around *in utero* during my dissertation defense and now trumpets with pride that 'Mama wrote a book!' to her classmates: thank you for being my center. And above all, to my parents, Barbara and James Solheim: so much love and infinite gratitude for all of the heavy lifting.

CHAPTER ONE

Introduction

The Call to Listen: A Cultural Phenomenon

This book considers the interplay of hearing, listening, and understanding in postcolonial Francophone literature and culture more broadly from North Africa and the Middle East. *The call to listen*—the cultural theory introduced in this book—is informed by the works of some of the most popular and critically acclaimed artists of the half-century following French decolonization: Algerian novelists Assia Djebar, Leïla Sebbar, and Yasmina Khadra; Lebanese playwright Wajdi Mouawad and avant-jazz trumpeter/visual artist Mazen Kerbaj; Iranian graphic novelist Marjane Satrapi; and Algerian Kabyle singer-songwriters and political activists Djura and Idir. These writers and artists have enjoyed great success not only in France but also with a global audience.

While sound and silence are the objects of inquiry in this book, the central question that drives this study takes a somewhat different tack: What compels us to listen? Why do some cultural works *speak* to so many, when there is a surfeit of choices in form and medium in contemporary global culture? From the 1960s through the first decade of the twenty-first century, the predominant use of analog sound and radio shifted to the digital age. The digitized movement of media made cultural works (including literature, graphic novels, film, theatre, and music) and journalistic enterprises (first including newspapers, and eventually blogs, news aggregates, and social media) more accessible to the general public. The shift from analog recording and radio broadcasting to digital media allowed for a more efficient transmission of national and regional cultures, as well as the immediate transmission of historic events and cultural works. Gone are the days when the only stories one hears are passed directly from voice to ear, from generation to generation. Stories are mediated, on the page, the tablet, on mp3, or in digital video format. The choice of what kinds of stories to hear, and in what medium, feels infinite.

So how do we choose which stories to hear? For it is not simply media that has changed: the content of stories, and the storytellers themselves, have changed too. The evolution from analog to digital sound technologies took place alongside the social and political shifts from colonialism to globalization. One of the major cultural shifts to occur alongside these social and political changes has to do with who tells stories, and whose stories will be heard. No longer are storytellers exclusively from one's own family or local social network. While male voices still dominate cultural marketplaces, women continue to gain traction, and cultural works written by women and minorities of centuries past continue to be recovered and disseminated. So the choices are manifold: what, when, where, and to whom do we choose to listen? Indeed, how and why do we choose to listen to the stories we do?

While the call to listen embeds sound technologies as part of the cultural phenomenon—none of these narratives could be constructed without the use of or reference to recording and/or communication technologies available from the advent of radio and telephone onward—the struggle to be heard has been motivating protagonists for millennia. In Ovid's *Metamorphoses*, Philomel wove a tapestry and had it smuggled to her sister Procne in order to reveal that Procne's husband, Tereus, had raped Philomel, then cut out her tongue and imprisoned her so that she could not reveal what happened. Arachne the spinner angered the goddess Athena with her weaving that depicted the cruelty of the gods to humans, and Athena ripped the tapestry to shreds, then transformed Arachne into a spider. Finally, listening prevention is perhaps the most famous narrative strategy of all when it comes to voices yearning to be heard: Odysseus orders his crew to block their ears with beeswax and lash him to the mast so that he can hear the Sirens' song as his ship passes their island without fear of being lured there by their dulcet tones. The *Odyssey* gives more space to the content of the Sirens' song than the qualities of their voices—here, we see how 'listening,' 'hearing,' and 'understanding' are terms, acts, *and* states of being, all of which can be conflated. Odysseus's 'hearing' does not have the effect desired by the Sirens: his ship, steered by the deafened crew, sails on.

If we are to talk about listening, we must necessarily describe who speaks, who is silent; what is heard, what is silent; when and where things are heard, when and where there is silence; and why some things are heard, and others silenced. In other words, the cultural works that give shape to the 'call to listen' phenomenon issue a stylistically compelling call, but the story told once the listener pauses to listen is rich and substantive. The stories that follow the call to listen in a text bring new understanding to bear on once-marginalized experience—*and* the call engages audiences in such a way that the story being told has universal qualities within its particularity. For example, loss is a predominant theme within all the narratives signaled by the call to listen. Loss is often followed by voices that go unheard—in other words, voices that, from a narrative strategic perspective, are performatively silenced.

The Performance of Listening in Postcolonial Francophone Culture intersects with both Francophone and sound studies, but its primary home is the interdisciplinary field of performance studies. Informing this study further is the sociocultural terrain of French and Francophone inquiry into how to listen and, in some cases, the suggestion that France as a society has a duty to listen to immigrants and minorities in an engaged and responsive manner. What follows in this introduction is an overview of how these different lines of inquiry, questions, and methodologies helped me expand upon the central claim of this book.

The call to listen is a cultural phenomenon that allows marginalized voices to weave into the social fabric alongside the reactionary, blanket statements of right-wing social and political figures in France like Eric Zemmour and Marine Le Pen. Their polemics assert innate and irreversible tendencies toward violence, oppression, and religious fundamentalism amongst immigrants and French citizens with ethnic backgrounds from former French colonies. Since this study took shape in the years before the Arab Spring, the Syrian Civil War, and the rise of Daesh (the Islamic State), when I cite sociologists and anthropologists in this study, I most often draw from works that were published in the first decade of the twenty-first century. For example, I follow the lead of sociologist Riva Kastoryano in her work addressing the 2005 riots in France by using the term 'assimilation' as equivalent to the French notion of *intégration*. John Bowen's chapter 'Remembering Laïcité' in *Why the French Don't Like Headscarves* (2007) offers a rigorous assessment and analysis of the legacy of assimilation and French Republicanism from a perspective that predates the dismantling of dictatorships in North Africa and the Middle East; the global refugee crisis that has resulted from the Syrian Civil War; the rise and spread of Daesh; and the attacks in Paris of January 7 and November 13, 2015. Accordingly, I have organized chronologically the following select bibliography of sociocultural works and cultural criticism on the importance of listening.

In one of the foundational works of sound studies, *The Tuning of the World: Toward a Theory of Soundscape Design* (1980), R. Murray Schafer notes that 'while we may use the techniques of modern recording and analysis to study contemporary soundscapes, for the foundation of historical perspectives, we will have to turn to earwitness accounts from literature and mythology' (8). Schafer goes on to describe the 'authenticity of the earwitness,' a kind of authenticity that I suggest is intrinsic in the call to listen:

> When Chateaubriand tells us that in 1791 he heard the roar of Niagara [Falls] eight to ten miles away, he provides us with useful information about the ambient sound level, against which that of today could be measured. [...] We trust [Erich Maria Remarque's earwitness in *All Quiet on the Western Front*] when he describes unusual sound events—for instance, the sounds made by dead bodies. 'The days are hot and the dead lie unburied. [...] Many have their bellies swollen up like balloons. They hiss, belch, and make movements. The gases in them make noises.' (8–9)

As Schafer suggests, the sensory description of the sounds of dead bodies brings the reader into an unexpected yet wholly believable— and, as a result, a seemingly authentic—experience of the First World War trenches: we imagine the hiss of gas emitted from a bloated body, and this sound triggers the image of beating sunlight, the sensation of heat. We may imagine the stench of rotting human flesh, and the taste of revulsion, nausea, and fear in the mouth. With imagined sensory experience comes an *empathic* response, an engagement not just as the reader or listener to a story, but as one human being imagining another human experience.

Imagination is always a facet of interpretation. In *Listening in Paris: A Cultural History* (1995), James H. Johnson asserts that a work cannot be heard today as it was heard in the artist's lifetime. Of a Haydn symphony, Johnson argues that '[a work] resides in the particular moment of reception, one shaped by dominant aesthetic and social expectations that are themselves historically structured. [... and] there is no musical meaning without interpretation' (2). To elaborate on Johnson's point, the way we listen to culture is informed by social context, aesthetic (or other) content, cultural form, and the interplay of all three aspects. Franz Fanon implores readers to consider this interplay in his 1959 essay 'Ici la voix d'Algérie' ['This is the Voice of Algeria'], in which he shows how Radio-Alger exemplifies 'les attitudes nouvelles adoptées par le peuple algérien au cours de la lutte de Libération, à l'égard d'un instrument précis: la radio' (51) ['new attitudes adopted by the Algerian people in the course of the fight for liberation, with respect to a precise technical instrument: the radio' (69)]. In the preceding and early years of the Algerian Revolution, Radio-Alger served as an instrument of oppression. For example, once the revolution was underway, Radio-Alger stopped provided simultaneous Arabic translations for commentary, instead taking up the formula 'les Français parlent aux Français' (81) ['Frenchmen speaking to Frenchmen' (96)]. This left Algerians unaddressed in the listening audience, and literally voiceless in radio broadcasts.

Furthermore, Fanon heard from many Algerians that the sexually charged commentary on the radio undermined indigenous 'traditions de respectabilité' (52), making it uncomfortable if not morally unacceptable for Algerian families to listen to radio broadcasts together. In Fanon's central claim about Radio-Alger in the early days of the revolution (italics original): '*Le poste de T.S.F., en Algérie occupée, est une technique de l'occupant qui, dans le cadre de la domination coloniale, ne répond à aucun besoin vital de "indigène"*' (55) ['*The radio in occupied Algeria is a technique in the hands of the occupier which, within the framework of colonial domination, corresponds to no vital need insofar as the "native" is concerned*' (72–73)]. In other words, the French broadcasting on Radio-Alger fostered psychic alienation among Algerians; their only moments of personal recognition were delivered in social and cultural differences, which Fanon's subjects found humiliating: 'il nous est pratiquement impossible d'écouter en famille les programmes radiophoniques. Les allusions érotiques, ou même les situations burlesques, qui veulent faire rire, évoquées à la radio, provoquent au sein de la famille à l'écoute des tensions insupportables' (52) ['it is practically impossible for us to listen to radio programs in the family. The sex allusions, or even the clownish situations meant to make people laugh, which are broadcast over the radio cause an unendurable strain in a family listening to these programs' (70)]. In Fanon's conceptualization of psychic alienation throughout *Peau noire, masques blancs* (1952), a French 'voice' overrides any indigenous one, and indeed, to be heard, an indigenous person must not only speak French, but *sound* French: 'En France, on dit: parler comme un livre. En Martinique: parler comme un Blanc' (16) ['In France they say "to speak like a book." In Martinique they say "to speak like a white man"' (4–5)]. Bringing these two works of Fanon together, then, we can understand Algerian silence as *French-sounding*; in other words: Francophone. On the radio, the voices on the air speak French, and assert the perspective of the colonial power; if an Algerian voice is to be heard, that voice must not only speak French, but an educated, literate, even literary French.

The estrangement Fanon describes from colonized people's own languages, linguistic styles, and oratory traditions (formal aspects of speech) and their distinct set of social, cultural, and historical perspectives (the content of that speech) suggests an erasure of voice. Herein lies the definition of silence in *The Performance of Listening in Postcolonial Francophone Culture*: silence is not an absence of sound or voice. Silence has both form and content; silence arises from that which goes unheard. Put another way, *silence* is the imposition of a dominant narrative upon narratives of marginalized peoples; *to silence* is to not listen.

While Fanon focuses on the imposition of the colonizer narrative upon Algerians, in 1975, Hélène Cixous's hallmark feminist essay 'Le Rire de la méduse' ['The Laugh of the Medusa'] issued a call to women to speak, to write, to express themselves creatively, intellectually, and politically, as women. Here, Cixous describes women's fear of speaking, which can be understood to function in tandem with Fanon's concept of psychic alienation:

> Toute femme a connu le tourment de la venue à la parole orale, le cœur qui bat à se rompre, parfois la chute dans la perte de langage, le sol, la langue se dérobent, tant parler est pour la femme—je dirai même, ouvrir la bouche—en public, une témérité, une transgression. Double détresse, car même si elle transgresse, sa parole choit presque toujours dans la sourde oreille masculine, qui n'entend dans la langue que ce qui parle au masculin. (43)

> [Every woman has known the torment of getting up to speak. Her heart racing, at times entirely lost for words, ground and language slipping away—that's how daring a feat, how great a transgression it is for a woman to speak—even just open her mouth—in public. A double distress, for even if she transgresses, her words fall almost always upon the deaf male ear, which hears in language only that which speaks in the masculine. (880–881)]

Women's silence arises not only from the fear of speaking but also, and perhaps more importantly, the fear that that speech will fall on deaf ears. Ears that are deaf because they can only hear language that speaks in the masculine—this is to say, these ears can only *understand* a male narrative.

While 'The Laugh of the Medusa' suggests a binary opposition between the masculine and the feminine, this dialogic falls short for Cixous in describing women's historical silence within patriarchal society. Cixous argues that women's sexuality and expression exists on a spectrum: 'you can't talk about *a* female sexuality, uniform, homogenous, classifiable into codes—any more than you can talk about one unconscious resembling another' (876). Cixous also draws the comparison between women's oppression and the subjugation of women and the oppression and subjugation of Africans in describing as Africa as a dark continent penetrated by white men. This metaphor is extended over several paragraphs:

> Dès qu'elles commencent à parler, en même temps que leur nom, que leur région est noire: parce que tu es Afrique, tu es noire. Ton continent est noir. [...] Nous les précoces, nous les refoulées de la culture, les belles bouches barrées de bâillons, pollen, haleines coupées, nous les labyrinthes, les échelles, les espaces foulés; les volées,—nous sommes « noires » *et* nous sommes belles. (41)

> [As soon as they begin to speak, at the same time as they're taught their name, they can be taught that their territory is black: because you are Africa, you are black. Your continent is dark. [...] We the precocious, we the repressed of culture, our lovely mouths gagged with pollen, our wind knocked out of us, we the labyrinths, the ladders, the trampled spaces, the bevies—we are black and we are beautiful. (877–878)]

Throughout 'The Laugh of the Medusa,' Cixous confronts a particular problem when it comes to the silencing of women's voices: feminist language, feminist stories, and feminist narratives fall on deaf ears because they do not fit patriarchal expectations of what women should say. As Cixous opens up the qualities of women's silence— again, *silence* is an imposition of a dominant social narrative upon marginalized voices—she describes its qualities through comparison to the domination of colonized people. Cixous's work begins to hint at the ways in which women's silence can speak, suggesting that at the assertion of strict lines of distinction between men and women, between European and African, white and black, these very lines of distinction start coming undone.

Naturally, it must be acknowledged that with Cixous's strict lines of distinction between men and women, she represents women's experience from a perspective that has been largely interpreted (and criticized) as both white and European. Three social categories—woman, white, and European—inform one another in ways that are intrinsic to Cixous's argument and the metaphors of silence that she deploys. Cixous indicates that there is the potential for the women to whom she addresses this essay to speak: it is from the moment that these women open their mouths and are taught their names that they are instructed in their 'blackness,' in other words, that their voices are not valued and will go unheard. As such, silence is qualified as intrinsic to black experience, leaving white, male experience unmarked, and the double silencing of black women unrecognized.

The abstract, silent voices at the intersection of gender, race, and ethnicity in Cixous's essay are embodied in Tahar Ben Jelloun's *Hospitalité française* (1987), in which he describes the phenomenon of silence as a strategy of social resistance among immigrants in France with whom he worked as a psychologist: 'Ils témoignent par leur silence de la nostalgie de l'époque où ils "n'existaient" pas, où on ne parlait pas d'eux, on les ignorait, et où personne ne venait déranger leur misère, leur solitude tissée d'amertume et de fatalité' (27) [In their silence, they bear witness to a time when they 'didn't exist,' when no one talked to them, when people ignored them, and when no one came to disrupt their misery, their solitude woven from bitterness and fate (my trans.)]. To silence, Ben Jelloun suggests, is to *not listen*. To not listen includes anticipating what will be heard, or validating only certain ways of relating immigrant experience in advance of hearing them. In a sense, the immigrants in Ben Jelloun's care might as well have their mouths gagged with pollen, to borrow Cixous's metaphor: their particular voices—their stories—are silenced before they even begin to speak. This is to say that, even if immigrants are granted the right to speak, if no one is listening or granting the speaker's narrative the room to be heard, what is articulated goes *unheard*. As a result, silence became an act of refusal for many immigrants. Ben Jelloun politicizes this particular kind of 'silence' as a gesture of refusal: silence opens up space in which to bear witness to the social erasure and marginalization of immigrants in France.

Both social critique and cultural narratives bear a burden of responsibility in representing voices from the margins of society, whether at the local, regional, or global level. A focal element of the call to listen as a cultural phenomenon is that these works tell particular, individual stories, but the narratives suggest that there are universal ways in which we can listen to accounts of marginalized experience. But what does it mean to listen? How does listening constitute a cultural practice? And what are the cultural effects of this practice? Can listening produce a cross-cultural effect, or a multicultural effect? And in the context of contemporary French society—keeping in mind the legacy of French colonialism and the *mission civilisatrice*, as well as the ways in which French universalism as a social value can, in practice, serve to exclude minorities in socioeconomic and political contexts—what would be a productive effect of the call to listen?

Since I define silence throughout this work as the imposition of a dominant social narrative upon expressions of marginal experience, it can be helpful to consider if, when, and how rhetoric plays a role in cultural works. In *Rhetorical Listening: Identification, Gender, Whiteness* (2005), Krista Ratcliffe defines rhetorical listening in the context of the United States as 'a trope for interpretative invention and as a code of cross-cultural conduct, [it] signifies a stance of openness that a person may choose to assume in relation to any person, text, or culture' (1). This definition is fairly close to what I argue is advocated by the call to listen as a cultural phenomenon—there is an element of persuasion at play in the cultural works considered in the call to listen corpus. And yet, the term 'cross-cultural' is a sticky one in French society, as is 'multicultural.' French universalism as a social value that parallels multiculturalism in the United States and Britain suggests that the French people should aspire to view one another as citizens of the Republic, *point*—the French are a unified and universal people, undifferentiated in society by gender, race, religion, or ethnic background. *Mixité* is the applied practice of universalism as a French social value, and its aims are admirable: *mixité* is intended to level gender, ethnic, and religious difference. But many immigrants to France and their descendants find that their identity does not fit neatly within the universalist narrative. So the concept of 'cross-cultural listening' would not be productive in the French context—in fact, it could prove to be more divisive than engaging.

The call to listen does demonstrate openness, however. In *Time Signatures: Contextualizing Contemporary Francophone Autobiographical Writing from the Maghreb* (2006), Alison Rice's spelling and pronunciation of Francophonie proves helpful:

> My new spelling of 'Francophony' could be pronounced Francophony, in accord with the word 'cacophony.' Contemporary writers from the Maghreb are not always concerned with creating harmony, either in theme or form. In fact, recent writing has been increasingly marked by dissonance [...] While 'cacophony' often carries negative connotations, writing that may initially impress readers as discordant and arrhythmic

can strike unique chords if we approach the text in new ways, learning to 'read by ear.' (27)

An openness to 'reading by ear' could be understood as part and parcel of Francophony. If, within French society and culture, universalism is a preeminent social aim, and *mixité* serves as a dominant social practice, then the call to listen cannily weaves minority voices into a French narrative: universalism as a value can be maintained, but its social dimensions have become more complex. (I consider this in detail in Chapter 5, which examines the idea of covering, or interpreting, French universalism to accommodate those represented by world music in France.) The idea of leveling difference borne from the Republican opposition to monarchical rule and divine right is starting to accommodate narratives of colonial oppression, postcolonial rifts and strife, and ideological clashes between French and Francophone societies. In other words, French Republicanism (or universalism) is a perpetual process, not a fixed state of being, and *how* social differences can be accommodated depends in large part on the ways in which narratives of different experience are heard and heeded—in other words, the ways in which a society and culture listens to narratives of social difference. This is where the call to listen enters the scene as a cultural phenomenon.

So how does this phenomenon take shape?

Sounding the Text:
One Critical Methodology, Multiple Modes of Analysis

As the title of this book suggests, the call to listen as a cultural phenomenon is a performance of listening that traverses genres and media. In this section of the introduction, I lay out the defining elements of the call to listen and how to identify and differentiate various calls to listen depending on the type of cultural work whence the call arises.

In *Story, Performance, and Event: Contextual Studies of Oral Narrative* (1986), Richard Bauman's concept of the 'performance event' considers how a story is told, the situation in which it is related, and the vocal and physical dynamics of the orator and listeners. Borrowed as a literary concept, the performance of listening within cultural work first establishes the *narrative as a listener*. In other words, it is the narrative of the work itself that intercepts sounds and silences. How this interception takes place depends largely on the medium and genre of an individual work, but before we consider media and genres, it is important to establish the first defining feature of works that issue the call to listen: in all cases, there are (1) a socially—if not politically—specific *mise en scène*, (2) a sound source, and (3) a listener.

These three narrative elements are in keeping with Bauman's notion of the performance event: without a specific context, further meaning (in other words, the performance event itself) cannot arise from a story told. Further qualities and narrative details of the performance event are revealed through both the speaker's and listener's respective vocal tics, pauses, facial expressions, and gestures. Accordingly, in sounding the text for a call to listen, these three elements must also be present. In a sense, sounding the text is like sounding a body of water: it is a critical measurement of sonic length and depth within a cultural work. The *mise en scène* provides the 'body' through which sonic elements resonate from sound source to listener. How and if the sound source responds, then, suggests whether the performance of listening in the narrative can be *heard* (this is to say, understood and heeded), or must be *traced*. Gayatri Spivak's concept of tracing silenced voices in 'Can the Subaltern Speak?' (1991) is an obvious point of departure here: in her examination of the absence of a subaltern voice in both history and intellectual discourse, she writes:

> When we come to the concomitant question of the consciousness of the subaltern, the notion of what the work *cannot* say becomes important. In the semioses of the social text, elaborations of insurgency stand in the place of 'the utterance.' The sender—'the peasant'—is marked only as a pointer to an irretrievable consciousness. (287)

Here Spivak establishes a relationship between the sender (or the irretrievable consciousness of the subaltern speaker), the social text (a metaphorically sonic field of intellectual inquiry), 'the utterance' (the voice of the sender, which can only be traced rather than heard), and the intellectual, who makes a choice to listen or not to listen to the utterance of the speaker upon the social text (here referred to as 'we,' which rolls Spivak, Michel Foucault, Gilles Deleuze, Jacques Derrida, and the community of deconstructionist thinkers into an assemblage of intellectual listeners). Later, in her analysis of the suicide of Bhuvaneswari Bhaduri in 1926, Spivak demonstrates that the utterance of the subaltern speaker can only be heard in *traces*: Bhaduri waited to hang herself until the onset of menstruation in order to disprove conjecture that her suicide 'would be diagnosed as the outcome of illegitimate passion' (307). Those who speak in this social text, however, write over Bhaduri's assertion: 'One tentative explanation of her inexplicable act had been a possible melancholia brought on by her brother-in-law's repeated taunts that she was too old to be not-yet-a-wife' (307). In Spivak's exploration, two of Bhaduri's nieces assert that 'it appears that it was a case of illicit love' (308). Spivak's analysis thus registers a voice silenced by the reverberations of more dominant voices in the social text about Bhaduri's suicide. In her conclusion, Spivak suggests that 'Derrida marks radical critique with the danger of appropriating the other by assimilation. [...] He calls for a rewriting of the utopian structural impulse as "rendering delirious that interior voice that is the voice of the other in us"' (308). Spivak's tracing of the utterance in 'Can the Subaltern Speak?' stands as part of a tradition of thinkers whose works suggest that listening *is* understanding—in other words, narratives can perform acts of hearing—understanding—or acts of silencing—the impossibility or refusal of understanding. Put another way, if the metaphor 'I have a voice' suggests personal and political agency, then the complementary metaphor 'I am listening' can assert either hearing (understanding) or silencing (the impossibility or refusal of understanding).

Regarding this latter claim, consider J.M.G. Le Clézio's children's story 'Lullaby' (1980), the gentle account of the eponymous young girl who plays truant from school for an extended period of time. (While Lullaby's name is not a focus of my analysis, it is worth noting that even the name of both protagonist and story suggest that there is a song to be heard if one listens.) The first day that Lullaby decides not to go to school, she writes a letter to her father, who is not with Lullaby and her mother; it is not clear where he is gone, only that he has been away for some time. She writes to him about the weather and the approaching winter. Lullaby spends glorious days near and on the beach, and revels in the sun, sings songs, tells stories. In one passage, she thinks about her math teacher, M. Filippi, who seems a kindred spirit in Lullaby's wandering imagination. She encounters a boy with whom she has guarded but playful conversations.

When she turns up at school again, she is marched straight to the Principal's office. Following a stern reprimand for Lullaby's absence, the Principal states that she is listening for Lullaby's explanation. This is the moment where the text issues a call to listen:

> « Je vous écoute », répéta la Directrice. L'indifférence de Lullaby semblait la mettre peu à peu hors d'elle. C'était peut-être aussi la faute du vent, qui avait rendu tout électrique.
> « Où étiez-vous, pendant tout ce temps? »

Lullaby parla. Elle parla lentement, en cherchant un peu ses mots, parce qu'elle n'avait plus tellement l'habitude maintenant, et tandis qu'elle parlait, elle voyait devant elle, à la place de la Directrice, la maison à colonnes blanches, les rochers, et le beau nom grec qui brillait dans le soleil. [...] La Directrice écoutait, et son visage prit pendant un instant une expression de stupéfaction intense. [...] Quand elle s'arrêta de parler, il y eut quelques secondes de silence. Puis le visage de la Directrice changea encore, comme si elle cherchait sa voix. Lullaby fut étonnée d'entendre son timbre. Ce n'était plus du tout la même voix, c'était devenu plus grave et plus doux.

« Ecoutez, mon enfant [...] Mon enfant, je suis prête à oublier tout cela. Vous pourrez retourner en classe comme avant. Mais vous devez me dire ... »

Elle hésita.

« Vous comprenez, je veux votre bien. Il faut me dire toute la vérité. » (116–117)

['I'm listening,' the Principal repeated. Lullaby's indifference seemed to set her more and more beside herself. It was, perhaps, also the fault of the wind, which had electrified everything.

'Where were you all this time?'

Lullaby spoke. She spoke slowly, searching a bit for her words, because she was out of the habit now, and while she was talking, she saw before her, in place of the Principal, the house with white columns, the rocks, the handsome Greek name that glittered in the sun. [...] The Principal was listening, and for a moment her face took on a look of thorough astonishment. [...] When she stopped talking, there were a few moments of silence. Then the Principal's face changed again, as if she was looking for her voice. Lullaby was surprised to hear her tone. It was no longer at all the same voice, it had become more serious and more gentle.

'Listen, my dear [...] My dear, I'm ready to forget all of this. You may go back to class like before. But you need to tell me ...'

She hesitated.

'You understand, I want the best for you. It is imperative that you tell me the truth.'] (my trans.)

Lullaby tells her about the beach, the sun, the rocks, and the columned house she found. These fantastical descriptions seem to soften the Principal, but she does not believe what Lullaby is saying. She wants the truth. She says that she is listening. But the Principal will only 'hear' (this is to say, believe) the narrative that she has imposed upon Lullaby:

« Vous avez un petit ami, n'est-ce pas? »
Lullaby voulut protester, mais la Directrice l'empêcha de parler.

« Inutile de nier, certaines—certaines de vos camarades vous ont vue avec un garçon. »

« Mais c'est faux! » dit Lullaby; elle n'avait pas crié, mais la Directrice fit comme si elle avait crié, et elle dit très fort:

« Je veux savoir son nom! »

« Je n'ai pas de petit ami! » dit Lullaby.

[...]

« Il faut me dire la vérité, mon enfant, c'est pour votre bien. »

Puis son timbre redevint dur et méchant.

« Je veux savoir le nom de ce garçon! »

Lullaby sentit la colère grandir en elle. C'était très froid et très lourd comme la pierre, et cela s'installait dans ses poumons, dans sa gorge; son cœur se mit à battre très vite, comme lorsqu'elle avait vu les phrases obscènes sur les murs de la maison grecque. (117)

['You have a boyfriend, don't you?'

Lullaby wanted to protest, but the Principal kept her from talking.

'It's useless to deny it, certain—certain schoolmates of yours saw you with a boy.'

'But it's not true!' said Lullaby. She had not yelled, but the Principal made as if she had yelled, and she said very forcefully:

'I want to know his name!'

'I don't have a boyfriend!' said Lullaby.

[...]

'You need tell me the truth, my dear. It's for your own good.'

Then her tone became hard and threatening again.

'I want to know the name of this boy!'

Lullaby felt the anger rise in her. It was very cold and very heavy like stone, and it lodged itself in her lungs, in her throat; her heart started beating very fast, as when she saw obscenities on the wall of the Greek house.] (my trans.)

Lullaby is supposed to be one thing—a troubled young girl—and the Principal won't hear any interpretation of her truancy but that the boy whom she encountered near the sea is her boyfriend. Lullaby and the Principal exchange accusation and protest until, finally, the Principal tells Lullaby that she knows her mother has been sick—this is new knowledge for the reader. She also knows that Lullaby is a good student: she doesn't want this promise to go to waste. Her imposed narrative is also sexist: if Lullaby was seen with the boy she encountered on the beach, he was, of course, her boyfriend; there is no other possible reason why she would be with a boy. The Principal cannot fathom a young girl dallying on the beach alone in order to alleviate anxiety; a boy could be the only lure from school. Had Lullaby been a boy, would the Principal have been so concerned if he had been seen with a girl?

To return to the story, Lullaby falls silent, which seems to appease the Principal. She orders Lullaby to class, with the warning that their conversation is not finished. But Lullaby has already warned her that she will not return to this or any school if the Principal tells her parents that she has a boyfriend.

Lullaby makes her way to M. Filippi's class, and outside the classroom she runs into the teacher taking a break and smoking a cigarette. The difference between their dialogue and that between the Principal and Lullaby is notable:

> « Eh bien? Eh bien? » dit-il. C'est tout ce qu'il trouvait à dire.
> « Je voulais vous demander … », commença Lullaby.
> « Quoi? »
> « Pour la mer, la lumière, j'avais beaucoup de questions à vous demander. »
> [...] M. Filippi la regarda d'un air amusé.
> « Vous avez fait un voyage? »
> « Oui … », dit Lullaby.
> « Et … C'était bien? »
> « Oh oui! C'était très bien. »
> « Je suis bien content [...] Vous n'allez plus partir en voyage, maintenant? »
> « Non », dit Lullaby.
> « Bon, il faut y aller [...] Je suis bien content [...] vous me demanderez ce que vous voudrez, tout à l'heure, après le cours. J'aime beaucoup la mer, moi aussi. » (120)

> ['So?' he said. It was all he could think of to say.
> 'I wanted to ask you …' Lullaby began.
> 'What?'
> 'About the sea, and the light, I had lots of questions to ask you.'
> [...] Mister Filippi gave her an amused look.
> 'You went on a trip?'
> 'Yes …' said Lullaby.
> 'And … was it good?'
> 'Oh, yes! It was very good.'
> 'I'm happy for you [...] You're not going on any more trips?'
> 'No,' said Lullaby.
> 'Okay, we need get going [...] I'm happy for you [...] you can ask me what you want later, after class. I love the sea too.'])

M. Filippi speaks in a way that assures Lullaby that her words are taken at face value. In other words, with this gesture of listening (as opposed to the statement, 'I'm listening'), Lullaby decides that she will no longer go 'traveling,' to follow M. Filippi's euphemism for skipping school.

So here is a young girl singled out as potentially troubled due to the absence of her parents, vulnerable to those who dominate the school where she is enrolled. There is one authority figure, the Principal with a capital P, who *silences* her: despite her assertions to the contrary, she is not listening. But here comes a second figure of authority, M. Filippi, who brings her back into the fold by demonstrating that he listens. By *listening*, I mean that he offers a sympathetic space in which Lullaby can tell him where she has been. Instead of interpreting her explanation to satisfy conventional expectations, he wants to hear more about her trip and answer her questions in turn. If the power dynamic between Lullaby and M. Filippi is not equal—for this, of course, is not possible between student and teacher—he nonetheless finds an equilibrium, a means through which Lullaby can speak.

The performance of listening, then, allows for the interception of both sound and silence based upon the configuration of sound source, listener, and setting. The listener's reaction to the sound source is crucial in the call to listen as a narrative performance: how the listener reacts determines whether the sound source resonates through sound or silence. In the encounter between Lullaby and the Principal, even though Lullaby spoke, she was effectively silenced by the Principal's refusal to hear her story on her terms. Yet when M. Filippi spoke with Lullaby, he listened. The performances of listening in 'Lullaby' thus tell stories of power dynamics between students and teachers—and what can be effective in working with a child in potential distress. It is notable that Principal's statement, 'I'm listening' is contradicted by her behavior. Spoken by someone in a position of power, 'I'm listening' is less an invitation than a command to speak. The performances of listening in 'Lullaby' offer a moral for both children and adults.

The call to listen, however, is not simply about texts that can be sounded. 'Lullaby' is written in such a way that the story could be about any coastal town in southern France, and it is almost impossible to situate temporally. As a cultural phenomenon, the call to listen is issued from postcolonial settings grounded in specific times and places. These specific settings are not accidental. Political and technological contexts are essential to cultural works that issue the call to listen, because they signal social difference in narrative perspective. For instance, in Djebar's 'Femmes d'Algers dans leur appartement' (1978) ['Women of

Algiers in Their Apartment'], the 1960s and '70s are clearly marked in different ways from different points of view. For Sarah, the Algerian protagonist, her experience of torture during the Algerian War colors everything that has happened since, and it is an inextricable element of the struggle to literally give voice her own experience. Meanwhile, Anne, Sarah's childhood friend and the daughter of a French diplomat, is recovering from a divorce in which she lost both husband and children. Anne's experience seems unmarked by the Algerian War, based on how Djebar relates her concerns. Later, Sarah's colleague Irma, a German woman, reinforces the idea that Europeans can move through Algeria with relatively little concern for negotiations of the state following the Algerian War. Sarah tunes Irma out as she sets to work in her research as an ethnomusicologist on *haoufis*, traditional songs of Algerian women. It is the act of strapping on the headphones and pressing play on the cassette deck that allows Sarah to dismiss Irma in a way that echoes her dismissal of Anne's lament about her divorce.

Significantly, in the novella's denouement, when Sarah does find a way to speak, Anne listens as Sarah asks:

> Une femme qui parle devant une autre qui regarde, celle qui parle raconte-t-elle l'autre aux yeux dévorants, à la mémoire noire ou décrit-elle sa propre nuit, avec des mots torches et des bougies dont la cire fond trop vite? Celle qui regarde, est-ce à force d'écouter, d'écouter et de se rappeler qu'elle finit par se voir elle-même, avec son propre regard, sans voile enfin ... (122)

> [A woman speaking in front of another one who's watching; does the one who's speaking tell the story of the other one with the devouring eyes, with the black memories, or is she describing her own dark night with words like torches and with candles whose wax melts too fast? She who watches, is it by means of listening, of listening and remembering that she ends up seeing herself, with her own eyes, unveiled at last ... (47)]

This description of testimony and bearing witness is entirely bound up in Sarah's experiences as both an Algerian revolutionary and a feminist. The way that Anne listens—still and silent, nonjudgmental and empathetic—embodies the call to listen. I analyze this passage at length in my analysis of Djebar's work (Chapter 2), but here, it provides an apt example of how the political and technological can be bound up in the call to listen as a cultural phenomenon.

The Performance of Listening in Postcolonial Francophone Culture proposes three modes of listening in culture. These three modes are bound to their media: *cut sound* in literature, the *citational hook* in film and theater, and *covering* in music.

First, in my proposal of *cut sound* as a literary device, I demonstrate that silences can be woven into literary narratives through the interplay of dialogue and characters' reactions with characters' thoughts. To develop *cut sound* as a literary mode of listening, I draw from Djebar's theorization of women's silences in the essay 'Forbidden Gaze, Severed Sound' (1978), from her collection *Femmes d'Alger dans leur appartement*, as well as oral folklore and performance studies scholar Richard Bauman's concept of the performance event. Music recording production techniques serve as a critical metaphor for how to listen for silences in literary narratives. The characters' thoughts either belie their reactions to what other characters say, or their thoughts efface parts of dialogue altogether, effectively erasing what other characters say from the text. In my readings of Djebar's novella 'Femmes d'Algers dans leur appartement' and Leïla Sebbar's novel *Shérazade* (1982), I demonstrate how cut sound weaves dialogue with thought in order to articulate cut sound, or the gendered silences of postcolonial subjects. With my reading of Yasmina Khadra's novel *The Sirens of Baghdad* (2006), I demonstrate that listening is not a given in any social exchange across either ethnic or gender lines: if no motive or desire to listen is present, voices go unheard and are, in effect, silenced. My analysis of Khadra's work is framed by a discussion of both visual and aural sirens in pop culture and media. I conclude with an analysis of how sirens redirect narrative focus and argue that, as literary cut sound, sirens are emblematic of the call to listen—they demand focus and attention.

The discussion of sirens in cultural narratives gives way to an introduction to the concept of the *citational hook* (a term I use to describe, within a cinematic or theatrical narrative, the interpretation of a popular song that imbues the lyrics with new and subversive or transgressive meaning), which is introduced through sing-along performances to Anglophone rock songs in Marjane Satrapi's film *Persepolis* (2007) and Wajdi Mouawad's play *Incendies* (2003). Working with Judith Butler's concept of citation, or the act of filling a dominant form with subversive content; Roland Barthes's essay 'The Grain of the Voice,' in which he argues that the most compelling and seductive elements of a singing voice are its human eccentricities and flaws, rather than technical flawlessness; and Michel Chion's analysis of image and sound with cinematic syncresis (the way that sound informs image), I demonstrate how the performances in Mouawad's and Satrapi's respective works can be heard as subversions of French universalist stereotypes of Middle Eastern femininity and masculinity that are linked to the symbols of the veil and the gun. I contextualize the performances through the universalist representations of immigrant men and women in France that have led to strictures on Arab women's dress and the social marginalization of Arab men. The sing-along performances demonstrate that it is imperative to look beyond received symbols of Middle Eastern women's oppression, such as the veil, and the stereotype of Middle Eastern men as inherently violent, such as the machine gun, and to allow for a broad range of possibilities for how masculinity and femininity are expressed within Middle Eastern ethnic identities. How, for example, does our interpretation of a young Arab man wielding a machine gun in *Scorched* shift as he sings along to Supertramp's 'The Logical Song'?

Third, readings of the CD liner notes of Idir's *Identités* (1999) and the lyrics to his song 'La France des couleurs' ['The France of Colors'] (2007) as well as the memoir *The Veil of Silence* by feminist singer-songwriter Djura (1991), demonstrate how these musicians of Algerian-Kabyle origin who live and work in France have created an alter-globalist culture within French world music. As Paul Gilroy argues of African-American culture in *The Black Atlantic*, Kabyle music in French is often introduced to the public with a 'split consciousness,' with one address to a French-speaking audience and another to a Kabyle audience. While this split consciousness in framing can be seen as a conscious act of promotion, it also creates the rhetorical problem that Abdelkebir Khatibi might call *dédoublement*, a splitting and fragmentation of public identity. Nonetheless, I argue, Idir and Djura play ably on universalist representations of North African immigrants in France—the men as violent toward and oppressive of women, the women as either victims or complicit aggressors toward other women—in order to call these representations into question. But by introducing their music to a wide audience through written texts, these artists offer an alternative vision of French universalism—an act of 'covering,' or reinterpreting French universalism, much like one interprets a song in a cover version. The alter-globalist 'cover' expands the definition of *French* to include a range of languages and cultural practices.

The Performance of Listening in Postcolonial Francophone Culture thus asserts that in assessing identity and belonging, societies must to not only look—but listen. I have refrained from referring to listening as either a duty or an ethics; this is a cultural study, rather than a philosophical one. And yet, for the artists whose works comprise the listening corpus, the problem of how to be heard as a minority voice certainly can be seen as a philosophical issue that all of the cultural works here have not only considered, but to which they have offered an embodied response. Hence, while *The Performance of Listening in Postcolonial Francophone Culture* engages with scholarship in French and Francophone studies as well as performance and sound studies, the call to listen, as a cultural phenomenon, arises from the literary, cinematic, theatrical, and musical works themselves.

PART I

The Performance of Listening in Literary Narratives

CHAPTER TWO

Cut Sound

The Literary Staging of Silence

In the introduction to this work I touched on Tahar Ben Jelloun's *L'Hospitalité française*, which describes his experience as a psychologist working with immigrant patients in France. He explains the change in the patients when they realized that their interlocutor believed their accounts of phantom-like physical pain:

> Je remarquais que l'expression de leur visage changeait. Une lueur traversait leur regard. Ils n'étaient plus démunis dans le silence. Ils pouvaient bouger, se déplacer et parler de leur corps malade parce qu'un aucun cri n'en surgissait, aucune colère ne s'en dégageait. [...] La consultation était une sorte de vérification, une entorse au silence. (89–90)

> [I noticed that the expression on their faces changed. A light came into their eyes. They were no longer silent and helpless. They could move and walk about and talk of their bodies, which were ill from being unable to utter a cry or give vent to anger. (...) For them, a consultation was a kind of verification, a breaking of the silence. (59–60)]

Through this passage, it is evident that silence can be performed, not only by the speaker, but also by the listener. If the listener does not take seriously what they hear, in essence, the voice goes unheard in favor of different sounds (or narratives) privileged by the listener.

Ben Jelloun suggests that we have a moral duty to listen that is part and parcel to the moral duties to feed, clothe, and give shelter to our fellow human beings (13). However, as Ben Jelloun demonstrates throughout *L'Hospitalité française*, he listened to the voices of immigrants due to a range of motivations: professional, intellectual, political, and personal. What happens when such motivations to listen fall away? While it may seem an obvious point, it is important to make clear that silent, marginalized voices signal not an absence of voice, but the absence of a motive or desire to listen on the part of those who stand closer to the center.[1]

In two literary works that came out of the French feminist movement and early postcolonial social awareness, exposition rendered through reflections of the character, from whose point of view the scene takes place, 'interrupts' people speaking or thinking. In other words, in these passages, thought trumps voice. Silence is thus staged—and, interestingly, both Assia Djebar's novella 'Femmes d'Alger dans leur appartement' (1978) and, in a passage depicting band practice in a squat, Leïla Sebbar's novel *Shérazade: 17 ans, brune, frisée, les yeux verts* (1982) [*Sherazade: missing, aged 17, dark curly hair, green eyes*] make use of sound technology to help mix silence into the narrative.

The literary staging of silence emerges from the specific contexts in which these voices and silences are situated. In the case of 'Femmes d'Alger,' this situation is the conflict that arises from the utopian inversion of the Algerian voice over the French hegemony, in a case where both voices are also distinctly feminist. The ways in which feminism and postcolonial awareness complicate one another prove especially productive in considering questions of 'what next?' once a marginalized voice has asserted itself. In *Shérazade*, the silenced voice of the otherwise quite outspoken eponymous character is marked within the narrative by a surrogate, a concept I have adapted from Joseph Roach's work on rituals of mourning in New Orleans. In the scene from Sebbar's novel, when the brash Rachid, Shérazade's squat-mate and fellow *Beur*, steals her place as lead singer in band practice, his ensuing thoughts as he sings demonstrate lacunae in his knowledge of French history, as well as the voice of a Jewish ex-girlfriend. This passage in *Shérazade* thus complicates marginalized women's silences by drawing increasingly wider lines around the social space of the squat rehearsal, until both feminine and masculine *Beur* voices are silenced within broader French society.

The aim of this chapter is not to recuperate voices so much as to formulate a methodology of listening to literary silence—in other words, to be able to analyze *cut sound*. Texts represent sounds: voices, silences,

---

1   Throughout this reading, the *motive* to listen is foregrounded in social and rational explanations of why we should listen—we should listen, for example, due to professional or intellectual aims. The *desire* to listen is rooted in the subjective and the personal. In either case, the motives and desires to listen are unstable and fluid, depending on, for example, shifts in social climate or personal perspective.

music. As different kinds of sound are woven together in a literary text (in the same way that in recorded music, sounds and silences are woven together), some sounds are privileged over others. All voices are marked by gender, ethnicity, nationality, and the ways that these categories inform and change one another, through which the privilege to be heard is often constituted. This is a given in literary texts: not all sounds can be heard at the same time, and not all voices can be equally loud. The question here is what emerges when we listen for what has been lowered in the mix.

'No other way out': Assia Djebar's 'Femmes d'Alger dans leur appartement' (1978)

'Femmes d'Alger' is the eponymous novella in a collection of Djebar's stories and essays. In the afterword, 'Regard interdit, son coupé' ['Forbidden Gaze, Severed Sound'], Djebar offers a range of interpretations of the 'son coupé' of Algerian women's voices, a kaleidoscope of images and sounds structured through two historical narratives: one reads Delacroix's painting 'Femmes d'Alger' alongside Picasso's cubist interpretation of it, and finally puts the two paintings in dialogue with one another. The other narrative looks at the social role that Algerian women played near the battlefield during the 1830 French invasion of Algeria, then skips to the militant role that women played both under and liberated from the veil during the Algerian War. Finally, Djebar examines how the widespread rape of Algerian women during the revolution was used to silence women's voices once more in the revolution's aftermath.

While the term 'son coupé' has been translated as 'severed sound,' I believe that the term 'cut sound' is not only more apt, but a more precise translation, give the common French usage of the term. 'Couper le son' means to cut, or turn off, the sound of a radio, a PA system at a concert, and so on. Rendering 'son coupé' as 'cut sound' represents the common French understanding of the term more precisely. More importantly, by using this expression, it becomes clear that Djebar's work engages with the idea that silence is never literally silent: rather, there are always sounds, voices, and music that *go unheard*, often in favor of other privileged sounds, voices, musics.

Djebar begins with the argument that feminine cut sound is a social construct: in Delacroix's painting, 'flotte donc, entre ces femmes d'Alger et nous, l'interdit. Neutre, anonyme, omniprésent' (244) ['What floats between these Algerian women and ourselves, then, is the forbidden. Neutral, anonymous, omnipresent' (137)]. Delacroix had been snuck into the harem (the apartment) in order to sketch and then paint the Algerian women. As a rule, harems are *haram*, forbidden to men (as opposed to *halal*, permissible). It is not merely the space that is forbidden to Delacroix but, more importantly, Djebar suggests, the gaze between men and Algerian women that is forbidden. Thus cut sound is represented by women's absence (both in body and voice) in public space and discourse. Here, then, the use of 'appartement' in Djebar's work becomes clear: 'appartement' resituates private space, since a harem is not *haram* to women. The term 'appartement' thus maintains the notion that women are separate from men, but offers the possibility of women's subjective experience within the space forbidden to men, which neither *haram* nor harem as social constructs allow.

It follows, then, that cut sound—the presence of sound rendered through structured absence—can be also represented through the veil. Djebar describes veiled women's furtive glances at men in cafés and Medinas: 'le fantôme blanc passe irréel mais énigmatique' (245) ['the white phantom, real but enigmatic, passes through' (138)]. Notably, the veil does not prevent the feminine gaze. Rather, it *hides* what Djebar calls the feminine eye, and the other eyes of the female body, including the breasts, the sex, and the navel. The veil bars women's many eyes from public view. In this explanation of cut sound, sensual forms of feminine expression are excised from public view—and, by extension, public discourse.

Yet modernity offers no means of recuperating cut sound. Djebar continues by describing the particular cut sound of modern, 'self-emancipating' young women as a movement away from the traditional:

> L'éloignement revient à déplacer le lieu de son mutisme: elle troque la gynécée et la communauté ancienne contre un face-à-face souvent fallacieux avec l'homme [...] Soudain la réalité présente se dévoile sans fards, sans passéisme: le son est vraiment coupé. (258–259)

> [The distancing amounts to shifting the location of her muteness: she exchanges the women's quarters and the old community for an often deceptive one-on-one with the man (...) And just as suddenly, the reality of the present shows itself without camouflage, without any addiction to the past: sound has truly been cut. (148)]

What Djebar points to as 'shifting the location' encapsulates two things: first, the cutting of sound (represented by the gaze) through both the harem and the veil while in the women's quarters and, second, the impossibility of articulating that experience once outside of it. This kind of cut sound cannot be reconstructed.

In a final explanation of cut sound, Djebar's reading of Delacroix's painting continues: she describes 'deux des femmes comme surprises à converser, mais leur silence ne finit pas de nous parvenir' (253) ['two of the women as if surprised in their conversation, but their silence has not stopped reaching us' (144–145)]. Djebar reaches an impasse between subaltern speaker and dominant listener in this description of cut sound. The notion that silence is sound that never stops reaching for a listener presages Spivak's formulation of silence as 'what the work *cannot* say' in 'Can the Subaltern Speak?' (285–286). If we use Djebar's description of Delacroix's painting as an example, what is lacking is neither sound source nor listener. The problem in this case is that the space between the two is impassable, *haram*. The sound of women's voices is cut by the oppression of women, which takes shape through the harem as a space forbidden to men. In the context of the intellectual and his subaltern subject, Spivak writes: 'The problem is that the subject's itinerary has not been traced so as to offer an object of seduction to the representing intellectual' (285). In this case, there is nothing offered to the intellectual that would lead to a motive (or desire) to listen (or read) for the traces of the subaltern subject's itinerary. Thus, to follow Djebar's explanation of the harem in Delacroix's painting as a site of cut sound, visual entrance into the harem satisfies forbidden desire. Without further desire, the women's voices continue to reach, and yet perpetually go unheard. Throughout the essay, Djebar suggests that women's voices are cut under the veil too.

In other words, Djebar's cut sound is not lost in the drafts or the sketches, for although the sounds of women's voices have always been present, they have never been recognized as being there in the first place. Cut sound cannot be located in the negative of an image, or in the silence that surrounds other sounds. Rather, cut sound always exists elsewhere; yet, as Djebar writes, it is also neutral, anonymous, and omnipresent.

As is the case with most of Djebar's œuvre, one of the central concerns in 'Femmes d'Alger' is the representation of women's voices, particularly those of Algerian women in the aftermath of the revolution, in this case through feminine silence. Listening to Algerian women's voices is one of the overarching aims and themes of Assia Djebar's œuvre. Yet it is from women's silence that Djebar takes her most frequent point of departure, for it is from silence that voices can—and perhaps must—originate. In her introductory statements on Djebar's work, Mireille Calle-Gruber describes the silence in her œuvre:

> Silence. Mais tissé de rumeurs, de bruits, voix et chuchotements. C'est depuis le silence qu'il faut tenter de lire et relier les récits d'Assia Djebar: ils enseignent l'écoute. (7)

> [Silence. But woven from murmurs, noises, voices, and whispers. It is from the silence that we've needed to try to read and make connections between Assia Djebar's stories: they teach us to listen. (my trans.)]

Born in Algeria of Arab and Berber parentage, Djebar was educated in France and was widely lauded in France and the United States throughout her career as a writer. She is considered a champion of breaking Algerian women's silence through literature and film, and writing in French has been her most critically acclaimed means to this end. Djebar became a member of the Académie Française in June 2006, which secured her both recognition and honor as a writer in French and as a voice for Algerian women in France. Since her death in February 2015, she has become even more widely recognized and celebrated in France, by, for example, an episode of the France Culture podcast 'Une vie, une œuvre' in February 2016.

Yet Djebar's work is not without its critics within feminist circles. In *The Eloquence of Silence: Algerian Women in Question* (1994), sociologist Marnia Lazreg derides Djebar's first novel, *La Soif* (1957), for the fact that

> Djebar's character evolves out of space and time, oblivious to the constraints of the war. Perhaps this novel reflected the author's own sheltered and privileged life as the daughter of a well-to-do family who physically could blend easily into French society but could not erase her Algerian origins. (200)

As either discussed or alluded to in several critical analyses of Djebar's work (including Woodhull 1993, Hayes 2000, Donadey 2001, Elia 2001, Ringrose 2006, and Murray 2008), the French press proclaimed Djebar the Algerian Françoise Sagan when *La Soif* was published. This was due not only to her youth at the time she wrote the work but also the subject matter: women's exploration of sexuality. The novel came out in 1957, at the height of the Algerian War, and in Algeria she received ample (and unsurprising) criticism from Algerian nationalists for her focus on women's sexual liberation. The revolution, it was argued, was far more urgent. This anecdote serves as a springboard for many critical discussions of the embodied and/or historical and political nature of Djebar's writing on women's expression.

Lazreg's criticism is thus notable, coming as it does not from a nationalist rationale but a patently Algerian feminist one: Djebar's novel, Lazreg suggests, lacks the appropriate social and political context to properly treat its subject. Lazreg goes on to level a similar criticism at the collection *Femmes d'Alger dans leur appartement*, as written from a 'feminist perspective that is remarkable for its decontextualized, uncritical and abstract character' (201), particularly in 'Regard interdit, son coupé.' Lazreg also claims that the collection 'constitutes another way of silencing women, this time by a woman' (201). Here, finally, is the nail in the coffin of Lazreg's assessment: Djebar 'evince[s] strong signs of colonial nostalgia' in her work (202–203).

So why is it that, on one hand, Djebar has been canonized within French and Francophone literary studies as a voice representing Algerian women, and on the other, she is so severely criticized by an Algerian feminist sociologist whose object of inquiry is the social conditions for women in both women's country of origin? The following close reading of 'Femmes d'Alger' takes up Lazreg's concerns, and demonstrates that Djebar's text issues a call to listen to her readers. The interplay of voices and silences in this literary work gives silence narrative shape, and allows readers to trace further, unspoken concerns about the problem of representing silence.

In the following reading of Djebar's 'Femmes d'Alger,' I analyze silences that arise from the conflict between feminist aims and post-Algerian War struggles with French hegemony in order to listen for what falls into the background. And, just as in a pop song, what goes on in the silence often packs as much of a wallop as what readers can hear in the foreground.

The process of silencing in 'Femmes d'Alger' relates to the narrative interplay of the thoughts and actions of Sarah, an Algerian woman, with the dialogue of her Algerian husband, Ali; with her good friend, a French woman named Anne; and with Irma, a German woman who works as a technician in the audiovisual center lab where Sarah does her research. In my analyses of this work, I consider the intellectual motive to listen through the shifting dynamics of feminist and counterhegemonic aims within the text. Furthermore, I highlight the problematics of listening by analyzing textual moments in which Sarah's interlocutors speak. For although these characters talk to Sarah, their voices are literally written over by Sarah's thoughts frequently in the text. These particular representations of silence in 'Femmes d'Alger' demonstrate the social and political issues that extend beyond the assertion of marginal voices. It is never simply a matter of talking. It is a matter of who—if anyone—listens when one speaks.

In this way, Djebar's text shifts the burden of responsibility to break the silence from the speaker to the listener. For 'Femmes d'Alger' represents silence not as absence, but as a willful overwriting of the voice of a speaker on the part of the listener. It follows, then, that it is the responsibility of the listener to ensure that the speaker's voice is not silenced—and this leads us to the issue of motives and desires, which is the critical overture that gives shape to the narrative conclusion.

Through the shifting dynamics of Sarah's roles as speaker and listener, it becomes clear that silence never refers to the literal absence of sound or a literal aphasia in Djebar's work. Interestingly, Djebar represents silence in 'Femmes d'Alger' through characters for whom the issue of claiming one's voice seems to be less contested than it is for Sarah. Anne and Irma, Sarah's two female interlocutors, are European women. Their social identities seem uncomplicated in comparison, for Sarah embodies three social identities: she is a postcolonial woman; she is a survivor of torture during the Algerian War who seeks a way to articulate her experience; she is also an intellectual, an ethnomusicologist who researches the songs of subaltern Algerian women. Thus Sarah's role as both listener and speaker shifts depending on which facet of her identity takes the fore in any given situation.

In 'Femmes d'Alger,' when voices go unheard, or are spoken over or cut off, this is the result of Sarah as a listener imposing either distracted thoughts or a refusal to listen to the specificities of what Anne and Irma say. In reading for the silences, we can see how ellipses, dialogue tags, and thought interweave with—and at the same time, cut off the sound of—voices within the text. Interwoven in this way, the text embodies the act of silencing, thus making an implicit argument for the importance of listening. More importantly, this work offers measures of motives and desires to listen; how to gauge the absence of the motive or desire to listen; and how to recognize this absence as *not listening*, rather than a silent voice.

The problem of representing silence in 'Femmes d'Alger' is established in this way: the voices of the two European women, Anne and Irma, are assumed by Sarah to lack political or intellectual value. This is revealed through the interplay of Sarah's dialogue, thoughts, and actions, an interplay that is a part of women's expression through both voice and body that Djebar elaborates throughout the collection *Femmes d'Alger dans leur appartement*. As one of a large ensemble of critics who have made comments to this effect, Nada Elia writes that Djebar's 'writing, like that of many feminists, is a validation of sensual and intuitive knowledge, of a history passed down orally and through the body, for it is not to be found in textbooks' (1). This practice lends subversiveness to Djebar's writing in French: 'decentering, deterritorializing, and stripping [French] of its exclusive membership rights' (19).

As Sarah's radar shifts between feminist and counterhegemonic concerns, the narrative forecloses upon Anne and Irma's voices. Foreclosing upon these European women's voices points to an inherent contradiction in the recuperation of women's voices: when any voice speaks, it requires a listener to make it heard, regardless of the social power dynamics between speaker and listener. Djebar's text thus opens and renews the debate over the competing concerns of feminism versus the postcolonial recuperation of a national Algerian voice.

'Femmes d'Alger' opens on a workday morning. Following a nightmare that seems to be a traumatic memory of torture, Sarah has leapt from bed and busies herself in the kitchen, making breakfast for her husband Ali, a surgeon. The phone rings. It is Anne, imploring Sarah to come help her: 'Je ne suis pas bien … (suspens; Sarah appelle, chuchotant) … Pas bien du tout' (64) ['"I'm not well …" (suspense, Sarah calls, whispering) … "Not well at all"' (6)]. Without a word to Ali, who is exercising in the bedroom, Sarah leaves breakfast unprepared, puts on her shoes, takes the car keys, and leaves the house. Ali grumbles about his son as Sarah leaves, but his concerns are cut as the front door to the house closes: 'Et Nazim, toujours ailleurs? (derrière elle, la voix d'homme bougonne). On pourrait avoir besoin de lui ici, maintenant que …' (64) ['"And Nazim, still out?" (behind her the man's voice grumbles). "We might need him here, now that …"' (7)].

The structure of Anne's and Ali's dialogue and the dialogue tags are parallel to one another. But there are fundamental differences between the ways in which the two characters speak, and the ways that Sarah listens to them. In Anne's case, the first set of suspension points denotes that she has trailed off. The parenthetical aside that follows suggests that Sarah is listening intently and urges her to continue. Her second statement, 'not well at all,' underscores the first, and marks her request as urgent. By contrast, Ali's voice persists through the parenthetical aside and suspension points. It is for Sarah as a listener that the dialogue trails off into grumbling; Ali continues talking. The suspension points at the end of the dialogue represent the cut sound of his voice as 'la porte claque dans le courant d'air' (64) ['the door slams in the breeze' (7)], and Sarah drives to Anne's house.

As Sarah drives, she worries about her inability to listen:

> Est-ce seulement avec Ali, est-ce avec eux tous? ... Quand les autres me parlent, leurs mots sont détachés ... Ils flottent avant de me parvenir! ... Est-ce pareil quand je parle, si je parle? Ma voix ne les atteint pas. Elle reste intérieure. (64)

> [Is it only with Ali, is it with all of them? ... When others talk to me, their words aren't connected ... They float around before they reach me! ... Is it the same when I talk, if I talk? My voice doesn't reach them. It stays inside. (7)]

Sarah's fretful thoughts echo Ali's dialogue: the two questions frame an elaboration on Ali's dialogue as it becomes nonverbal grumbling. 'My voice doesn't reach them' parallels the second set of suspension points in Ali's dialogue, which marked his dialogue as interrupted by the door slamming in the breeze. Just as Ali's voice stayed inside the house, Sarah's voice stays inside her. Furthermore, this passage indicates that when given a choice between listening to a male voice and a female voice, Sarah will choose the woman's.

Given the privileging of feminine over masculine voices as a base assumption in the novella, the question becomes, *which* feminine voices should be privileged? Some character background will be helpful before I address the first scene between Sarah and Anne. Sarah survived imprisonment and torture in the Barberousse prison during the Algerian War, and at the time that 'Femmes d'Alger' takes place, she is working at a musicology institute on an Arabic-French translation of and a documentary project on *haoufis*, traditional women's songs from Tlemcen. Sara's friend Anne is a French woman living in Algiers who is either divorced or separated from her husband, with whom she has three children. The daughter of a magistrate, she spent her early childhood in Algeria before her father was transferred to another colony. She and Sarah had run into each other at Algiers airport, and rekindled the childhood friendship that ended when Anne's family moved. The women's respective testimonies bookend the narrative; several Algerian women's stories are interspersed, perhaps most famously the story of

Fatima, the masseuse from the Turkish bath whose story is related in a series of contrapuntal narratives.

When Sarah arrives at Anne's apartment, she realizes that Anne has taken an overdose of pills. She apologizes to Sarah as she vomits; Sarah sees herself in the mirror, 'debout: derrière la Française aux cheveux trop longs' (65) ['standing behind the Frenchwoman whose hair is too long' (7)]. Indeed, to read Sarah's thoughts, she has little sympathy for Anne: she snickers at the crisis, belittling it as 'Un coup de cafard! … un vrai mélo' (66) ['a fit of the blues … a real soap opera' (8)]. Telling Sarah that she realized that she has come to Algiers to die, Anne recounts '"son" histoire; le mari, les trois enfants, quinze années d'une vie étrangère contenue dans une heure de mots: est-ce banal? C'est banal' (66) ['"her" story; the husband, the three children, fifteen years of a strange life contained in one hour of words: Is it trite? It's trite' (8)]. Sarah's summary and dismissal of Anne's story keeps the reader from being able to hear the story in Anne's own words.

But Sarah's gestures contradict her dismissive thoughts: she cleans Anne's face after she vomits and reorganizes the cushions and mattress so that Anne can rest. After Anne relates her story, Sarah goes to open the curtains. It is clear that Sarah wants to appear empathetic to this female friend, even as she dismisses her story as trite. Anne breaks down, sobbing, 'Je ne supporte pas la lumière!' (67) ['I can't bear the light!' (9)]. In Sarah's physical response, it is hard to tell where Sarah ends and Anne begins: 'Sarah, de nouveau accroupie sur la natte, l'enlace, la berce en cadence, tandis qu'elle continue à se défaire, à se refaire dans une fatigue différente' (67) ['Sarah, once again crouched on the mat, takes her in her arms, rocks her rhythmically while she continues to come apart, to put herself back together in a different kind of weariness' (9)]. With the repeated use of subject and direct object pronouns, it is unclear whether it is Anne or Sarah who continues to come apart and put herself back together. And is it, like the cut sound of the modern, self-emancipated young woman, a different kind of weariness between the two women? Or is it that Sarah's weariness has changed in bearing witness to Anne's attempted suicide and breakdown? These questions go unanswered, perhaps intentionally, for the overt intention of this passage is to convey Sarah's feelings of disconnectedness from the people to whom she is closest, due to her own inability to speak. My voice stays inside, Sarah laments to herself, yet because of the narrative structure of this passage, the reader 'hears' more about Sarah than Anne: through Sarah's counterhegemonic critique of

Anne's story, Anne's agency as a speaker and the reader's agency as listener are obscured.

Sarah's sense of a disconnectedness between her thoughts, speech, and actions is viewed through the optic of Sarah-as-intellectual in the following passage at the musicology institute:

> Assise, elle manipula le magnétophone habituel, prépara les écouteurs, sortit de sa boîte un rouleau magnétique. Irma, l'ingénieur du son responsable du laboratoire, se mit à raconter avec volubilité le dernier week-end musulman qu'elle passait toujours avec son mari et ses trois garçons dans une petite ville conservatrice de l'intérieur du pays.
> [...]
> Sarah, par politesse, gardait les écouteurs sur les épaules. Elle profita du silence pour les mettre à ses oreilles. Elle s'excusa d'un geste du doigt et reprit l'étude des 'haoufis' de Tlemcen, chants des femmes d'autrefois.
>
> Près de l'appareil, elle disposa deux feuilles de couleur différentes. Sur papier rose, elle écrivit, nerveusement, ce qui l'habitait tous ces jours tandis qu'à pied ou en voiture, elle parcourait, l'air apparemment absent, les rues de la ville:
>
> 'Comment mettre en musique une ville entière'
> project de documentaire. (77–78)

> [Sitting down, she worked the usual tape recorder, got the headphones ready, took a tape out of its box. Irma, the sound engineer in charge of the laboratory, effusively began to recount the last Moslem weekend, which she always spent with her husband and three boys in an old-fashioned little town in the interior of the country. (...)
> Out of courtesy, Sarah kept the headphones on her shoulders. She took advantage of the silence to put them on her ears. With a motion of her finger she apologized and went back to studying the *haoufis* of Tlemcen, women's songs of times gone by.
>
> She put down two sheets of paper in different colors, near the machine. On pink paper, she wrote nervously what preoccupied her every day now while she ran around the streets of the city, whether by foot or by car, seemingly absentminded:
>
> How to put an entire city to music
> projected documentary. (16)]

In this passage, the relation between the motives of the listener and what is heard becomes clear. There are two sound sources in this passage: the tape recorder and Irma. In the excised paragraph, Irma describes new regulations for raising and slaughtering pigs, and laments the loss of independent farms.

As with her reaction to Anne's breakdown, if one reads only Sarah's affect and gestures in reaction to Irma's banter, she has carefully hidden her disdain for the banal details of the other woman's experience. In the third paragraph, there seems to be a shift in the locus of disconnectedness that concerned Sarah in the car on her way to Anne's. Where in the first passage Sarah seems to be reflecting upon Djebar's cut sound, in this passage, the preoccupation that leaves her seemingly absentminded in her day-to-day life is of an intellectual nature: how to represent a vocal subject that is difficult to trace, the women singing the *haoufis*.

As the passage in the musicology institute continues, Sarah listens to the *haoufis*, and the melodies conjure childhood memories as she translates the lyrics from Arabic into French. The sum of these narrative details offers a critique that contradicts the explicit goal to represent cut sound. Sarah's subject position (whether that of silenced woman or intellectual) is no longer clear. Is she struggling with her own voice, or is it that in her quest to trace the itinerary of the *haoufi* genre and her own childhood, she cannot be bothered with the voices of those around her?

Sarah's disconnection intensifies through the description of the way Irma speaks Arabic. Irma speaks in a too-thick German accent, which 'masqua la sollicitude du ton' (80) ['masked the concern in her voice' (18)] when she saw Sarah looking faint after she received a phone call about Nazim. The sense that Irma's concern is masked by her German accent presages the way that, in *L'Amour, la fantasia* (1985), Djebar would later describe her own emotional experience of a man whose native tongue was Arabic making advances in French: 'Lorsqu'un homme de ma langue d'origine pouvait, me parlant en français, se permettre une approche, les mots se transformaient en un masque que, dans les préliminaires du jeu esquissé, l'interlocuteur se résignait à prendre' (145–146) ['Whenever a man whose mother tongue was the same as mine ventured to make advances, speaking in French, his words formed a mask which the interlocutor had willy-nilly to adopt in the opening moves of the game' (128)].

As the passage weaves seamlessly back and forth between details that Sarah notices about Irma, her progressing thoughts on the *haoufi* project, and Sarah's memories, it becomes clear that the passage has been written over Irma's ongoing banter:

Une crise d'adolescence ..., concluait Irma qui avait dû dire plusieurs autres phrases, sans que Sarah levât la tête. Elle fixa Sarah de l'air gêné de ceux qui présentent leurs condoléances, reprit ses fiches arabes traduits puis sortit du laboratoire dignement. (82)

['... an adolescent crisis,' concluded Irma, who must have said several things without Sarah having raised her head. She stared at Sarah with the embarrassed look of those who come to offer their condolences, picked up her Arabic cards, now translated, then left the lab with dignity. (19–20)]

This passage at the musicology institute offers a different interpretation of the cut sounds of Ali's and Anne's voices, as well as Sarah's feelings of disconnectedness both from her own volition to speak and from the voices of others. Sarah's exchanges with Irma are experienced through very different barriers than the ones Djebar describes in 'Regard interdit, son coupé': Sarah muses over her work and childhood memories, and while Irma thinks that Sarah is about to faint when she receives the call about Nazim, the reader knows nothing of the content of that phone call, nor what Sarah's reaction was. Irma's voice, meanwhile, is masked—or cut off from Sarah—by her European accent. There is a further, if convenient, miscommunication here (more precisely, in French this would be called a *mésentente*, a misunderstanding that works to the advantage of both parties): Irma thinks that Sarah is distracted because she is worried about Nazim. This adds an additional layer to the intervention that Sarah's work at the musicology institute offers the reader: it is not clear whether she is distracted by trying to give voice to her past, or by her intellectual work.

Curiously, Sarah's intellectual work seems informed, if not entirely motivated, by the cut sound of her own voice. In the opening passage of the final chapter of 'Femmes d'Alger,' she begins to articulate her experience of prison during the revolution. Throughout the text, there are oblique references to her imprisonment: for example, Anne notices the black and blue torture scar on Sarah's abdomen when it is exposed in the Turkish bath. This variant on voice offers the ultimate embodied representation of cut sound: the torture scar is a corporeal gag that not only stifles her body's expressiveness, but also represents an attempt to force Anne to speak. In the opening nightmare sequence of the story, Ali dreams of Sarah being tortured. This opening sequence could be said to inform all of the passages in which Sarah cannot seem to listen to others, but it also offers a distraction from the more elusive unspoken point made by Djebar's novella about the tensions between feminist and counterhegemonic recuperations of silence.

In the opening passage of the final chapter, Sarah and Anne are back in Anne's apartment. Sarah smokes and paces nervously as she proclaims, 'Je ne vois pour nous aucune autre issue que par cette rencontre' (122) ['I see no other way out for us except through an encounter like this' (47)]. She goes on to describe the possibility of a verbal encounter between two women that parallels the moment when Sarah sat on the floor with Anne, rocking her:

> une femme qui parle devant une autre qui regarde, celle qui parle raconte-t-elle l'autre aux yeux dévorants, à la mémoire noire ou décrit-elle sa propre nuit, avec des mots torches et des bougies dont la cire fond trop vite? Celle qui regarde, est-ce à force d'écouter, d'écouter et de se rappeler qu'elle finit par se voir elle-même, avec son propre regard, sans voile enfin … (122)

> [a woman speaking in front of another one who's watching; does the one who's speaking tell the story of the other one with the devouring eyes, with the black memories, or is she describing her own dark night with words like torches and with candles whose wax melts too fast? She who watches, is it by means of listening, of listening and remembering that she ends up seeing herself, with her own eyes, unveiled at last … (47)]

Rather than the bodies and emotions of two women entwined, here is a description of the testimony and memory of two women interconnected. These two passages, interwoven through the parallel of voices and bodies, serve as the opposite ends of the sieve through which the rest of the story passes: Anne is amazed that only a few days have passed since it was she who 'avait déroulé en mots hâtifs sa propre vie' (126) ['had unraveled the story of her own life in a rush of words' (49)]. As their stories become unraveled, the disconnect Sarah describes is also undone. They work in inverse proportion to one another: it is in the unraveling that the speaker and listener become entwined.

The ways in which the two women's stories are revealed are mirror images, however. The cut sound of Anne's voice is part of her introduction to the narrative, while Sarah's voice assumes a central place in the narrative conclusion. This opening and closing of the sounds of voices is intrinsic to understanding how cut sound becomes part of the textual weave in 'Femmes d'Alger.' In the first scene depicting Anne and Sarah together, when Anne is mid-crisis, Anne unravels her story without any prompting from Sarah. Sarah reacts through gesture, comforting Anne as she cleans her face, straightens her room, and holds her while she weeps. Yet, as the reader knows, Sarah feels disconnected from Anne's voice. Anne's story is reduced to a four-line synopsis in the narrative, concluding with the critique that her story is trite. In Sarah's case, Anne prompts her to talk, asking for the first time about her imprisonment. Sarah's story unravels, first through the story of the day she was told that her mother had died while she was in prison. Incarcerated and unable to mourn, Sarah reflected on her mother's life. The story she tells Anne over the course of a multi-page monologue is primarily concerned with her mother's entrapment in her marriage, her subservience to Sarah's father, and the shadows in which she lived her life. As Sarah tells her story, Anne sits still, and listens; nothing about her own thoughts is revealed.

Over the course of her monologue, Sarah elaborates on women's imprisonment in everyday life, a variation on the primary theme of 'Regard interdit, son coupé.' Sarah reflects on the generations of women who came before her, and then turns to the continued silence of women in the aftermath of the revolution, exclaiming, 'Oh mon Dieu! ... Quel nouveau, quel offensif harem! (elle cria) justement sans "haram," sans interdit! Au nom de qui? Au nom de quoi?' (128) ['Oh, my God! ... What a new, offensive harem! (she cried out), precisely without *haram*, without taboo. In the name of whom? In the name of what?' (50)]. Notably, it is through the absence of Anne's thoughts in the narrative that Sarah reconnects with her own voice. It is not clear in the novella's conclusion whether this attenuated the disconnection Sarah felt between herself and the broader world. But it is an example of what Sarah seems to have been trying to articulate from the first pages of 'Femmes d'Alger': for the voice to come out, for words to be connected, the listener needs to be engaged as much as the speaker, and feel as implicated in what the speaker is saying as the speaker is—and thus committed to social change for both the speaking woman in particular and silenced women in general. Although Djebar chose not to reveal Anne's thoughts explicitly, given the way the two passages in which the women tell their stories mirror one another, there is the implication that Anne's thoughts were focused on Sarah's story—not her own critique of that story as banal.

It is difficult (and sometimes impossible) for Sarah to listen to those around her in the committed way she advocates at the end of the novella. Take the case of Anne, who was voluble from the start, vomiting, too-long hair hanging in the way, weeping, gesticulating, and above all talking—for an hour. If Sarah's story in the final chapter is a transcription, she wrapped up what she felt she needed to say in far less time. Yet we know very little of Anne's story: indeed, Sarah seemed to cut the sound of Anne's voice, rather than listening in the way she later advocates. Sarah does not watch, listen, and remember in such a way that she ends up seeing herself. The narrative writes off Anne's story as trite, and both mocks its familiar details and distances Sarah from it through the use of quotation marks ('her' story).

Certainly, Sarah struggles with the fact that she feels disconnected from Anne's story. As with Irma, Sarah's gestures and movements are suggestive of one who is listening, who is sympathetic. Sarah represents one possible mode of engagement, but it is not through the committed kind of listening that Sarah herself suggests is necessary if women's voices are to find their way out from inside. Anne's voice is cut in the narrative by Sarah's struggle to listen to what European women have to say about their lives.

Through its theorization of how women's voices can resonate from silence, 'Femmes d'Alger' offers an unspoken radical break from utopist feminist discourse on dialogical power struggles. Sarah, who seeks to trace her own itinerary through intellectual and political pursuits, can neither listen in the way she insists is necessary to break outside of the anonymous, neutral, and omnipresent *haram*, nor can she say that there is the motive to listen to the other—in this case, Anne. *I don't wanna hear it*, Sarah effectively moans to herself as Anne tearfully reconstructs the story of her marriage. Sarah cannot articulate a certain paradox in the imperative that oppressed women speak: to listen to the other speak might be politically or intellectually motivated, but it is not a desire. To listen to the other can be a struggle, and takes effort. If one is tired or distracted, as Sarah often is in 'Femmes d'Alger,' listening in the way she describes as 'the only way out' is impossible.

Through the cut sound of Anne's story, cut off by the narrative synopsis and Sarah's dismissal of the story as trite, an unspoken axiom emerges: listening is not easy for any of us. Women fare no better than men, the colonized no better than the colonizer, in this regard. Djebar's solution to the question of silence may be an optimist one, but it resists utopian conclusions through serious complications. By reversing the listener/speaker power dynamic as the colonized woman listens to the colonizing woman first, a question emerges in 'Femmes d'Alger' that can be traced in the silence of what this novella cannot say: without a motive to listen to the other, who will? Will we? In this way, Djebar's novella evades a simplistic utopia. Instead, 'Femmes d'Alger' presents the reader with further questions to consider what we mean when we talk about the act of silencing, and the state of being silenced.

'en rocker, en teddy-boy, en rebels':
Cut Sound and Literary Surrogacy

Leïla Sebbar's *Shérazade: 17 ans, brune, frisée, les yeux verts* (1982) tells the story of Shérazade, the French daughter of Algerian immigrants. She is a teenage runaway who lives in a squat near the Barbès neighborhood north of Paris's right bank. She comes home one day to find her squat-mates Krim, Basile, and Pierrot about to start band practice. They ask Shérazade to sing, and her improvisations over their playing impress them. They say they want to hire her for their next gig, and Pierrot suggests that she take some free voice lessons at the municipal center. It is at that moment that Rachid, another squat-mate who is also *Beur*, like Shérazade, bursts into the room and takes over as singer.

In 'Femmes d'Alger' the characters of Sarah and Anne embody the conflict between feminist aims and postcolonial counterhegemony. In the squat band rehearsal scene in *Shérazade*, the corporal difference is gendered, and both feminine and masculine *Beur* voices are silenced through different intersections of gender and ethnic identity in broader French society. At first, it might appear that Rachid unceremoniously silences Shérazade, and that no one questions this (both characters are Kabyle and *Beur*). Yet, as the social context is broadened in the passage from the squat rehearsal to rock culture in France and into Rachid's meditation on French historical memory, it becomes clear that, depending on how broadly the social circle is drawn, both characters are effectively silenced due to their marginalized status as *Beur*.

Where 'Femmes d'Alger' offers an embodied bridge between the women's respective Algerian and French identities, in *Shérazade* the eponymous character is situated in Paris, at the center of the French metropole, yet she is also searching for a path to pursue an identity quest: she spends much of the novel scheming and in consternation about whether or not to leave Paris in order to go find her roots in Algeria. Rachid, meanwhile, seems less concerned with his Algerian roots than with finding some place in French society and culture. His concerns are woven into his rehearsal performance: as he sings, a stream-of-consciousness narrative of his thoughts leads him from music genres to Nazi punks to a Jewish ex-girlfriend who questions his involvement with the punks, to the connections Rachid sees between the Holocaust and the Algerian War due to the gaps in his knowledge about both historical events.

Of particular interest to me in the squat band practice passage is the way in which silenced voices are represented by surrogates. Joseph Roach's theorization of surrogates that stand in effigy for the dead in order to reproduce collective memory proves helpful in this second formulation of cut sound:

> Culture reproduces and re-creates itself by a process that can be best described by the word *surrogation*. In the life of a community, the process of surrogation does not begin or end but continues as actual or perceived vacancies occur in the network of relations that constitutes the social fabric. Into the cavities created by loss through death or other forms of departure, I hypothesize, survivors attempt to fit satisfactory alternates. Because collective memory works selectively, imaginatively, and often perversely, surrogation rarely if ever succeeds. (2)

Surrogation in the squat rehearsal scene of *Shérazade* functions to fill vacancies left by marginalized voices that have been silenced by dominant social narratives. In the passage, surrogation plays out in the following way: Shérazade is the first to sing, and the band is excited about her vocal improvisations. Rachid interrupts, and without any explanation or apology, takes Shérazade's place as singer. Shérazade falls uncharacteristically silent. In the Kabyle immigrant community, of which Shérazade and Rachid are both part, Rachid's vocal performance represents a surrogate for Shérazade's voice, an unceremoniously silenced Kabyle woman's voice. Within Rachid's stream-of-conscious narrative, however, it becomes clear that when the Kabyle immigrant community is considered within the broader fabric of French culture, Rachid's voice is also silenced. This is in evidence also in the fact that Rachid imitates other performers, rather than offering his own interpretation or style. It is the voice of conscience of Rachid's Jewish ex-girlfriend within the stream-of-consciousness narrative that serves as a surrogate for Rachid's silence.

In sum, what I demonstrate in the following reading is that surrogates can mark cut sound (in other words, silenced voices) within literary narratives. As Roach notes, surrogation does not work to recover these voices. The surrogate fills the vacancy left by the silenced voice, in this way marking a narrative with the silenced voice even if it is no longer literally present within the text. In marking the silences in a text, there remains, nonetheless, the possibility for marginalized voices to be heard, since the narrative space is occupied by the surrogate in order to fill the space that was voided by a voice that was present, and then silenced.

In the squat rehearsal scene, Shérazade's silence is constituted through the absence of her usual brash outspokenness. In the shift from Shérazade to Rachid as singer, Shérazade's silence in this passage is *marked* in the particular sense that Cixous gives to women's silence in 'The Laugh of the Medusa.'[2] That these silences are marked as feminine has specific implications for not only Shérazade's silence, but Rachid's silence as well.

Typically, Shérazade is not one to go quietly under any circumstances. She flies into a rage when, upon moving into the squat, Pierrot asks her for identity papers. She is attacked by pimps on rue St-Denis, and as she angrily describes the attack to Krim, Basile, and Pierrot, one of them asks her, 'Et qu'est-ce que tu foutais dans cette rue? C'est pas ta place' ['And what the hell were you doing there? That street's no place for you']. She replies, 'Je vais où je veux, quand je veux et ma place c'est partout' (88) ['I go where I want to, when I want to, and my place is everywhere' (92)]. When Shérazade and her friends Zouzou and France launch a guerrilla attack on a porn photographer who is about to do a soft-core shoot of the three girls in jungle garb, it is Shérazade who speaks for the group:

> Il y en a un sur les trois qui est chargé. C'est comme la roulette russe vous connaissez? On va tout foutre en l'air et on se tire. Si vous ouvrez votre gueule on porte plainte pour incitation à la prostitution [...] On a des preuves. On vous connaît. D'ailleurs je me demande si on devrait pas vous descendre comme un chien. (155–156)

> [One of the three (guns) is loaded. It's like Russian Roulette, you know what that is? We're going to screw up the whole show and scram. If you shoot your mouth off we'll bring a charge against you for inciting to prostitution (...) We've got proof. You're well-known. Besides, I'm wondering if we shouldn't just shoot you like a dog. (167)]

As Dorothy S. Blair writes of the eponymous protagonist in the introduction to her English translation of *Shérazade*, 'she is wayward, insolent, impulsive, exploitative, fearless and totally amoral.' Hayes argues further that 'She is [...] a model of feminist subjectivity and the embodiment of feminist resistance [...] the paradigm of an urban

---

2   Cixous writes: 'il y a des écritures marquées [...] où la femme n'a jamais eu *sa* parole, ceci étant d'autant plus grave et impardonnable que justement l'écriture *est la possibilité même du changement*, l'espace d'où peut s'élancer une pensée subversive, le mouvement avant-coureur d'une transformation des structures sociales et culturelles' (42) ['there is such a thing as *marked* writing [...] where woman has never *her* turn to speak—this being all the more serious and unpardonable in that writing is precisely *the very possibility of change*, the space that can serve as a springboard for subversive thought, the precursory movement of a transformation of social and cultural structures' (879)].

feminist guerrilla in *la lutte des sexes* as well as the struggle against racism in France' (215). It is thus notable that Shérazade says absolutely nothing when Rachid bursts into the practice space and takes over, and Basile, Krim, and Pierrot play as his backing band without a word. Singing with the band could have been an opportunity for Shérazade to give voice to the poetry she writes in secret. While Rachid's performance certainly doesn't preclude future rehearsals, he unceremoniously steals her thunder in the rehearsal passage.

Given Shérazade's confrontational reactions in social situations, her quiet disappearance from the passage following Rachid's abrupt entrance is most certainly marked as an uncharacteristic silence, and this uncharacteristic silence is situated in the text in the following way. Shérazade's silent disappearance from the rehearsal passage offers a notable silence in which she never has her turn to speak through song. Shérazade has a chance to sing, it is true: the narrative suggests that this comes to pass casually following a typical series of sassy quips between the four squat-mates about black women from Africa and Martinique:

> Basile fit un large geste pour signifier n'en parlons pas et ils se mirent tous les trois à leurs instruments. Krim dit à Shérazade de chanter. Shérazade improvisa. Elle avait une belle voix et les copains lui promirent de l'engager pour leur prochain concert. (162)

> [Basile made a vague gesture indicating don't let's talk about that and all three began playing. Krim told Shérazade to sing. Shérazade improvised. She had a good voice and the squatters promised to engage her for their next gig. (174)]

Given how casually this happens and the fact that there is no mention beforehand in the text that Shérazade is a singer or has any vocal training, her improvisation seems more of a caprice than a conscious attempt at creating extemporaneous music or lyrics. Nevertheless, the band is clearly excited by what they hear since they promise to bring her on for their next show.

That Shérazade is seriously considering the possibility of singing can be extracted from her response to Pierrot's advice, 'En attendant … tu devrais prendre des cours de chant' ['Meanwhile … you ought to take singing lessons'] to which she replies, 'Où ça?' (162) ['Where?' (174)]. This is atypical of any exchange between Pierrot and Shérazade in which Pierrot tries to give Shérazade advice. (For example, in an earlier passage, Pierrot tells her that he thinks she looks like a tart in red stilettos and black fishnets, and she retorts, 'Bien sûr un vieux militant comme toi, c'est sérieux' (36) ['You would, wouldn't you, a square old militant like you' (35)]. The re-emergence of her voice at the end of the squat rehearsal scene, which I will address in the conclusion, is also a case in point.) That Shérazade only asks him where to go for voice lessons suggests that she is taking their praise and promise seriously. Finally, the fact that she never sings again in the novel suggests that we can mark her singing as cut, and the cut sound of her voice is marked by Rachid as singer-surrogate.

Why have I been insisting upon the significance of Shérazade's fleeting stint as a singer in this passage? Consider the use of cameras and the literary lens that is trained upon Shérazade throughout Sebbar's trilogy: Julien spies on her throughout the early chapters of *Shérazade* before he is able to convince her to hang out with him. He tries, to Shérazade's ambivalence, to exoticize her by comparing her to the odalisques in Delacroix's paintings. When Shérazade is attacked by pimps on rue St-Denis, they threaten to force her to work in a peep show. In the passage with the porn photographer, she wields a gun (and, as I've pointed out, her voice) to render him powerless. In the second volume of the trilogy, *Les Carnets de Shérazade*, the French truck driver Gilles 'remembers colonial postcards to imagine Shérazade dead' (Hayes 226). Finally, in the third novel, *Le Fou de Shérazade*, film crews await her return to the H.L.M. because she has been cast as the star in Julien's film but, as her family and entourage in France learn in bits and pieces through photographs of Shérazade printed in the newspapers, she is being held hostage in Lebanon.

Her brief stint as a singer in practice thus offers the tantalizing possibility for another sort of utopian subversion: had Shérazade pursued this path as singer, she would have subverted the privileging of her image through the use of her voice. Had she chosen this path, the trilogy would have told a very different story. Shérazade's aim in this first novel is to get to Algeria on her own, not to become a riot grrl prototype.[3] Had the

---

3   The argument could be made that Shérazade embodies the 1990s riot grrl spirit, while Rachid's posturing could be said to presage hipster culture of the 2000s. These two comparisons follow a social logic: while feminism was the *raison d'être* for riot grrl culture, Rachid's aggressively apolitical stance seen in this passage seems like a harbinger of the hipsterism that rose in the US under the presidency of George W. Bush. At times, hipster culture is understood as a protective shell against world events of such a horrifying and grand scale that one cannot grapple with them, much as we will see in Rachid's attempt to dismiss considerations of the Holocaust and the Algerian War.

narrative pursued the possibility of success through finding a voice as a singer, the conclusion might have been utopian or prescriptive, and the tense narrative thread of Shérazade's search for her identity might have changed course: as a singer with a platform, she would have remained in Paris. Instead, the text introduces us to her singing voice as one of many possibilities set aside in favor of the journey upon which she embarks at the end of *Shérazade*.

Rachid's voice, which is distinctly *Beur* and masculine, serves as a surrogate for Shérazade's cut sound: feminine *Beur* silence. As the passage progresses, however, Rachid's voice is silenced, too, requiring another surrogate (this time a Jewish, feminine voice of conscience) to mark his silence. There is the question, first, of whether we ever hear Rachid's real voice in the text. Krim, Basile, and Pierrot never take Rachid seriously as a singer, but rather as a performer: after he sings, Basile says, 'Tu devrais t'engager dans un café-théâtre ... C'est des petits théâtres où on fait des sketches, des imitations' (164–165) ['You ought to get taken on in café-theatre ... They're little theaters where they put on sketches, improvisations' (177)]. The other squat-mates, the second-generation Polish immigrant Pierrot, the Guadeloupian Basile, and the *Beur* Krim, listen as a band. As a band, their social differences are leveled, and they can appreciate Shérazade's singing. *Beur* man to woman, however, Rachid is having none of Shérazade's singing. Or perhaps he is simply oblivious to it.

This narrative detail opens to a specific context of social tension through the *Beur* community, and through which Shérazade's silence might be read. A memoir such as Kabyle feminist singer-songwriter Djura's *Le voile du silence* (1991), which I discuss in Chapter 5, suggests that Kabyle women's voices are often silenced by men of the same origins, while French men can be seen as champions of women's voices. Yet, as one among many other scholars, anthropologist Miriam Ticktin points out, 'Algerian men are depicted in the French public imaginary as violent and deceitful, and oppressive to women' (185). Notably, this passage from *Shérazade* cannot be pinned down as one or the other.

Indeed, what is particularly interesting about the passage in which Rachid sings is that the silence goes unremarked upon in the text: it neither diagnoses nor vindicates. It simply suggests the possibility of a gendered tension as Rachid takes over as singer and Shérazade's silence passes unnoticed. This is in direct contrast to Djebar's 'Femmes d'Alger,' throughout which silences are registered and analyzed, and the very denouement comes through the possibility of finding a solution, a way out of women's silence that crosses national lines between Algeria and France. Intellectual and political motives on the part of the characters and Djebar's readers are assumed in the way the text is framed by 'Regard interdit, son coupé.' *Shérazade*, instead, contextualizes feminine and masculine *Beur* silences through the desires to listen and to be heard, through both the scope of the *Beur* community and the writing of history in the turn to broader French society. Furthermore, Rachid also performs in readerly silence. His voice is written over by his consideration of recent French history through what he does not know. Rock culture and the shared knowledge of musical gear with other men replace the lacunae in his historical knowledge.

How, then, does the shift from Shérazade to Rachid as singer mark silence? As a performer, Rachid can be read as a particular kind of surrogate to the historical absence of women's voices, and Shérazade's voice in particular. Meanwhile, the way he fills the gaps in his French historical knowledge with rock history and music tech talk constitutes a kind of double surrogation. Rachid's thoughts during his performance serve as a surrogate for women's silence by measuring those silences through history—while, in turn, measuring Rachid's own silence through musical knowledge, which acts as a surrogate for his place in French social history.

Marginality is a crucial aspect of Rachid's stream-of-conscious thinking as both surrogate for women's silence and the double surrogation of *Beur* voices, both masculine and feminine.[4] The focus on Shérazade as a surprisingly good singer, and Rachid's abrupt interruption followed by Shérazade's silence before, during, and after his performance, cues his thoughts as veering between center and periphery. Rachid bursts into the room, in a foul mood and alone, without his hairdresser girlfriend, Véro. He seems to be offering a corrective to Shérazade's improvisation as he keys the rehearsal to a rock genre that had recently emerged in France at the time this novel was published in 1982: 'Alors, les Beurs on singe *Carte de Séjour*? Il vous faut un chanteur arabe. Moi je chante; je sais pas très bien l'arabe, je suis kabyle, mais je peux faire un mélange ...

---

4 Roach writes: 'In the creative scope of liminal categories, periphery and center may seem to change places. What results is a contradictory push and pull [...] as communities construct themselves by both expanding their boundaries and working back in from them. They pull back by excluding or subordinating the peoples those larger boundaries ostensibly embrace. Such contradictory intentions remain tolerable because the myth of coherence at the center requires a constantly visible yet constantly receding perimeter of difference' (39).

Tout le monde sera content. On y va?' (163) ['Right, you Beurs, shall we do a take-off of *Carte de séjour*? You need an Arab singer. I can sing; I don't know much Arabic, I'm a Kabyle, but I can do a mixture ... That'll satisfy everyone. Shall we try?' (175)]. Carte de séjour, a band from Lyon, was at the forefront of *Beur* music from its inception in the 1980s, and launched the career of its singer and founder, Rachid Taha. The term *Beur* here refers not only to the children of immigrants in France who comprised *Beur* bands, but also to the particular mixing of musical genres that defines *Beur* music.[5]

Interestingly, the only actual noise from the performance that is represented in the text is 'on y va' (translated by Blair as 'shall we try?'), the French equivalent of an Anglophone rock singer saying, 'Let's go!' before counting off. Rachid suggests that he will mix Arabic and Kabyle, but in the performance that follows, he imitates European and American rock singers: 'Il connaissait tout sur le rock, les groupes anglais, américains, français' (163) ['There was nothing he didn't know about rock, all the English, American, French groups' (175)]. As he sings, he meditates upon his lack of historical knowledge through a surfeit of rock n' roll culture. This keys his performance as both surrogation and double surrogation—in this passage, around and through which historical narrative as center and *Beur* men's and women's voices in its margins can circulate:

Il avait fait partie de bandes de loubards et s'était successivement habillé en rocker, en teddy-boy, en rebels [...] Rachid avait connu des bandes auxquelles il ne s'était pas intégré—les Hells—à Crimée, Créteil ... Il les rencontrait souvent mais leur crâne rasé et les insignes S.S. qu'ils affichaient lui déplaisaient. Il avait eu une petite amie juive qui lui avait reproché son intérêt pour des bandes qui reprenaient à leur compte, même si comme certains le prétendaient, c'était pour s'en moquer, les emblèmes du nazisme. Il l'avait écoutée. Elle parlait souvent de ces histoires des juifs et de Hitler, il avait vu ça à la télé, *Holocauste*, ça s'appelait [...] Il pensa à la guerre d'Algérie dont il ne savait rien parce que personne ne lui en avait jamais parlé, ni son père, ni sa mère, ni les familles chez qui il avait été placé, ni les assistantes sociales, ni les éducateurs des foyers où il

5 In this passage, Rachid distinguishes himself linguistically from Arabic-speaking *Beurs* and thus informs the reader that he is of Kabyle, rather than of Arab, extraction. Although the term *Beur* is *verlan* slang for *arabe*, the term commonly refers not only to second-generation immigrants of Arab extraction, but to those of North African extraction more generally, thus including Berbers and Kabyles.

était passé. Son amie juive l'avait quitté parce qu'elle en avait marre d'être traînée dans ses bandes de rockers où ils parlaient toujours de la même chose, les fringues, les boutiques pour les insignes, les badges, les groupes rocks elle connaissait tout ça par cœur: Gene Vincent, Eddie Cochran, toujours Presley, Matchbox, Crazy Cavan, Chuck Berry, Stray Cats ... Ces fans de Rockabilly, et du rock n' roll qui parlaient de révolte et de violence, mais qu'elle voyait plus inquiets de la laque pour leurs cheveux et de ce qui manquait à leur panoplie. (163)

[He'd been a member of gangs of young hoodlums, dressing successively as rocker, teddy-boy, weatherman (...) Rachid had known gangs he'd never belonged to—Hell's Angels—in the suburbs of Crimée, Créteil. He often bumped into them, but he didn't like their skinheads and the SS badges they flaunted. He'd had a Jewish girlfriend who'd reproached him for his interest in gangs that adopted Nazi badges, even if, as some of them claimed, it was just for a joke. He'd taken notice of what she'd said. She often talked about what happened to the Jews and about Hitler, he'd seen it on the telly, *Holocaust* it was called. (...) He thought of the Algerian War that he knew nothing about as nobody had ever talked to him about it, neither his father, nor his mother, nor the foster families he'd been put with, not the staff at the various homes he'd been in. His Jewish girlfriend had left him as she was sick of being dragged into his gangs of rockers where they never talked of anything but gear, shops where you could buy badges, rock groups, she knew all that by heart: Gene Vincent, Eddie Cochran, everlasting Elvis, Matchbox, Crazy Cavan, Chuck Berry, Stray Cats ... Rockabilly fans, rock n' roll fans who talked about revolt and violence but who were more worried about the lacquer for their hair and things they needed for their gear. (175–176)]

First, Rachid's thoughts reveal new knowledge to the reader: he has been in and out of foster care and homes. Elsewhere in the novel, we learn that he was born to a Kabyle mother and a father of unmentioned origins (in a suggestion of his class origins, Rachid notes at one point that his father worked at an auto plant in Lyon, similar to Shérazade's and Krim's fathers, who work at the Citroën plant in Aulnay-sous-Bois). In this passage, however, the gaps in his historical knowledge are filtered specifically through these details about his past. And he is, like Shérazade, living in the squat. Thus the fact that this is a shift from female to male *Beur* singer is further complicated: within French society, Rachid is a similarly marginal figure to Shérazade. They are not only *Beur*, but Kabyle; they are also runaways, and they live in an illegal squat.

Despite their similar social status, because of his distinctly masculine identity within the Kabyle community, Rachid's performance serves as a surrogate for Shérazade's silence. Throughout the novel, Shérazade's thoughts on her place in French society as both a woman and a *Beur* are interwoven with her actions and dialogue. So there is a parallel established when Rachid takes the mic, but instead of a description of his singing, the reader learns his thoughts. With his meditation on music, French history, and his two girlfriends, Rachid's performance becomes a double surrogation of his own voice (a masculine, *Beur* voice) and Shérazade's (a feminine, *Beur* voice). Rachid's thoughts further reveal his own marginalized status. Finally, his privileging of music culture and Véro over French history and his Jewish ex-girlfriend resolves these absences in Rachid's life, rationalizing the position in which he finds himself during the moment when he sings. Embodying as he does the spirit of Carte de séjour (he sings in a mixture of Kabyle and Arabic, but imitates the singing styles he's learned from rock music), this passage is no simple reduction of masculine voice singing over the feminine. Rachid's voice as surrogate, and the double surrogation that takes place in his thoughts while he sings, are rendered through social and cultural layers that are simultaneously both gendered and ethnic.

Rather than representing music in the text, historical and political references are situated in the framework of rock culture. The restlessness and rebellion of rock gives way to contemplation about, first, the absence of the Algerian Revolution and, second, the vicissitudes of the Holocaust in French collective memory.[6] In Rachid's performance as surrogate for Shérazade's silence, he glides across a variegated sonic surface as a performer who skillfully integrates styles and techniques from different national musical traditions and subcultures in a transnational performance.

Meanwhile, hovering in the past is Rachid's Jewish ex-girlfriend who insisted upon the importance of preserving the historical memory of the Holocaust by contesting the appropriation of Nazi symbolism by a skinhead punk band. He listened to this ex-girlfriend; she remains

6   Throughout this reading of *Shérazade*, I have used the term 'French' to describe history as it relates to the Hexagon, specifically Vichy, the Shoah, and the Algerian War. I have used this term rather than 'French and Algerian' or 'European' to underscore the fact that Rachid's silence emerges not within the squat setting, but once he situates himself in a society that regards Paris as the center of the Metropole in the stream-of-consciousness passage: his experiences and knowledge are informed by his identity as young, male, and *Beur* within a universalizing society that levels social difference in favor of the somewhat messy and uncertain category of 'French,' which is to say, white, European, French-speaking, and male.

nameless, but Rachid's conversations with her sparked something. The meditation on Rachid's oblique understanding of the Holocaust gives way to thoughts on the Algerian War, but this leads to Rachid's reflections on his marginal social status. These references ultimately complicate this passage from *Shérazade* as a narrative that embodies social complexities and marginalized identities. It is through the Jewish ex-girlfriend's conscience, articulated in his stream-of-conscious narrative, that Rachid's silenced voice in French society is marked.

The musical gear motif adds an additional layer to the sociocultural complexities of this passage. Shared knowledge and the discussion of musical gear among Rachid and the 'bandes de rockers' gives form to the exclusion of women's voices. The Jewish ex-girlfriend expressed frustration to Rachid that gear talk is privileged over discussing the historical and social issues that have informed different rock cultures. This is an example of what Spivak might call the 'slippage from rendering visible the mechanism to rendering vocal the individual' (285). The talk that privileges musical gear over history constitutes a body of knowledge shared by Rachid and his entourage, part of Rachid's veering from center to periphery. His lack of knowledge is supplanted by a surfeit of knowledge shared among subversive musicians.

The ex-girlfriend, Rachid's meditation reveals, eventually left Rachid with a letter: 'une lettre gentille où elle lui expliquait qu'elle avait envie de regarder ailleurs. Il ne l'avait pas revue. Avec Véro, c'était facile. Elle était moins tourmentée' (164) ['She'd written to him quite nicely, explaining she wanted to look around a bit. He'd not seen her again. With Vero, it was easy. She didn't agonize so much' (176)]. 'Tourmentée,' or 'agonizing,' refers to the girlfriend speaking. This brings the passage back full circle to a variation on Shérazade's silence, for Rachid's critique of his ex's social and political engagement as 'agonizing' is also a form of silencing. However, it is significant that Rachid contemplates his ex-girlfriend in this passage. Were she absent, it would go without saying that her comments left no mark upon him—she would have been erased. Indeed, it is in her contrast with the ex-girlfriend that Véro is easy to live with. Véro is locked in constant battle with Rachid's funky fashion sense and hairstyles. Recall that Rachid's annoyance over Véro's criticisms was where his meditation opened before he turned to think about music, the ex-girlfriend, and French history. So there is a thematic revolution here: Rachid casts off his frustration at Véro as he begins performing, and this in turn leads him to think back to his other girlfriend by tracing his musical influences. Her 'dear John' letter can be read, then, with Rachid's regret. The letter is followed by Rachid's rationalization of Véro's presence in his life through his ex's 'agonizing.' The performative dimensions of Rachid's meditation as surrogation and double surrogation thus oscillate widely.

As a final point of elaboration, recall that Rachid's actual voice is absent from the narrative. It is true that the reader is given an idea of the style in which Rachid might be singing, compared to no description of Shérazade's improvisation. This is in part because Rachid has played with bands before—he is a performer. For Shérazade, this is all a possibility, but her singing was more a caprice than a preconceived act. But, aside from a list of the range of rock singers he might be imitating, we know nothing of how Rachid actually sounded. We know nothing of the range, tone, color, and other qualities of his particular voice— nor what language or languages he was actually singing. Thus we see again how the meditative surrogation of Rachid's performance in fact constitutes a double surrogation of both feminine and masculine *Beur* silences. Rachid cannot participate in what he does not know—in this case, French history. As a surrogate, then, we see the liminal place in which this performance takes place: his musical knowledge is the surrogate for his absent historical knowledge, but his meditation upon his marginalization—represented by his lack of historical knowledge— eclipses (as a double surrogate) his vocal performance, which is a demonstration of his musical knowledge. And so, the reader's desire to hear both singers goes unfulfilled.

Rachid's performance as surrogate and meditation as double surrogation end at this point; this is made clear through the squat-mates' critique of his performance, when they advise him to try his hand in café-theaters. And this is where Shérazade returns to the passage, her usual cheeky self: 'Vous, dit Shérazade, en s'adressant à Pierrot et Basile, vous savez toujours ce qu'il faut pour les autres. Et pour vous?' (165) ['"You two," said Shérazade to Pierrot and Basile, "you always know what's good for other people. And what about yourselves?"' (177)]. The surrogation that marks women's silence can be dropped within the narrative, because Shérazade's voice is back. She could have retorted verbatim to Pierrot when he suggested that she take voice lessons. Her rejoinder after his performance is a crack at Pierrot and Basile, with no commentary on Rachid stealing the mic from her. As many critics have shown, Shérazade is constantly asserting her right to speak throughout the trilogy. To sing would have been a more fully conceptualized mode of expressing her sense of injustice. That idea left her speechless, and brings to mind Cixous's description of women's torment at getting up to speak.

While, initially, this passage could be read as a missed opportunity for Shérazade's voice to sing, Rachid's performance and meditation on his past in fact articulate the absence of women's voices in history. And Rachid, too, is absent from the historical narrative: it is structured through his scant knowledge of the Holocaust and the Algerian Revolution. With the initial absence of one woman's voice in the narrative, we find that through surrogation, *Beur* silences ring out in distinctly masculine and feminine tones and assert their presence.

Cut Sound: A Literate Silence

'Femmes d'Alger' and *Shérazade* are interwoven with voices and silences as part of their textual fabric. The recuperation of Algerian women's voices and experience was central to Djebar's early fiction. The motive to listen and desire to be heard resonates throughout both her fiction and her autobiographical writing. In the case of Sebbar's work, representing the experiences of minority, immigrant, and *Beur* men and women serves as a prism through which narratives are refracted. While the recuperation of voices does not prove to be as central a motif as it does in Djebar's work, a complicated theme runs throughout *Shérazade*: it is as if the eponymous character is under perpetual visual surveillance, and often she is interpreted through her looks rather than what she says. In this way, the scene in which her singing is supplanted by Rachid's underscores this thematic, rather than undermining it. Yet this musical moment also provides the occasion with historical context, as well as Jewish and masculine *Beur* voices, to resonate as surrogates. Surrogation in the squat band practice underscores a problem posed through a central motif in the novel which is faced not only by Shérazade, but by many of the marginalized characters in the novel: no one wants to listen.

What becomes clear in both works, however, is that literary silences can be woven into a text, and serve as either theme or motif to issue a call to listen to the other, even when the motive or desire might not be readily apparent. The following visual representation demonstrates silence as a voice written over in 'Femmes d'Alger':

Sarah's thoughts——————————————————————

Anne's story ——————————————————————————...

Here, Anne's story is the substrate to Sarah's thoughts in the narrative. We know that Anne is talking the entire time Sarah has her disdainful thoughts about the banality of Anne's story—and that, if Anne's story had been transcribed as dialogue (as it is suggested that Sarah's story is at the end of the novella), it would have taken up far more space on the page that Sarah's thoughts. By weaving in Anne's story as substrate to Sarah's thoughts, Anne's voice is silenced not only through the writing over, but also through circumscription in literary time.

By contrast, this visual representation of the squat band practice demonstrates the way in which surrogates mark Shérazade's and Rachid's silences:

Rachid thinks about musical genres——neo-Nazi
1. Shérazade sings—Rachid comments—Rachid sings——————————

punks—Jewish ex-girlfriend———Véro—break-up letter from Jewish ex-girlfriend—Véro—
2. Rachid sings——————————————————————

Interestingly, in these moments of silencing in 'Femmes d'Alger' and *Shérazade*, voices are substrate to thought. That those thinking could be said to have minority voices serves different ends in the two works. In the case of Sarah, this is, of course, the representation of a utopian postcolonial hegemony that is complicated by feminist intentions, thus ably demonstrating the tension between the political aims of formerly colonized people with feminist activists. Is it possible to balance the two, to work for the liberation of both minority populations and women both within and without those populations?

By contrast, in the case of voice substrate to thought in *Shérazade*, Rachid's thoughts are written over his own voice. Does this suggest a Fanonian psychic alienation on Rachid's part? It seems that the outspoken *Beur* runaway is beyond the oppression suffered by his progenitors: Rachid suffers no sense of shortcoming in his abilities as a singer and impresario. Nonetheless, in his brazen sweep into the room to take the mic from Shérazade, a *Beur* woman, the stream of consciousness that follows assumes the aural space for, first, Rachid's meditation on Vichy and the Algerian War. Then comes the voice of his Jewish ex-girlfriend, the conscience within his stream of consciousness, ringing forth even as Rachid reminds himself how much 'simpler' it is with Véro, who doesn't 'agonize' like his ex. The ex's voice punches through, nonetheless, and the fact that his lack of knowledge about

Vichy and the Algerian War follow one from the other in Rachid's thoughts offers a reason why it is easier to silence voices such as Rachid's rather than listen to them. To listen would be to recognize the historical and social gaps into which marginalized figures like Shérazade, Rachid, and the Jewish ex-girlfriend fall.

On a final note, it is worth considering the fact that in neither text is a voice *literally* silenced. They have been silenced in the narrative, thus is it the reader who cannot hear the voices, for whom they have been silenced, rather than the other characters. Within the scenes, both Anne and Rachid are heard by the other characters. The problem in 'Femmes d'Alger,' of course, is that Sarah is dismissive of Anne's story as banal—as addressed, this is part of the reason why Anne's dialogue is written over with Sarah's thoughts. Rachid, meanwhile, writes over his own singing with his thoughts. Basile and Krim both listen attentively to his singing, so much so that they are able to suggest ways that he could make use of his voice, quite different from their suggestions to Shérazade. It should also be reiterated that while Rachid is complimented as an impresario, it is the possibility of Shérazade as singer that excites Basile and Krim. And this is based on her off-the-cuff improvisations. These texts lure us to listen: the voices are there to be heard. The narrative silences, in turn, speak for themselves.

CHAPTER THREE

Visual and Sonic Imagery
in
Postcolonial Francophone Culture

J'ai lu avec beaucoup d'intérêt votre article, 'A la recherche de modernités non occidentales' que j'ai trouvé tout à fait pertinent. En effet, celui-ci rappelle une réalité souvent oubliée: celle de la multiplicité possible des modernités. [...] Dans toutes les études réalisées sur cette question, l'expérience occidentale de la modernité est toujours érigée en modèle indépassable, comme si la modernité de tel ou tel pays ne pouvait exister que par rapport à cette modernité-là. La dimension universelle du concept si riche de modernité a été, semble-t-il, tout bonnement confisquée par l'Occident.

[It was with much interest that I read your article 'In Search of Non-Western Modernities,' and I found it very topical. This piece brings up an oft-overlooked reality: that of the possible multiplicity of modernities. (...) In all the studies conducted on this question, the Western experience of modernity is always erected as an unachievable model, as if the modernity of this or that country could only exist in relation to Western modernity. The universal dimensions of a concept as rich as modernity has been, it seems, confiscated by the West. (my trans.)]

—Meriem, Paris, Letter to the Editor, *Le Courrier de l'Atlas: le magazine du Maghreb en Europe*, September 2008.

Nothing to See, Hear?

On February 2, 2008, Wajdi Khalifa, the DJ and blogger for the Belgium-based Arab music radio show and blog *Arabesque* (http://arabesque48fm.blogspot.com/) reported that Lebanese singer and national icon Faïrouz would perform eight sold-out shows in Damascus, Syria. This news—which was reported on websites, television, and in newspapers worldwide—stirred enormous excitement and contentious debate throughout the Arab world. Faïrouz had not performed live in Syria for nearly twenty years.

The *Arabesque* blog entry describes Faïrouz as the 'plus grande chanteuse arabe depuis la disparition d'Oum Kalsoum' ['the biggest Arab *chanteuse* since the death of Umm Kulthum'].[1] A little less than a year later, in an obituary for Mansour Rahbani (who co-wrote most of Faïrouz's biggest hits with his brother Assi), the *Arabesque* blog stated that Faïrouz and the Rahbani brothers' music had 'révolutionné l'Histoire de la musique au Liban, ainsi qu'au Moyen-Orient' ['revolutionized Lebanon's musical History, as well as that of the Middle East'].

These sorts of descriptions of Faïrouz are widespread, and not hyperbolic. In the introduction to *Popular Culture and Nationalism in Lebanon: The Faïrouz and Rahbani Nation* (2008), Christopher Stone describes the singular importance of Faïrouz as both singer and national icon and the legacy of her work with the Rahbani brothers:

> No artistic family or individual in Lebanon comes close [in the second half of the twentieth century] to the influence of Faïrouz and the Rahbanis' thousands of songs and tens of musical-theatrical works.
>
> Faïrouz and the Rahbani brothers came to prominence at a time of increased internal and external migration and a global expression of mass media technologies. It was a time, in other words, when representations of the nation were particularly potent. [...]
>
> It is my contention that Faïrouz and the Rahbanis were and continue to be key players in the protracted struggle over the identity of this new nation. Faïrouz and the Rahbani Brothers (Assi and Mansour) have always been thought of as unifying forces in Lebanon and beyond, and this seems to have been their intention. (1)

Accordingly, the focus of the *Arabesque* blog report on Faïrouz's live shows is not on the performances themselves. A photograph of Faïrouz dressed in pale green at the first show in Damascus is embedded just

---

1   All translations from the *Arabesque* blog are mine.

below the date and time of the blog entry. But the entry itself centers around the debate over whether or not these performances in Damascus were meant to be a political transgression, given that they took place just three years after the end of the three-decade-long Syrian military presence and occupation of Lebanon. *Arabesque* quoted Faïrouz's press representatives at the end of the blog entry: 'l'art n'a rien à voir avec la politique. Faïrouz présente son œuvre au public syrien, et non pas à un chef politique' ['Art has nothing to do with politics. Faïrouz is performing for the Syrian public, not for a political leader']. This is an odd assertion, given the many ways that Faïrouz has been long identified with Lebanon as a nation and a culture (Stone 139–169), as well as with the political tensions between Syria and Lebanon. In the *New York Times* article 'A Lebanese Diva, Performing in Syria, Creates Drama in More Ways than One,' Robert Worth noted:

> Others say that she came here to deliver a veiled message. The musical comedy she chose, 'Sah el Nom' is about a cruel and corrupt dictator, with Faïrouz in the role of a woman who speaks truth to power and reforms him […] 'I think some of the people represented in this play were sitting in the front row,' [actor Rafed Zaqout] said, noting the presence of several high-ranking Syrian officials in the audience.

Faïrouz herself did not make a public statement regarding her intentions for the performances, which is typical of the artist. As Stone writes, 'Faïrouz's voice, outside of the context of her onstage performances, was and remains seldom heard' (155). In the *New York Times* article, Faïrouz's position on the political nature of the performances is related second-hand:

> The singer had initially refused to come to Damascus for the festival, Ms. Hassan said, and had cited the political tensions between Syria and Lebanon as the reason.
>
> 'I told her, that's been the situation for 20 years—we can't wait forever,' said Ms. Hassan, who has known Faïrouz for years. Finally, the singer relented.

Faïrouz never spoke directly to the press about these concerts, but images from them, as well as sound and video clips, were disseminated worldwide at a rate that would have been unthinkable when the tidy 3- to 5-minute average length of the Rahbani brothers' recordings helped revolutionize advertising on Lebanese radio in the 1940s and 1950s (Stone 43–49).

Arabesque devotes one sentence to the description of Faïrouz's first performance in Damascus. It was, Khalifa writes, electrifying despite the fact that she was lip-synching, a performance mode typical for the septuagenarian.[2] As such, Faïrouz's impact as an aging and venerated performer is staked upon her visual presence: she offers herself up formally as a singer, but through lip-synching, she remains silent. In effect, Faïrouz ventriloquizes herself. This combination of visual presence and physical silence establishes a space within the live performance for the recorded vocal performance. Thus, an enthralling hybrid form of spectacle and recording—Faïrouz's 'real-life' visual presence and 'real-life' physical silence, combined with the recorded sounds of a past vocal performance of the same woman onstage in the present—constitutes her performance.

The *Arabesque* blog entry about Faïrouz's performances in Damascus thus serves as a representative nexus of Faïrouz's physical presence, recorded voice, live silence, and finally, the circulation of this particular kind of performance within global culture. Her name and image raise political debate worldwide even as she remains silent on the issues at hand. Globalized media circulate her name and the images of her silent, visual accompaniment to recordings of her own voice, recordings extracted from a different political time and place. Her voice and image are quite literally produced and reproduced through historical time and transnational space. Thus, Faïrouz's music and performances assume shifting meanings as they circulate from one historical moment and political context to others.

Keeping in mind the potential mutability of what Faïrouz's music and performances can signify, I turn to the culminating statement of the *Arabesque* blog entry, which includes a common and in this case telling French expression: 'l'art *n'a rien à voir avec* la politique.' *N'avoir rien à voir avec* translates into English as 'to have nothing to do with.' But where English employs the verb 'to do,' as if to describe the impossibility of two things working together in tandem, French uses the verb *voir*, to see. *Voir* is also used, along with *entendre* [to hear], as common synonyms for *comprendre*, to understand. For example, as in English, *vous voyez?* is a typical rhetorical question posed to a listener after a speaker has related a situation or a story. The expression *bien entendu*, meanwhile, lets a speaker know that the listener has understood.

So in situations in which it seems *il n'y a rien à voir*, how can *l'entendement* come to pass? In this chapter, I wrestle with this question

---

2   'Faïrouz a électrisé la salle de l'opéra, même si elle se produisait en playback' (Khalifa).

by claiming more specifically that sound can intervene to blur presumed social distinctions, such as modernity and tradition (or, perhaps, sound simply reveals that these distinctions were always imbricated). In literary texts, when images are used to represent the idea that there seems to be *rien à voir* between two people, cultures, etc., auditory cues intervene and offer points of contact between the two. These ostensibly silent texts both represent and embody the primary contention of the letter to the editor of *Le Courrier de l'Atlas* in the epigraph of this chapter: there is no sharp line of distinction between cultures that are respectively categorized as modern and traditional. These respective categories are fluid, and cannot be categorized one way or the other.

Yasmina Khadra's novel *Les Sirènes de Bagdad* (2006) is the third instalment in a trilogy depicting the wars that ravaged the Middle East in the 2000s. But to begin, Khadra himself is a fascinating literary personality to consider. Yasmina Khadra is the *nom de plume* of Mohammed Moulessehoul. Moulessehoul was an officer in the Algerian army who began writing 'ethno-thrillers' (*ethno-polars*) in French in the 1990s. His Commandant Llob trilogy met with great critical success both in Algeria and in France.

Moulessehoul adopted not only a feminine pseudonym but a female identity to protect himself and his family: assassinations of writers and journalists in Algeria were far from uncommon in the 1990s, and Khadra's Llob trilogy offers potential criticisms of the fundamentalist movement and terrorism in Algeria. Louiza Kadari suggests that Khadra's Llob subscribes to an '"islam fictionnalisé" de l'assise fondamentaliste capable de générer une violence totalitaire' (55) ['fictionalized Islam' based in fundamentalism (that is) capable of generating a totalitarian violence (my trans.)]. This fictionalized Islam could have easily been interpreted as a critique of Islamic fundamentalism in Algeria.

Khadra left Algeria with his family in 2001. After a brief stay in Mexico, France promised hospitality to him and his family: his books had met with enormous success there, not the least of the reasons for which was his assumed identity. Readers and critics in France believed Khadra to be a new voice for Arab women until 2001, with the publication of his autobiographical work *L'Écrivain*, in which he revealed his story of a lifetime in the army and his reasons for choosing to write under an assumed female name and identity. This did not dampen France's enthusiasm for Khadra's work: his new novels are always critical events.

The settings of Khadra's subsequent fictional trilogy mirrored his own migration, which circumvents the Mediterranean in his identity as an Algerian writer, writing fictional works about Middle Eastern content that was originally published in French and in France. *Les Hirondelles de Kaboul* (2002) portrays life in Afghanistan under the Taliban and the American invasion, while *L'Attentat* (2005) tells the story of an Arab Israeli surgeon who is on emergency call when a suicide bomber attacks a Tel Aviv restaurant, and he learns that his Palestinian wife was the suicide bomber. Subsequently, *Les Sirènes de Bagdad* offers a variation on the Bildungsroman as it traces the effects of the early years (2003–05) of the second Iraq War on the Iraqi Bedouin narrator. It is in this final novel of Khadra's Middle Eastern trilogy that the issue of blurring social boundaries becomes apparent. The narrator, as we will see, differentiates himself from his reader from the first passage of the novel. He assumes his interlocutor-reader to be, at the very least, not of the same fictionalized Islamic bent that supports his moral judgments, and quite possibly Western rather than Middle Eastern. It is in this polarization of narrator and interlocutor-reader that *Les Sirènes de Bagdad* introduces its call to listen.

Sounding Textual Imagery

Les Sirènes de Bagdad is divided into four parts that are rooted in specific places and temporally situated through both historical events and the use of specific verb tenses. The untitled introduction takes place in Beirut and is written in the present tense. The second part, 'Kafr Karam,' named for the home village of the narrator, a 21-year-old Iraqi Bedouin whose education at the University of Baghdad was abruptly ended in 2003 with the U.S. invasion of Iraq. This section is written in the *passé composé* and *imparfait*, and describes, primarily through sight and sound, three violent events that lead to the narrator's alienation from his hometown, and establishes a sound-image chronotope in the novel.[3] 'Kafr Karam' also establishes Faïrouz's music as a musical

---

3   Bakhtin explains the chronotope in the essay 'Forms of Time and of the Chronotope in the Novel: Notes Toward a Historical Poetics': 'We'll give the name *chronotope* (literally, "time space") to the intrinsic interconnectedness of temporal and spatial relationships that are artistically expressed in literature. This term (space-time) is employed in mathematics, and was introduced as part of Einstein's Theory of Relativity. The special meaning it has in relativity theory is not important for our purposes; we are borrowing it for literary criticism almost as a metaphor (almost, but not entirely). What counts for us is the fact that it expresses

chronotope that propels the narrative of political and social extremism within this literary work of mobility.[4] Part three, 'Bagdad,' written in the *imparfait* and *passé simple* tenses, depicts the cultivation of the narrator as a terrorist. Part four, 'Beyrouth,' shifts from past tenses back to the present, establishing a cyclical temporality and spatiality in the novel. This fourth section depicts the narrator's 'coming of age' as a terrorist when he accepts to be the vessel for a virus that he will spread through London via excrement. Ultimately, hearing Faïrouz on the radio in a taxi on the way to catch his flight to London and the memory of talking about an unheard song, 'Les Sirènes de Bagdad,' lures him away from the plot, both in the sense of the potential terrorist act and the plot of the novel itself.

I lay out my argument for how sound functions in *Les Sirènes de Bagdad* in two parts. First, I consider the narrator's recounting of sounds and images through descriptions of three violent events in 'Kafr Karam' as an underlying pattern that results in a variegated sensory experience of events within the narrative. The narrator's physical and emotional reactions are plotted upon this sensory grid. The ineffable is expressed through the narrator's resistance to—and horror of—the sights and sounds of violence and its aftermath, and the sights and sounds of Western modernity that the narrator understands to be harbingers of future violence and social and cultural decay.

In the third part of this chapter, I argue that both the music of Faïrouz and conversations about a song called 'Les Sirènes de Bagdad' serve as a chronotope, an imbrication of time and space, throughout the novel. The memory of this unheard song and the promise to hear it ultimately lure the narrator away from terrorist plans. Faïrouz's music acts as a trigger to 'Les Sirènes de Bagdad' and appears in the narrative through radio and Walkman headphones. 'Les Sirènes de Bagdad,' meanwhile, is carried in the narrator's memory.

Les Sirènes de Bagdad opens as night falls on Beirut, described using an idiom for closing one's eyes to go to sleep: 'Beyrouth retrouve sa nuit et s'en voile la face' (7) ['Night veils Beirut's face again' (1)]. Night falls as

the inseparability of space and time (time as the fourth dimension of space). We understand the chronotope as a formally constitutive category of literature; we will not deal with the chronotope in other areas of literature' (84).

4 'The study of what some would call "travel literature," of what others (in more neutral, ahistorical terms) dub the 'literature of mobility' [...] allows an opening up of cultures predominantly viewed hitherto as discrete' (Forsdick 523).

the narrative opens using a metaphor of veiling one's eyes, which works in curious tension with the narrator's subsequent lament: 'Je l'imaginais différemment, arabe et fière de l'être. Je me suis trompé. Ce n'est qu'une ville indéterminable, plus proche de ses fantasmes que de son histoire, tricheuse et volage, décevante comme une farce' (7) ['I'd imagined a different Beirut, Arab and proud of it. It's just an indeterminate city, closer to its fantasies than its history, a fickle sham as disappointing as a joke' (1)].

Here, I point to the narrator's inability to pin down Beirut as one thing or the other. As his scathing commentary on the city mounts, it becomes clear that Beirut can be viewed through these descriptions as an amalgamation of identities and allegiances shifting between Oriental and Occidental, traditional and modern, Arab and European/American. And all of these categories are qualified through a difference—in the narrator's estimation, Beirut cannot be Arab and proud of it precisely because of its constant shifting:

> Je la hais de toutes mes forces, pour ses sursauts d'orgueil qui n'ont pas plus de cran que de suite dans ses idées, pour son cul entre deux chaises, tantôt arabe quand les caisses sont vides, tantôt occidentale lorsque les complots sont payants. (9)

> [I hate it with all my heart for its gutless, illogical pride, for the way it falls between two stools, sometimes Arab, sometimes Western, depending on the payoffs involved. (2)]

Interestingly, the narrator's perspective on what makes Beirut a Westernized city is more than reminiscent of Orientalist representations of the Arab: a collaborator who moves between two cultures, shiftless, sneaky, and not to be trusted. Yet the narrator doesn't seem to recognize the irony in his contentions: he establishes himself as someone bound to Middle Eastern tradition who abhors all things modern and Western, without questioning these distinctions, even as Beirut represents the blurring of these distinctions within the narrator's own descriptions.

Just as important to the details that the narrator conveys is the fact that this is a first-person narrative. In *Les Sirènes de Bagdad*, the narrator speaks directly to an interlocutor whom he situates as outside his social milieu through narrative details. Because of this narrative perspective, *Les Sirènes de Bagdad* can be read as a performance event which encompasses the way in which this story is relayed from storyteller to listener. It is not simply the story that the narrator tells in *Les Sirènes de Bagdad*: it is also the *way* in which the story is being told—and the fact that he indicates that he is speaking to someone outside of his social milieu—that is important here.

Key to the reading of *Les Sirènes de Bagdad* as a performance event is an understanding of how the publication of Khadra's work constitutes a cultural event in and of itself, as delineated in the introduction to this section. So, while *Les Sirènes de Bagdad* could be read as a terrorist Bildungsroman, it is important to note, first, that the work is confessional in tone; second, the narrator often digresses briefly from the narrative into pseudo-religious and quasi-sociocultural explanations to justify why he believes what he believes, why a character behaves in a certain way, and why the narrator made the decisions he made. From these explanations, it seems at times that the narrator is speaking to not just his interlocutor but also an audience. And, of course, that is precisely what is happening if we take both textual and extratextual details into account: this narrative of a fledgling Iraqi terrorist was written by a gender-crossing writer renowned for his ethnographic detective novels. The narrator's audience is also Khadra's. And it is to this audience that the narrator explains his background and motivations for all that unfolds as the novel progresses. This is the performance event: as the narrator explains why he took the path toward terrorism, a dynamic between the narrator as speaker and reader as listener is one of the terms of the story's telling.

To establish the storytelling terms, the narrator's violent extremism is represented in the introduction through resistance to listening, which serves as a device that establishes the sensory grid of sound and sight. This grid allows the reader to listen, not only to the sounds represented throughout the text, but also to the narrator as storyteller. With his repeated references to sirens, listening is established as part of the performance event. Initially, he refers to the sirens of the Homeric tradition, who represent lying, stealing, and more generally the ways of the West, as we see in the narrator's first description of their tempting call: 'L'Occident n'est qu'un mensonge acidulé, une perversité savamment dosée, un chant des sirènes pour naufrages identitaires' (18) ['The West is nothing but an acidic lie, an insidious perversity, a siren song for people shipwrecked on their identity quest' (10)]. If one is not steadfastly rooted in Arab identity, he suggests, one risks being perverted by modern thought and practices. And those practices stay immobilized in his descriptions of the modern in a way of being that is opposed to honesty and integrity.

As he describes the hardships that have befallen his village since the outbreak of the war, he evokes sirens once more to explain in idealistic terms the villagers' refusal to steal or to give in to vice: 'Le chant des sirènes a beau claironner, l'appel des Anciens le supplante toujours—nous sommes honnêtes par vocation' (26) ['The call of the Ancients drowns out the sirens' song, no matter how loud. We're honest by vocation' (18)]. Through the siren metaphor, the narrator sets the terms of the modernity-tradition binary opposition by evoking sirens that represent modern moral decay, as opposed to the urging of these unnamed 'Ancients' to stand with traditional moral fortitude. Setting the terms as such underscores his criticisms of Beirut in the opening passage. If a person, place, or thing is not marked as clearly modern or traditional, then it is elusive, thus given to lying, manipulation, and thievery, all behaviors that he equates with modern thought and practices.

I return to the first line to pursue the idea of seeing and hearing as understanding. The narrator wants to be able to pin down Beirut as a consistently Arab space, and indicts it through visual metaphors for his inability to do so. The city refuses to 'see' this; Beirut 's'en voile la face,' effectively closing its eyes and continuing on the same somnambulistic path of greed and destruction, if we are to believe the narrator: 'Si les émeutes de la veille ne l'ont pas éveillé à elle-même, c'est la preuve qu'elle dort en marchant. Dans la tradition ancestrale, on ne dérange pas un somnambule, pas même lorsqu'il court à sa perte' (7) ['If the tumults of the evening haven't awakened her, that just proves she's sleepwalking. According to ancestral tradition, a somnambulist is not to be interfered with, not even when he's headed for disaster' (1)]. Beirut acts like a sleepwalker, unable to wake from its march to destruction.

Somnambulism is a recurring trope throughout *Les Sirènes de Bagdad*. In the introduction to the novel, Beirut is asleep, elsewhere, in the face of all it has lost. This establishes a sleepwalking motif, a state the narrator enters with every act of wartime violence he experiences in the first part of the novel. This is one of the primary ways in which the narrative shuts down: the sudden absence of the narrator's sensory perceptions. As a result, sounds and images are thrown into relief.

In this introduction, however, observation seems to lead to no further understanding for the narrator. 'Sa nuit' might refer to nightfall, but it might as easily refer to Beirut's obliviousness to and oblivion within the Arab world. But if the narrator criticizes Beirut for not seeing its errant ways, keeping an eye on the city doesn't seem to be doing any good: 'Plus je l'observe, et moins j'arrive à la suivre. [...] Ses airs affectés ne sont qu'attrape-nigauds' (7) ['The more I observe the place, the less I get it.

[...] Its affected airs are nothing but a con' (1)]. These details suggest that the narrator is both trying to explain Beirut to someone who has never been there, and to justify his own position within Arab society and as an extremist.

If seeing Beirut as a means of understanding is constantly undermined through the city's own shiftiness and voluntary blindness, then what are we to make of the narrator's resistance to listening? The sensory stakes of *Les Sirènes de Bagdad* become clear in this initial description of Beirut as the narrator describes: 'Le matin une sourde aversion me gagne lorsque je reconnais le charivari de souk' (8) ['In the morning, when its souklike din begins again, I'm overcome with silent loathing' (2)]. *Sourd* in this context could refer to deafness, voicelessness, or the unnameable. The word evokes the impossibility for the narrator to represent these noises. The tension between the din of the *souk* and the narrator's dull aversion to this noise is notable as well: he describes the noise in order to foreclose his susceptibility to it. The sounds of evening revelry bode no better in the narrator's estimation: 'Le soir, la même colère lève en moi quand les fêtards viennent frimer à bord de leurs bolides fourbis, les décibels de leurs chaînes stéréos à fond la caisse' (8) ['In the evening, when the party animals show off their gleaming high-powered cars and crank up their stereos to full blast, the same anger rises inside me' (2)]. The cars may gleam, but it is their owners' blasting stereos that allow them to attract attention. The sound is what irks the narrator, too.

Between the sonic descriptions of morning and night, sounds emerge in this passage through the narrator's resistance to listening. Morning noise is represented through *charivari*, or the 'souklike din.' But come nighttime, noises that offer a fused embodiment of the modern with the traditional world fare no better. A tension between narrative details and the narrator's perception of those details thus mounts: the narrator's resistance to hearing can only be described by representing the very noises to which he is resistant within the narrative. This is also part of his justification to the reader: he offers these details not to tell a story, but to justify his hatred of Beirut as a neither strictly modern nor strictly traditional, neither strictly Western nor strictly Arab city.

The importance of the narrator referring to Beirut as a somnambulist, as well as his voluntary deafness, becomes evident in the second part of *Les Sirènes de Bagdad*, 'Kafr Karam.' As the narrator sets the scene and describes his family and the villagers around him, we learn that he was a student at the University of Baghdad until the American invasion in

2003, when he was forced to leave the university and return home. In 'Kafr Karam,' the narrative establishes a sonic landscape to accompany the three spectacular and horrific events that precipitate the narrator's exile and in turn lead him to engage with terrorist circles. The narrator is party to all three incidents to varying degrees. In all three cases, the events (distilled down to sound and sight) are followed by descriptions of the narrator's extreme bodily reactions: he faints after the first, he experiences intense nausea following the second, and throughout and after the third event, he veers between brutal lucidity and sickening, hallucinatory disbelief.

In the first incident, Souleyman, a mentally challenged Kafr Karam villager, has chopped two fingers off one of his hands. The narrator is driving Souleyman and his father, the local blacksmith, to the closest medical facility. They are stopped by American GIs who refuse to listen to either the narrator or Souleyman's father, and Souleyman panics and runs into the desert. The GIs shoot and kill him as he flees; in the narrator's description of his death, violent visual imagery is grafted over silence. The silence, note, is situated through sounds of violence:

> *Mike!* aboya le sergent, *ce fumier porte un gilet pare-balles. Vise la tête* ... Sur la guérite, Mike posa un œil sur la jumelle de son fusil, ajusta sa ligne de mire, retint sa respiration et appuya délicatement sur la détente. Il fit mouche du premier coup. La tête de Souleyman explosa comme un melon, freinant net sa course débridée. Le ferronnier se prit les tempes à deux mains, halluciné, la bouche ouverte sur un cri suspendu; il regarda le corps de son fils se décrocher au loin, pareil à une tenture, s'effondrer à la verticale, les cuisses sur les mollets, puis le buste sur les cuisses, puis la tête en lambeaux sur les genoux. Un silence d'outre-tombe submergea la plaine. (69)

> ['Mike!' the sergeant barked. 'He's wearing a bulletproof vest, the little prick. Aim for his head.' In the sentry box, Mike peered through his telescopic sight, adjusted his firing angle, held his breath, and delicately squeezed his trigger. Bull's-eye, first shot. Sulayman's head exploded like a melon; his unbridled run stopped all at once. The blacksmith clutched his temples with both hands, wild-eyed, his mouth open in a suspended cry, as he watched his son's body fold up in the distance and collapse vertically, like a falling curtain: the thighs on the calves, then the chest on the thighs, and finally the shattered head on the knees. An unearthly silence settled over the plain. (57–58)]

Because of the narrator's point of view and distance from Souleyman when he is shot, the sergeant's order is the only sound represented as audible in this passage. The graphic image of Souleyman's head exploding and then his body collapsing is followed by the description of his father's open-mouthed, silent scream. Silence floods the passage as the narrative moves into the immediate aftermath of Souleyman's death.

While visual imagery conveys the bare facts of the situation at hand, sound and silence nuance this passage, lending it both desperation and urgency. Just prior to shooting Souleyman, the GIs bark orders to the narrator, the blacksmith, and his son in the car; they refuse to listen to the narrator's attempts to explain where they are going; and they threaten the three men with death if they defy any order. While the narrator obeys these orders to the letter, stepping slowly and silently out of the car with his hands behind his head, Souleyman and his father react through another kind of imposed silence. The father attempts to explain to the GI that his son doesn't understand, and the narrator explains the GI's reaction: 'il semblait excédé qu'on lui parlât dans une langue qui ne lui disait rien, et cela le foutait doublement en rogne' (67) ['the fact that someone would address him in a language he didn't know seemed to infuriate him, and so now he was doubly angry' (56)]. The expression the narrator uses to explain that the GI doesn't understand the language, 'on lui parlât dans une langue qui ne lui disait rien,' is particularly interesting. So, first, it is the very sound of the Arabic language being spoken to him that angers the GI. Second, it is not simply a language he does not know, but if the expression 'une langue qui ne lui disait rien' is taken literally, it is a language that *tells him nothing*. This phrase serves to write over—to silence—the three men in a way that elaborates upon Djebar's literary silences in 'Femmes d'Alger dans leur appartement.'

Souleyman audibly panics and, as the GIs pitch their orders and threats with increasing intensity, he flees, screaming all the while. The GIs shoot him several times in the back, and he continues to run. The fatal miscommunication is visual: the GI orders Mike to shoot Souleyman in the head, on the assumption that he is wearing a bullet-proof jacket because he continues to run after he has been shot.

The immediate aftermath is portrayed through the narrator's own physical collapse: his stomach retracts as he faints. This faint is rendered formally by a break between two paragraphs. As the narrator comes to, he pieces together himself and what has happened: 'Je revins à moi, morceau par morceau, les oreilles sifflotantes' (70) ['I regained consciousness slowly. My ears whistled' (58)]. The whistling sound in his ears is punctuated by the incensed and panicked tones of Souleyman's father as he berates the GIs, struck dumb, looking at the ground in silence.

After Souleyman has been killed and the narrator revives, it becomes clear that the misunderstanding has been resolved through the interwoven sound of Souleyman's father's voice and the GIs' silence—too late, of course, for Souleyman. The deafening silence, punctuated only by the GI's orders, established the chronotope of sounds and images of violence and despair that is pursued throughout 'Kafr Karam.' The images in this passage lend the sense that we are standing before a series of horrifying *tableaux vivants* mounted for display. Its centerpiece is a version of Edvard Munch's *The Scream*, which the shocked, open-mouthed, hands-at-temples silence of Souleyman's father immediately calls to mind. Unlike in the introduction, the narrator is not resistant to listening in this passage so much as he cannot hear (because he cannot comprehend) what has happened. Notably, these moments are devoid of the value judgments he makes about the characters and places he qualifies as either modern or traditional.

The spectacular and sonic dimensions of *Les Sirènes de Bagdad* deepen in the second violent incident in Kafr Karam, in which a plane crash annihilates a wedding party at a house situated among orchards some distance outside the village. The explosion from the crash is heard in the village before it is seen, since the incident occurs after night has fallen, and panicked reports about the crash pierce the darkness: "'C'est un avion," cria quelqu'un dans la nuit. "Je l'ai vu tomber"' (105) ["'It was a plane," someone cried out in the night. "I saw it come down"' (90)]. The headlights of an automobile speeding toward the village then appear on the horizon, to which the narrator's cousin, Kadem, reacts: "'Ça, c'est mauvais," me dit Kadem en regardant le véhicule fou tanguer sur la piste. "Ça, c'est très mauvais"' (106) ["'This is bad," Kadem said, watching the vehicle bound and pitch as it hurtled toward us. "This is very bad"' (90)]. Villagers rush to the scene to provide aid, and the catastrophe reveals itself through image and sound, but in contrast to the description of Souleyman's death in several ways. The narrator describes what he sees and hears upon his arrival following the crash:

> Les vergers baignaient dans une obscurité malsaine. Nous les traversâmes comme un territoire maudit. La maison des Haïtem était intacte. Des ombres se tenaient sur le perron, les unes effondrées sur les marches, la tête dans les mains, les autres appuyées contre le mur. Le lieu du drame se trouvait un peu plus loin, dans un jardin où une grande bâtisse, probablement la salle des fêtes, brûlait au cœur d'un amas d'éboulis fumants. Le souffle de l'explosion avait projeté sièges et corps à une trentaine de mètres à la ronde. Les survivants erraient, en haillons, les

mains en avant, semblables à des aveugles. Quelques corps étaient alignés sur le bord d'une allée, mutilés, carbonisés. Des voitures éclairaient la boucherie avec leurs phares pendant que des spectres se démenaient au milieu des décombres. Puis, des hurlements, d'interminables hurlements, des appels et des cris à couvrir la planète. Des femmes cherchaient leurs gosses dans la confusion; moins elles obtenaient de réponses, plus elles s'égosillaient. Un homme ensanglanté pleurait, accroupi devant le corps d'un proche. (108)

[The orchards were sunk in a malignant darkness. We raced through them. The Haitems' house looked intact. There were shadowy figures on the staircase leading to the entrance, some of them collapsed on the steps, their heads in their hands, and others leaning against the wall. The focal point of the tragedy lay a little farther on, in a garden where a building, apparently the hall the family used for parties, was burning at the center of a huge pile of smoking debris. The force of the explosion had flung chairs and wedding guests thirty meters in all directions. Survivors staggered about, their clothes in rags, holding their hands out in front of them like blind people. Some mutilated, charred bodies were lined up along the edge of a path. Cars illuminated the slaughter with their headlights, while specters thrashed about in the midst of the rubble. Then there was the howling, drawn out, indeterminable; the air was full of pleas and cries and wails. Mothers looking for their children called out into the confusion; the more they went unanswered, the louder they shouted. A weeping man, covered with blood, knelt beside the body of someone dear to him. (92–93)]

Where the passage relating Souleyman's death can be read as if the narrator witnessed the event through *tableaux vivants*, the passage here vividly describes near-constant movement through both sound and image. The car's headlights torpedo toward Kafr Karam to seek help, giving a visual hint to the emergency that resulted from the sound of the explosion in the dark night. As the narrator races toward the scene of the crash in the same car, the orchards are bathed in ominous darkness. The passage that describes the crash site flickers with the movement of darkness, shadow, smoke and flames, and a soundtrack emerges: mothers cry out for their children as they struggle to find them in the fire, smoke, and rubble. The children's silent responses give way to their mothers' wails. A man covered in blood crouches near the body of a friend and audibly weeps.

Where Souleyman's death is described as if the scene took place in deafening silence, a metaphor of blindness colors the scene of the plane crash. The narrator describes the survivors mimicking the blind with their hands as they stumble around. To describe the scene, the narrator attributes to survivors the inability to see in order to portray their reactions to the disaster. What it looks like is blindness. What it felt like, by contrast, was deafness. With this subjective oscillation between sight and sound, the narrative devises a grid-like chronotope of the interplay of the two senses. On this grid, the narrator plots his and others' physical reactions to the violence they see and experience.

In this second incident, the narrator is overcome by nausea, and he falls to the ground on all fours. Kadem tries to help him up, but quickly turns his attention to the wounded. The narrator then observes from the sidelines: 'Je me ramassai au pied d'un arbre et, les bras autour des genoux, contemplai le délire' (108) ['I crept over to a tree, put my arms around my knees, and contemplated the delirium' (93)]. The immediate aftermath of the plane crash is recalled through rapid flashes of movement and orders from those who came to help the wounded: 'Surtout ne t'endors pas' ['Don't go to sleep'] orders one of the helpers as he helps a victim stagger to a spot near the narrator. While the narrator was incapacitated at the scene of Souleyman's death, in the aftermath of the plane crash he enters a similar unconscious state, but in this case he then throws himself into the heart of the disaster and possibly joins the rescue effort, although exactly what he is doing remains ambiguous:

> Je me levai tel un somnambule et courus vers le brasier.
> J'ignorais depuis combien de temps j'étais là, à renverser et à retourner tout autour de moi. Lorsque je revins à moi, j'avais les mains en sang, boursoufflées d'ecchymoses, les doigts déchirés aux jointures; j'avais tellement mal que je tombai à genoux, la poitrine polluée de fumée et d'odeurs de crémation. (109)

> [I got to my feet like a sleepwalker and ran toward the fire.
> I don't know how long I was there, yanking, heaving, and turning over everything around me. When I came out of my trance, my hands were bruised and my fingers lacerated and bleeding; I sank to my knees, wretchedly sick, my lungs polluted with smoke and the stench of cremation. (93–94)]

At first, the narrator is aware of both visual and sonic action surrounding him. While in both cases he seems to be in shock before he loses consciousness, in the first passage he is incapacitated when he faints, while in the second, he seems to spring into unconscious action, presumably to help. In both cases, he describes a return to consciousness: 'je revins à moi' is used in both passages (70, 109). In both passages, he becomes aware that he is covered in bodily fluids: when he returns to consciousness following Souleyman's death, he finds himself face down in a pool of his own vomit. In the aftermath of the plane crash, his hands are covered with blood and bruises. The GIs bind his hands behind him; at the site of the plane crash, when he emerges from his delirium, his fingers are lacerated. And again, in both cases, he falls incapacitated to the ground.

I return then to his criticism of Beirut as a somnambulist in the face of decadent behavior transpiring on the streets. One of the attendants to the plane crash begged a wounded victim not to fall asleep. And yet the narrator, himself lost in a delirium, proceeds much in the way that he accuses Beirut of acting, as a sleepwalker. These different states of perception and awareness layer representations of sensory perceptions within the narrative and also highlight the narrator's hypocrisy. Thus, through the sleepwalking motif, the narrative offers an unspoken critique of making value judgments based upon social binaries, even if the narrator never explicitly articulates this contradiction. As the narrative progresses, this contradiction is articulated through a somnambulism that renders the narrator hopeless and suicidal before he heeds a particular siren's call, which I will address shortly.

It is revealed that the plane crash was the result of an errant American drone plane—another somnambulist of sorts. The third attack hits home both literally and figuratively, and leads the narrator to a self-imposed exile from Kafr Karam. The narrator introduces the third incident in a way that layers the first two events upon one another, and melds the three together in memory:

Et une nuit, de nouveau, le ciel me tomba sur la tête. J'avais d'abord pensé à un missile lorsque la porte de ma chambre avait volé dans un fracas. Une bordée d'invectives et de fuseaux éblouissants m'ensevelit. Je n'eus pas le temps de tendre la main vers le commutateur. Une escouade de GI venait de déflorer mon intégrité. *Reste couché! Bouge pas ou je t'explose ... Debout! ... Reste couché! Debout! Les mains sur la tête! Pas un geste!* Des torches me clouaient au lit tandis que des canons me tenaient en joue. *Bouge pas ou je t'explose la cervelle!* ... Ces cris! Atroces. Déments. Dévastateurs. À vous démailler fibre par fibre, à vous rendre étranger à vous-même ... (114–115)

[And then one night, the sky fell in on me again. At first, when the door to my room flew open with a crash, I imagined another missile. Then came shouted insults and cones of blinding light. I didn't have time to reach for the lamp switch. A squad of American soldiers barged into my privacy.

'Lie back down! If you move, I'll blow you up!' 'Stand up!' 'Lie down!' 'Stand up! Hands on your head! Don't move!' Flashlights nailed me to the bed; weapons were aimed at me. 'Don't move or I'll blow your brains out!' Those shouts! Atrocious, demented, devastating. Capable of unraveling you thread by thread and making you a stranger to yourself. (99)]

The first two lines in this passage recall the military plane falling from the sky and crashing onto the wedding party. American GIs have invaded the house, and as they storm the narrator's bedroom, he tells us, he doesn't have time to switch on the light—thus this third incident also begins in darkness. Their forced entry shakes the narrator from sleep, and awakens him not only from nighttime slumber but also from the delirious somnambulistic state in which the aftermath of the plane crash left him—yet their cries leave him undone, unrecognizable to himself.

I note specifically the sentence 'Une escouade de GI venait de déflorer mon intégrité' ['A squad of American soldiers barged into my privacy']. With this invasion of privacy, the narrative as a whole turns outward, contrary to the inwardness of the narrator's reactions to the previous violent incidents. And it is no accident, of course, that the narrator used the verb *déflorer* [to deflower] to describe the home invasion. This event represents a final loss of innocence for the narrator, a loss through force that is as violent as rape. It is here, too, that the descriptions of sound and image fall away, and the musical chronotope becomes predominant. In 'Bagdad,' the narrator describes how witnessing atrocities eventually inures him to violence, and then breaks his will to live. It is in this violation of privacy as the GIs break into the bedroom that this process begins, although this admission only foreshadows what is to come as the GIs continue. As the narrator flips his light on with the GI invasion of his bedroom, however, the sound-image grid is taken apart, and what remains in its place throughout the balance of the novel is music, transmitted through both radios and memory.

The allusions to Souleyman's death and the plane crash mount: the GI threatens to 't'exploser la tête' ['blow your brains out'], employing the same root word (*exploser*) that the narrator used to describe Souleyman's head upon the impact of the bullet. The orders are similar to those the GIs gave when the narrator was sitting in the car, before Souleyman fled. Finally, the screams of the GIs here are what pull the narrator apart; he suggests that these atrocious cries make you 'étranger à vous même' ['a stranger to yourself'].

With this expression the narrator makes it clear that the GIs invasion of his bedroom has shaken him in a different way than the other two events. But as this incident continues, the difference in his reactions to what he experiences and what he witnesses becomes clear. While he seems lucid as they search his room for weapons, he experiences being dragged out into the main hall of the house as a waking nightmare: 'je cauchemardais debout, tel un somnambule' (115) ['(I was) caught in a waking nightmare like a sleepwalker' (100)]. Although he evokes sleepwalking here as he did in the plane crash passage, as the GIs invade the house the sleepwalking reaction is rendered distinct from his delirium and fainting through the fact that his reactions to the other two events were caused by witnessing violence rather than experiencing it.

Once he has been dragged into the front hall, he sees that his sisters, nieces, and nephews have endured similar brutal awakenings. His oldest sister's breasts are exposed, while her daughter (who, the narrator related earlier, is bald due to a childhood illness) stands beside her without her wig. Bahia stands erect with a nephew in her arms, but a trickle of blood runs from the nape of her neck. The narrator describes the scene, and the detail about the blood on Bahia's neck is followed by an ellipsis and a paragraph break. This break seems to formally mark the narrator's reaction to surveying this scene: 'Je me sentis défaillir. Ma main chercha en vain un appui' (116) ['I felt faint. My hand searched in vain for something to hold onto' (100)].

The paragraph breaks again after these two short phrases, and the narrative returns to describing the action around the narrator. His mother attempts to protect the narrator's wheelchair-bound father, who has been pulled out into the main hall by the GIs. Seeing his mother helpless, his stoic and mysterious father utterly vulnerable, the narrator is

> hypnotisé par le spectacle qu'ils m'offraient tous les deux. Je ne voyais même pas les brutes qui les encadraient. Je ne voyais que cette mère éperdue, et ce père efflanqué au slip avachi, au bras ballant, au regard sinistré qui titubait sur les ruades. (117)

> [hypnotized by the spectacle the two of them presented to my eyes. I didn't even see the brutes who surrounded them. I saw only a distraught mother and a painfully thin father in shapeless underwear, his eyes wounded, his arms dangling at his sides, stumbling as the soldiers shoved him along. (101)]

The father is described in a way that mimics the survivors of the plane crash, in a seeming blindness. He tries to return to his room, but one of the GIs hits him with such force that he flies backwards, his genitals exposed to the room.

This is where the narrator experiences a visual upheaval that constitutes a shift in the narrative. He luridly describes the movement of his father's genitalia: 'le pénis de mon père rouler sur le côté, les testicules par-dessus le cul …' (117) ['my father's penis, rolling to one side as his testicles flopped up over his ass' (101)]. Then, he laments:

> Le bout du rouleau! Après cela, il n'y a rien, un vide infini, une chute interminable, le néant … Toutes les mythologies tribales, toutes les légendes du monde, toutes les étoiles du ciel venaient de perdre leur éclat. Le soleil pouvait toujours se lever, plus jamais je ne reconnaîtrais le jour de la nuit … Un Occidental ne peut pas comprendre, ne peut pas soupçonner l'étendue du désastre. Pour moi, voir le sexe de mon géniteur, c'était ramener mon existence entière, mes valeurs et mes scrupules, ma fierté et ma singularité à une fulgurance pornographique. (117)

> [That sight was the edge of the abyss, and beyond it, there was nothing but the infinite void, an interminable fall, nothingness. Suddenly, all of our tribal myths, all the world's legends, all the stars in the sky lost their gleam. The sun could keep on rising, but I'd never be able to distinguish night from day anymore. A Westerner can't understand, can't suspect the dimensions of the disaster. For me, to see my father's sex was to reduce my entire existence, my values and my scruples, my pride and my singularity, to a coarse, pornographic flash. (102)]

Folded into the narrator's personal reaction to seeing his father's genitals are generalizations which, along with his statement that a Westerner couldn't understand, might suggest that this incident runs against some common-knowledge social taboo in the Middle East. Returning to Kadari's theory of Khadra's fictionalized Islam, in *Les Sirènes de Bagdad* this fictionalized Islamic extremism is colored by a totalitarian mysticism that presupposes Khadra's fictionalized accounts of wartime violence and terrorist acts. This totalitarian mysticism, in turn, represents a sensory truth about extremist experience, rather than a factual recounting of motivations logically delineated.

Thus, the cartography of the narrator's moral universe: the reader's entry into the text is mediated by the narrator, a young Middle Eastern man who has been stripped of his personal and political agency and traumatized by events that are a part of the U.S. invasion of Iraq, and as a result takes up an extremist position that echoes Islamic militantism. The narrator's polarizing perspectives on Beirut as a city both modern and traditional in the introduction is undermined in the narrative by evoking the somnambulism motif in 'Kafr Karam' (for the narrator sleepwalks his way through the violence). The narrative offers an unspoken critique of both the narrator's polarizing perspective, and thus suggests that polarizing perspectives might always beget some form of violence. But 'Kafr Karam' also allows the reader to bear witness to the moments that lead to the construction of the narrator's extremism. In this way, the narrator, like Medea, forces us to bear witness to what happens when people are betrayed and they have no means of righting these wrongs. This is what happens when we do not listen.

To elaborate on this point through the rest of the home invasion passage, I highlight the metaphors of light and darkness that shoot through the narrator's lament. He qualifies his reaction to the event as something beyond Western comprehension. But his reaction is also subjective and his alone, 'pour moi' suggesting how deeply personal the experience is. *His* existence, values, scruples, pride, and singularity are brought to a brutish intensity by seeing his father's genitals—it's worth noting that he does not once refer to his father as being humiliated. That is not the issue at hand. Rather, it's the sight of his father's exposed penis and testicles—a 'pornographic flash'—that leads to this psychological turning point for the narrator. And it is with the representation of sight as both sense and understanding that the gravity of this personal shift for the narrator becomes clear.

Earlier in 'Kafr Karam,' he describes his distant relationship with his father, and comments on what a mystery his father is to him. This incident shatters that distance:

> Je regardais mon père, et mon père me regardait. Il devait lire dans mes yeux le mépris que j'avais pour tout ce qui avait compté pour nous [...]. Je le regardais comme du haut d'une falaise maudite par une nuit d'orage, il me regardait du fond de l'opprobre; nous savions déjà, à cet instant précis, que nous étions en train de nous regarder pour la dernière fois. (118)

> [I looked at my father, and my father looked back at me. He must have read in my eyes the contempt I felt toward everything that had counted for us [...]. I looked at him as though from atop a blasted cliff on a stormy night; he looked at me from the bottom of disgrace. At that very instant, we already knew that we were looking at each other for the last time. (102)]

This event clearly constitutes a personal turn for the narrator. It's not clear how the GI invasion of the narrator's home ends; the passage concludes as the narrator declares that '*à cet instant précis ... j'étais condamné à laver l'affront dans le sang*' (118, emphasis original) ['*at that very instant ... I was condemned to wash away this insult in blood*' (102)]. Where the narrator's physical reactions to witnessing violence were once rendered, in this third violent event physical reactions are supplanted by a call to militant action. This call to action gives structure to the second half of *Les Sirènes de Bagdad*, 'Bagdad' and 'Beyrouth,' but these two sections are propelled by music, in several ways: the songs of Faïrouz are represented in the text, along with the memory of a song that goes unheard throughout the novel.

Reading Sirens

Time is a given element in music: we measure music in time, whether in musical time or by clocking it on digital displays. Music is not measured spatially, but sound waves move through space, and the reach and speed of sound waves are used, for instance, to sound, or measure, the depth of water. In *Les Sirènes de Bagdad*, the movement of music through space and time acts as a narrative counterweight to the narrator's call to extremist action and ultimately thwarts the narrator's violent impulses in the final section, 'Beyrouth,' which leads to the undoing of both terrorist and narrative plot—the novel's dénouement.

This cycle established through the narrative structure of *Les Sirènes de Bagdad* is in keeping with the novelistic chronotopes that M.M. Bakhtin outlines. My analysis of the musical chronotope in *Les Sirènes de Bagdad* hinges upon the movement of music in the novel through a Walkman, a radio, and the narrator's memory. Sensory perceptions and memories of music in *Les Sirènes de Bagdad* demonstrate social complexities and contradictions within the brutal narrative universe established by the narrator in the introduction.

The music in *Les Sirènes de Bagdad* is an intrinsic part of the narrative process that thematizes these binaries. As part of the dénouement, the chronotopes undo the strict binary opposition that the narrator sets up in the introduction and first part of the novel. So the social heterogeneity and contradictions revealed through the chronotope of Faïrouz's music give both tension and texture to *Les Sirènes de Bagdad*. The narrator's confusion and negotiation of the multiplicities and overlaps of modernity and tradition is what drives the narrative. It is, as Gilroy might say, the 'changing same' (106), rendered formally through its cyclical and spatial temporality, that makes *Les Sirènes de Bagdad* exemplary in its use of the sensory perception of music as a literary device.

After Souleyman's funeral, the narrator finds himself incapacitated, unable to leave the house and subject to recurring nightmares. When

Souleyman was killed, the text suggests that the narrator bore silent witness. But in his dreams, 'Au moment où sa tête explosait, je me réveillais en hurlant' (82) ['At the moment when his head exploded, I woke up screaming' (69–70)]. To help comfort him, Kadem comes to the house with music cassettes.

Kadem, the narrator has explained earlier, is a lute player, who made his living primarily by playing at weddings. He is also twice widowed: his first wife died of pneumonia in a hospital, because the food for oil embargo had led to a dearth of medical supplies. His second wife, whom his father had forced him to marry to try to cure his melancholy over his first wife, died of meningitis eighteen months after they were married. The narrator explains that 'Kadem en perdit la foi' (34) ['Kadem lost his faith' (25)]—and when he comes to visit the narrator after Souleyman's death, he has some news that suggests that this loss of faith was symbolized by him giving up music: while the deaths of his wives silenced him, Souleyman's death—which, like that of his first wife, was also the result of violent Western intervention in Iraq—seems to have given him the impetus to play once more. Notably, his confession that he is playing again is preceded by his introduction of Faïrouz's music to the narrative.

> Kadem me passa alors les écouteurs de son baladeur. Je reconnus Faïrouz, la diva du Liban.
> —Est-ce que tu sais que j'ai repris mon luth? me confia-t-il.
> —Ça, c'est une excellente nouvelle. (83)

> [Kadem handed me the headphones attached to his Walkman, I recognized the voice of Faïrouz, the Lebanese singing star.
> 'Have I told you I've taken up my lute again?' he asked.
> 'That's excellent news.' (71)]

Faïrouz's music and public personality represent Lebanon as a nation, but her role as national icon was informed by Lebanon's past with France.[5]

---

5   'In Lebanon, the national identity formation projects in which the Rahbanis, Faïrouz, and others participated were, in fact, an extension of a discourse encouraged by Lebanon's French colonizers (Kaufman 2004). Faïrouz was, in other words, part of a national project that significantly was *not* predicated on difference with Europe. And though there was pressure for the French to quit the country ultimately, the national Maronite elite, as represented in the Baalbeck Festival committee members (the festival which launched Faïrouz to stardom), continued to look to Europe—and France in particular—as a cultural and civilizational model' (Stone 141–142).

And as a national icon for the country of which Beirut is the capital, her voice is key to *Les Sirènes de Bagdad*: its sound could have punctuated the narrative as a reminder of this impossible-to-pin-down urban space that so irks the narrator in both the introduction and 'Beyrouth' section of the novel. Yet the narrator is entranced by the sound of her voice.

In the novel's dénouement, Faïrouz's voice returns to cue the eponymous sirens of Baghdad, which arise not from Baghdad but from the rural village of Kafr Karam. I follow Kadem's lead by not qualifying Faïrouz as a siren herself. Kadem tells the narrator to listen to Faïrouz as a voice of redemption rather than the call of a siren: 'Ce n'est pas une sirène qui chante [...] si je devais mettre une voix sur la Rédemption, ce serait celle de Faïrouz' (96–97) [This is no siren song [...] if I had to put a voice on Redemption, it would be Faïrouz's (my trans.)]. This comment arrives the second time Kadem and the narrator listen to Faïrouz together. In this second passage, they listen to what is perhaps Faïrouz's most famous song: 'Passe-moi la flûte' ['A'tini al-nay' in Arabic, 'Hand Me the Flute' in English]. Here, Kadem offers his interpretation of Faïrouz's voice as one of redemption. It is significant that this song is playing through shared headphones as Kadem explains this to the narrator. Based on a poem by Kahlil Gibran, 'Passe-moi la flûte' is said to echo a Maronite liturgical principle with the line 'Song is the best prayer' (Stone 81). The loss and retrieval of Kadem's faith is represented by music. Faïrouz's voice, Kadem asserts, serves as a call for redemption.

So who or what answers that call? As Kadem tells the narrator that he has started to play his lute once more, he explains that before he was awakened by Souleyman's death, his mourning over his wives had taken on a moribund quality:

> Depuis des mois et des mois, ma tête ressemblait à une urne funéraire; sa cendre obscurcissait ma vision des choses, me sortait des narines et des oreilles. Je ne voyais pas le bout du tunnel. Puis, la mort de Souleyman m'a ressuscité. (84)

> [For months and months, my head was like a funeral urn. The ashes were obscuring my vision, coming out of my nose and ears. I couldn't see any way out. But then Sulayman's death brought me back. (71)]

The metaphor of the funeral urn full of ashes offers appropriately morbid embodied imagery, as the sensory experience that Kadem describes both echoes and foreshadows the narrator's experiences of violence at the hands of American military forces. Ashes obscure Kadem's vision much like shadows, fire, and smoke obscure the scene of the plane crash. The acrid smell of the ashes and the sounds they smother reflect back and forth between the narrator's experience of Souleyman's death and the aftermath of the plane crash. But Souleyman's funeral had the opposite effect on Kadem: it resuscitated him. The funeral urn metaphor stops there, and the narrative returns to the somnambulist motif, conveyed, paradoxically, through an awakening triggered by death. '"Comme ça," ajouta-t-il en claquant des doigts' (84) ['"Just like that," he added, snapping his fingers' (71)]. Souleyman's funeral triggered Kadem's awakening just as Faïrouz's voice triggered his admission that he was again playing music. And it is here that we learn about the sirens of Baghdad. Kadem continues:

> De retour du cimetière, alors que je me dirigeais machinalement vers mon muret, je me suis surpris en train de rentrer chez moi. Je suis monté dans ma chambre, j'ai ouvert le coffre serti de cuivre qui évoquait un sarcophage au fond du débarras, sorti mon luth de son étui et ... je t'assure, sans même l'accorder, je me suis mis aussitôt à improviser. J'étais comme emporté, ensorcelé. (85)

> [On my way back from the cemetery, I was automatically heading for the little wall and my rock, when I found myself entering my house. I went up to my room, searched the depths of the storage closet, located the trunk with the brass fittings—it looked like a sarcophagus—opened it, took my lute out of its case and, I swear, without even tuning up, I started composing. I was carried away—it was as though I were under a spell. (72)]

Note that the sirens have not yet been evoked by name. Kadem is lured not by sirens themselves. He is shocked, rather, out of a somnambulistic state by Souleyman's violent death at the hands of the American military. (The narrator's shocked awakening is echoed when the GIs invade his house and rouse him with violent threats, and subsequently when he sees his father's penis as his father is taunted and abused by the GIs.)

The narrator begs Kadem to play his new song: 'Je crève d'envie de t'entendre' [I'm dying to hear it (my trans.)], he says, and then asks Kadem what he calls it. Kadem hesitates, saying that he is superstitious and doesn't like to reveal too much about things yet unfinished. However, he decides to make an exception for the narrator and tells him that the name of the song is 'Les Sirènes de Bagdad.' The chapter concludes with the narrator's question: 'Celles qui chantent ou bien celles des ambulances?' and Kadem's reply: 'C'est à chacun de voir' (85) ['The ones that sing or those of ambulances?' ... 'That's for each of us to see' (my trans.)].

The song's content—that which the narrator is dying to hear—remains for each individual to *see*, not, as would be a direct response to the narrator's question, for the narrator to hear. By reading 'Kafr Karam' together with the introduction in Beirut, we can see how the narrative begins its perpetual veer between wakefulness and sleep, sight and blindness, hearing and deafness. It is all subject to interpretation, and to a willingness not only to look, but also to see, and not only to listen, but to hear—in other words, to understand. If we read 'Les Sirènes de Bagdad' as both the title of the song and the novel, the narrator's own subjectivity is highlighted. Polarized as his perspective is in a naïve and crude traditionalism, if we reverse this perspective, a critique of the narrator's strict distinction between modernity and tradition emerges. Does the perspective emerge as one qualified through tradition (the singing sirens) or modernity (ambulance sirens)? The ambiguous response to this question, 'C'est à chacun de voir,' refers not only to the narrator's interpretation of a song he has not yet heard, but to the sirens, which have a more seductive pull on him as the novel continues—the call to militant action or the call to elsewhere; the modern siren or the ancient one.

Superstrate to this critique is the textual universe constructed through the narrator's sensory experience: a world both modern and traditional, violent and civilized, a culturally multiple world that has been violently disrupted by the American invasions, as Kadem's mourning in silence and the narrator's stunted education attest. So in 'Kafr Karam,' a sensory pattern of sound and image emerges, upon which is plotted the narrator's physical reactions to the violence to which he bears witness. The resonance of Faïrouz's voice and the desire to hear Kadem's song 'Les Sirènes de Bagdad' prevails for the duration of the novel as it moves through both the narrator's and narrative memory. Based upon Kadem's awakening from mourning that led to the trance-like composition of 'Les Sirènes de Bagdad,' the sirens are introduced, and yet, seemingly, they were already there, and never really leave. Music and its promise trace the narrator's travels through both narrative and the narrator's memory as he moves from Kafr Karam to Baghdad to Beirut.

The culminating traces of sound arrive in the final section of the novel, 'Beyrouth,' as Faïrouz's voice filters back into the narrative. In the passage below, the narrator has already been infected with the virus, which is in incubation and scheduled to begin spreading some hours after he lands in London. He sits in the backseat of a taxi, and the taxi driver turns on the radio when they stop at a red light:

Faïrouz chante *Habbeytek*. Sa voix me catapulte à travers les âges et les frontières. Telle une météorite, j'atterris dans le cratère, près de mon village, où Kadem me faisait écoutait les chansons qu'il aimait. Kadem! Je me revois dans sa maison, contemplant le portrait de sa première femme. *Les Sirènes de Bagdad* ... Finalement, je ne saurai pas lesquelles. (328)

[It's Fairuz, singing 'Habbaytak Bissayf.' Her voice catapults me through space and time. Like a meteorite, I land on the edge of the gap near my village where Kadem had me listen to some of his favorite songs. Kadem! I see myself in his house again, looking at the portrait of his first wife. 'The Sirens of Bagdad' ... In the end, I will never know which ones they were. (my trans.)]

Again, Faïrouz's voice does not act as the siren here: she is a trigger to 'Les Sirènes de Bagdad,' Kadem's song, which the narrator remembers as Faïrouz's voice metaphorically catapults him through time and space. This is accompanied by a forceful longing to hear 'Les Sirènes de Bagdad'—and the narrator realizes, simultaneously, that he never will.

'Les Sirènes de Bagdad' lures the novel away from both terrorist and narrative plot to its sinister conclusion. He asks the taxi driver to turn down the radio, to which he responds, furrowing his brow, 'C'est Faïrouz' (328) ['It's Fairuz' (298)]. The narrator insists, and the taxi driver says that he won't turn it down but he will turn it off. In the absence of Faïrouz's music, the narrator, and—by extension—the narrative at first resist the recollection of the death of another character, Dr. Jalal, the day before: 'J'essaie de ne pas penser à ce qui s'est passé, la veille, et m'aperçois que je n'arrive pas à m'en débarrasser' (328) ['I try not to think about what happened last night, and I realize that I can't clear these thoughts away' (298, modified trans.)]. Contemplating the dying man's cries in the past, he looks, in the present, to the streets and the crowds outside the window: 'Les cris du Dr. Jalal résonnent à travers les douves de mon crâne, aussi tonitruants que ceux d'une hydre blessée. Je déporte mon regard sur la foule déambulant sur les trottoirs' (328) ['Dr. Jalal's cries resound through my skull, as thunderous as the cries of a wounded hydra. I shift my eyes to the crowds on the sidewalks' (299, modified trans.)]. 'Les Sirènes de Bagdad,' that song he was dying to hear, will never be heard, but its call lures him away from the plot nonetheless.

The passage in the taxi ends abruptly with a one-sentence paragraph: 'Je crois que je me suis assoupi' (330) [I think I dozed off (my trans.)]. In the subsequent paragraph, the narrator finds himself in the airport. So we find the narrator in a somnambulistic state once more in this one-sentence, transitional paragraph. This moment is key in *Les Sirènes de Bagdad*: recall the narrator's critique of Beirut in the opening pages of the novel. He finds himself in the same state, just as he had during the three violent events in Kfar Karam that precipitated his departure. This returning leitmotif suggests a kind of sympathy that develops in the narrator over the course of the novel. He introduces himself with disdainful thoughts about Beirut as sleepwalker. Yet he engages again and again in somnambulistic behavior when he encounters situations beyond his emotional and psychological comprehension. (And given that the introduction sets up a cyclical temporal structure for the novel, in expressing disdain for Beirut as a sleepwalker, the narrator expresses disdain for his own reactions as well.) More importantly, when it becomes clear in the subsequent paragraph that the narrator is suddenly in the airport, the one-sentence paragraph that serves as a transition between two spaces also becomes a shared understanding between the narrator and the interlocutor from whom he tries to distance himself in the novel's opening pages. In the transitional time during which he thinks he dozed off, he has paid the taxi driver, gathered his things, opened the taxi door, walked to the airport entrance, and entered. It is a simple series of events, one easily recognizable to anyone who has taken a cab to the airport (or seen a representation of someone doing so in film or on television). In this instance of somnambulism, thus, the narrator and his othered interlocutor come together through a shared understanding of an everyday experience.

The shared understanding and sonic disorientation continues when the narrator finds himself in the airport: 'Les guichets d'enregistrement sont pris d'assaut. Une voix féminine nasille dans les haut-parleurs' (329) ['The ticket counters are thronged. The public address announcer is a woman with a nasal voice' (299)]. Both narrator and narrative are suddenly in the airport. The lure of 'Les Sirènes de Bagdad' (and contemplation of the cries that signaled Dr. Jalal's death the day before) cleaves narrator from terrorist plot as Faïrouz's music comes together with the sensory pattern of sound and image. Once he has cleared security and waits at the gate, he looks around and marvels at seeing a man beaming at his pregnant wife, a girl waiting for a message on her cell phone. He even admires the affection between a young, blond European couple leaning against a vending machine: 'Leur étreinte était passionnée, belle, généreuse' (330) ['Their embrace is passionate, beautiful, generous' (301)]. He never makes that flight to London.

The restless sonority and the sudden outpouring of affection for those in the world around him extends into the final passage, as the narrator sits in a daze on a rock outside one of the terrorist headquarters hidden in the countryside. As he anticipates his death at the hands of the terrorists for whom he was once an honored vessel, Chaker, a member of the cell who had recovered him from the airport, tells him a secret: 'Je hais l'Occident comme c'est pas possible. Mais, à bien réfléchir, tu as bien fait de ne pas prendre cet avion. Ce n'était pas une bonne idée' (337) ['I hate the West more than it's possible to say, but I've thought about it, and I think you were right not to get on that plane. It wasn't a good idea' (307)]. Even terrorists are capable of reflection, apparently, and the narrator's response reveals that the extremism that drives him and drives the narrative has been diffused: 'Qu'ils fassent vite. Je ne leur en voudrai pas. D'ailleurs, je n'en veux plus à personne' (337) ['Let them be quick. I don't hold it against them. In fact, I don't hold anything against anybody anymore' (307)]. Just before he says this, the squeal of tires, signaling his murderers' arrival, is heard.

Immediately following the narrator's final line of dialogue, he tells us: 'Puis je me concentre sur les lumières de cette ville que je n'ai pas su déceler dans la colère des hommes' (337) ['I concentrate on the lights of the city, which I was never able to perceive through the anger of men' (307)]. So as the squeal of tires signaling his impending death marks the narrative conclusion, he continues to allow the lure of 'Les Sirènes de Bagdad,' triggered by the voice of Lebanese national icon Faïrouz, to entice him, although this time it is not through sound but through the lights of Beirut, punctuating the nighttime sky. The lights, the narrator tells us, are not discernable through anger, an anger that can be read as 'la même colère' he felt at the *charivari* of Beirut's souks in the morning, and the blasting car stereos in the evening. Kadem's response to the narrator's question about which sirens his song describes resonates through these noises, even as it goes unmentioned.

Thus Kadem's call to subjective interpretation of 'Les Sirènes de Bagdad'—'C'est à chacun de voir' (85)—supplants the narrator's extremism in *Les Sirènes de Bagdad*. The narrator's polarizing perspective on the elusive city of Beirut and its confounding combination of both modernity and tradition is undone, and with it, the perspective from the other pole (which might condemn Beirut for traditional elements woven into its urban modernity) is undone as well. Through the narrator's eyes, song and city bring together time and space in the final moments of *Les Sirènes de Bagdad*, coming full circle with the narrator: his extremist position, which is constructed through Western military violence and represented through his resistance to listening to the street sounds of a Beirut (which brings together both the modern and the traditional), comes undone. The many sirens of Baghdad issued a call to understanding when they were resisted by the narrator who, in turn, conveys these sounds to his interlocutor-reader as a speaker, in both senses of the term. So the sirens, in a way, move through him, even as he resists them. And in serving as the sonic vehicle for his interlocutor, the reader in turn is lured by the sirens as well.

Hear it with Your Own Eyes

February 26, 2009
I'm revising my reading of *Les Sirènes de Bagdad* when, as if on cue, an email arrives from the Musée de la Musique in Paris, announcing the museum's grand reopening. The subject line: 'Il faut le voir pour l'entendre.' This is the slogan for the reopening. Over the next several days, as I'm walking through the metro I see billboards with this slogan at almost every station. Beneath and at times intersecting with the slogan are Western musical instruments—a violin, a clarinet—digitally stretched into exaggerated shapes.

This slogan, 'Il faut le voir pour l'entendre,' plays on the same expression in French ('n'avoir rien à voir l'un avec l'autre') from which this chapter takes its theme: when it looks like two social concepts or situations have nothing to do with one another, before coming to any conclusions, we have a duty to listen—to hear out these concepts or situations through their specific contexts—in order to see if connections (*l'entendement*) between the two can be made. The subject line of the Musée de la Musique email announcement could be translated as 'You need to hear it with your own eyes,' and is playing on the idea that a museum devoted to the musical arts is something to be seen to be believed. And in fact, the reopening does not center around an exhibition (the museum is winding up a Serge Gainsbourg exhibit that opened last fall and has been extended through mid-March) but concerts. So this slogan is an apt one, since we talk about going to see concerts rather than going to hear them.

The interplay between sight and sound continues: among the concerts advertised in the email is a series of three shows that will take place the afternoon of March 22. The series is called 'Un Dimanche de Grande Nouba: 3 Villes, 3 Concerts: Tunis, Constantine, Rabat.' The musics at these concerts represent a range of Arab-Andalusian styles, but there is

Figure 1: Poster from La Grande Nouba

one image representing all three concerts on the poster: a woman's face is centered in the black-and-white photograph (see Figure 1). Her lips are painted with dark lipstick, and her eyes are lined with kohl. She peers through an ornate scrim face. It is framed by a headdress of jewels and pearls, and the headdress extends upward to a metalsmithed crown. An elaborately embroidered drape of fabric seems suspended and affixed to her pate behind the crown. Down her chest is a white bib with a dark, wide stripe down the center, laden with medallions and finally draped with strings of freshwater pearls. Her mouth is closed and she appears entirely still. This image, too, is all over the metro stops in Paris. This is not one of these uncanny interplays of sight and sound so much as a tantalizing promise that catches the passerby's eye. I see her in the poster and think of a silent siren, beckoning weary commuters to a harem of delights through these concerts. A friend of mine remarked that he had glanced at the poster and assumed that it was some sort of orientalist exhibition at the Louvre.

Indeed, this image reinforces orientalist representations of North Africa as exotic, and harkens to colonial history. It says little about the concerts themselves—of the three shows featured as part of the Grande Nouba concerts, only the first one features a female singer. A headshot of Dorsaf Hamdani from Tunisia smiles from the Musée de la Musique website once you click on the link in the email. As you scroll down past the orientalist poster, Hamdani's photo is the next image you see. Her headshot follows the conventions of most aspiring actors and models.

She is smiling, her head is at a three-quarter profile, and her hand is on her chin. Her hair has been styled straight, with a slight curl at the ends. She wears pearl earrings and a matching necklace. Her makeup is subtle—no kohl, lipstick only slightly darker than her skin tone. Her concert is the only one of the three for which there is no audio clip.

Images of ostensibly silent women encased in a *burqa* or tempting odalisques weighed down by ornate jewelry, their mouths painted with promises of sensual delight for those who come closer, do nothing to counter exotic representations of North African peoples. But the cultural phenomenon of the call to listen offers a range of counter-examples through sound. With the kind of engaged listening that sounding as a methodology advocates, the visual orientalist represen-tations of North Africa and the Middle East are readily undone. The way that Souleyman's father evokes Edvard Munch's *The Scream* in reaction to his son's death in *Les Sirènes de Bagdad* embodies the shared experience of parents who watch their children die: there are no words, only silence and gaping emptiness—sensory representations of the ineffable. Faïrouz's music as represented in *Les Sirènes de Bagdad* calls to the narrator, forces him to reconsider his extremist position on not only the Western world, but the multiple nature of Beirut as well.

Finally, there is the potential significance of Khadra's biographical and literary triangulations that circumvent the passage across the Mediterranean from Algeria to France. His ethno-thriller Llob trilogy was a direct import, portraying life in contemporary Algeria under the violent regime of fundamentalist Islamic forces for French readers. But despite the fact that *Les Sirènes de Bagdad* could be qualified as a terrorist Bildungsroman, for every representation of a violent man or meek woman of Middle Eastern extraction in *Les Sirènes de Bagdad*, there is a foil. Bahia may be subservient and docile, but the doctor's sister in Baghdad is independent, free-thinking, and free-willed. The narrator and other characters may be out for blood, but Kadem and, in the end, both Dr. Jalal and the narrator himself, suggest other ways of venting grief and anger. And then there is the siren herself, Faïrouz, singing for a wounded country, luring the narrator away from his quest for vengeance. He may die once the novel has concluded, but he takes no victims with him.

This is the effect of a siren: when we hear it, we stop. We might be in the midst of teaching, or sitting in a classroom, we might be walking down the street, we might be in a movie theater or chatting on the phone. But when we hear a siren, we pause, and wonder, and look. That ambulance siren wailing past the window, the fire alarm in the hallway, the warning siren that alerts the public to some potential emergency—these all lead us to stop and pay attention.

The same goes for singing sirens. When the narrator of *Les Sirènes de Bagdad* hears Faïrouz's voice, it triggers in him the desire to hear Kadem's song, 'Les Sirènes de Bagdad'—and he is lured elsewhere. Representations of music make us stop and consider, and defy the idea that there is no commonality between Western and Middle Eastern experiences of modernity and tradition, not to mention personal crisis and redemption.

The point is that when we hear a siren, we stop and pay attention. And, sometimes, that act of looking to see what's going on leads us on a markedly different path than the one we were on before. In the call to listen as a cultural phenomenon, this proves particularly interesting in the reversal of the sense which is first privileged. If the call to listen urges France to not only look, but also listen, here it is suggesting that vision can aid in the understanding of what is happening once a siren sounds its call. In the next chapter, I consider how the call to listen creates a narrative shift in two other art forms in which sound and image are necessarily entwined: theater and music.

PART II

The Performance of Listening in Film and Theater

Citational Hooks

Music and Middle Eastern Gender Identities in Postcolonial Francophone Film and Theater

Introduction: The Citational Hook

In the first two chapters of this book, the performance of listening in literary texts demonstrates how sound and silences can be embedded in a literary narrative. In the second half of this book, listening becomes part of a broader performance, whether on stage, on screen, or in music. Cultural interpretation—formulated in this chapter through the concept of the 'citational hook,' and in Chapter 5 as 'covering'—demonstrates a kind of meta-listening. To interpret, one needs to know the song, the ritual, the language—just a few examples of things that we interpret in culture—intimately.

Accordingly, the interpretation of a song by a new performer offers the possibility of a change in the meaning of the narrative constituted in the song's lyrics. This chapter explores two such performances, examples of a cultural mode of listening I call the 'citational hook.' First, I consider a performance of the song 'Eye of the Tiger' (1982) composed and originally performed by Survivor, which Marjane, the main character from Marjane Satrapi's autobiographical animated film *Persepolis* (2007), sings as part of a musical montage that portrays her re-entry into life in Iran following her teenage years in exile in Vienna. The second performance is of the Supertramp hit 'The Logical Song' (1979), which is sung by Nihad, the villain in Wajdi Mouawad's 2003 play *Incendies* [*Scorched*]. As Nihad, a Lebanese sniper in his late teens, listens to the Supertramp recording on his Walkman, he sings along to 'The Logical Song,' using his automatic rifle as an air guitar. The performances in *Persepolis* and *Incendies* rely on media and cultural representations of Middle Eastern femininity and femininity that define and are defined by respective Western and masculine identity (in form) and Middle Eastern and feminine and masculine identities (in content).

In analyzing these scenes from *Persepolis* and *Incendies* I consider how media representations of Middle Eastern femininity and masculinity are questioned and complicated in the performance of the citational hook. The lyrics to both 'Eye of the Tiger' and 'The Logical Song' are first-person narratives, and this is key to both Marjane's and Nihad's citations: they sing along to well-known and often-mimicked rock songs not to impersonate or imitate, but to embody gender transgressiveness and identity as a process through the citation of first-person narratives. In other words, these citations assert the particularities of each singer's experience of gender, ethnic, and national identity.

With the citational hooks in *Persepolis* and *Incendies*, I demonstrate how citations function within cinematic and theatrical narrative. Next, I show that these specifically gendered citations also draw their content from the singers' ethnic and national identities. Their citations thus challenge French cultural and media representations of Middle Eastern men with guns as inherently violent and Middle Eastern women wearing veils as necessarily oppressed. Finally, I unpack the hook, or the incongruity in these performances, in order to show the narrative power of these satirical and musical misfits. In so doing, these performances issue their own calls to listen that are particular to cinematic and theatrical works, rather than literary or musical.

Nihad in *Incendies* offers an example of a citational hook that complicates cultural representations of Middle Eastern masculinity as inherently violent. Lebanese-Quebecois playwright Mouawad's *Incendies* is the second play in *Le Sang des promesses* [*The Blood of Promises*] tetralogy. This tetralogy considers questions of origin and identity in its representations of the Lebanese Civil War and its aftermath (in *Littoral* and *Incendies*), the Second World War (in *Forêts*), and September 11, 2001 and its aftermath (in *Ciels*). Nihad, a Lebanese man in his late teens with a rifle strapped to his chest, is introduced about two-thirds of the way through *Incendies*, as he sings along to 'The Logical Song.' His performance offers comic relief only to yield to new tension when Nihad shoots a photographer. After Nihad wounds, verbally tortures, and then kills the photographer, he interviews himself, using the dead photographer's arm as a microphone. Nihad plays the part of two characters, a rock star Nihad, cast into some future time and place, and the interviewer from 'Star T.V. Show,' Kirk. Finally, the gun becomes a microphone as he launches into a performance of the Police song 'Roxanne' (1978), which I will address as part of my analysis of the narrative turn in *Incendies* that begins with Nihad's performance of 'The Logical Song.' Nihad's performance as a citational hook opens up questions about the character's identity in a way that resonates long after the play's conclusion.

The term 'citational hook' refers to two interdependent phenomena. Citation can be defined as the embodiment of a dominant form filled with subversive content. In the cases of *Persepolis* and *Incendies*, the content (the characters' performances) is subversive because it is inherently marginal, and yet claims centrality within and changes the very character of the dominant form it embodies. In *Bodies that Matter* (1992), Judith Butler conceptualizes citation in her analysis of Luce Irigaray's essay on Plato's *Timaeus*, 'Plato's *Hystera*,' from *Speculum de l'autre femme* (1974). Irigaray's reading of Plato, Butler explains, appropriates the form of the *Timaeus* in order to demonstrate its fallacy by subverting the original content in favor of feminist content. As she mimes and repeats the Platonic form using feminist content, the materiality of Irigaray's femininity inscribes itself within her critique while maintaining the original form. So citation can be understood, first, as a subversive upending of an original work with the uncanny appropriation of the original work's form by filling it with transgressive content.

While Butler's conception of citation concerns the construction of the feminine, I consider issues of intersectionality within the citations in this chapter as well, noting the particularities of the singers' gender identities in conjunction with their ethnic and national identities. My arguments hinge on the cultural interpretation of visual symbols that 'speak' for the Middle Eastern other. By looking at the intersections of gender, ethnicity, and nationality in these performances, I demonstrate how the citational hook undermines sociocultural assumptions about Middle Eastern gender roles and tendencies. In *Persepolis*, Marjane's citational hook challenges the notion that veils are the symbol *sine qua non* of Iranian women's oppression. In *Incendies*, Nihad appropriates his gun—both symbol and embodiment of French media and cultural representation of inherently violent tendencies in Middle Eastern men— as a guitar and microphone in addition to using his weapon for its intended use, all while questioning who he is and how he became this person. I read his citational hook as a critique of representations of violence as inherent to Arab masculinity: his citational hook opens up a consideration of the origins—or the impossibility of pinpointing the origins—of his motivation to behave violently and to subjugate others through violence. In turn, the considerations of Nihad's origins offer a reflection upon the difficulty of pinpointing the origins of the Lebanese Civil War and the Palestinian diaspora.

I qualify these citational performances further as 'hooks' in the sense of a catchy melody or guitar riff in a pop song. The citations in *Persepolis* and *Incendies* take their content from the characters' respective performances, which portray the giddy experience of singing along to a favorite song and performing one's own story while doing so. Both *Persepolis* and *Incendies* suggest that listening to marginalized voices can change the way that Middle Eastern gender roles and identity can be understood. In considering Middle Eastern gender construction in film and theater in French, how does what we hear change the way we see?

A common trait of both Marjane's and Nihad's citational hooks is the fact that they are essentially comedic performances that don't seem to fit: key to my analyses of these performances are the ways in which they are incongruous with the narrative contexts at hand. Furthermore, the way that these characters sing in English makes these performances incongruous. Marjane's off-key singing and heavy accent and Nihad's broken English render their songs humorously and sympathetically incongruous. In this chapter, I use 'incongruous' in two different ways to measure how these performances function: Marjane and Nihad's voices are both *out of step* with typical usage and *out of place* in their given context.

The incongruity of the sing-along performances, thus, is what renders them *hooks*, like a catchy melody in a pop song that draws in its listeners. It evokes, further, the narrative turn—the changes in tone and theme in these scenes signal the commencement of the respective narrative conclusions. So what is the hook in these performances? In both cases, a Middle Eastern character sings along in private, imitating elements of rock star posturing to a world-renowned pop song, unapologetically playing up vocal difference in order to create a humorous misfit. This misfit, or incongruity, marks a narrative turn in ways that complicate the social context presented in the story up until the moment of the performance.

Surprisingly, perhaps, the incongruity in these scenes has little to do with the English-language music as something out of the ordinary. Most of the music played and named in both *Persepolis* and *Incendies* is American and British rock, save the extranarrative use of traditional instrumental Persian music in *Persepolis* and some live percussion and ululation in Mouawad-directed productions of *Incendies*, which are not included in the stage directions of the play like 'The Logical Song' and 'Roxanne.' Within these textual works, English-language music, the musical genre of rock, and the Western instrumentation of rock music, are hardly incongruous.[1] These predominantly French-language works are rooted in the Middle East through their content and the origins of their writers, and were produced and released to great critical success in France. But the English-language songs in the citational hooks performed in *Persepolis* and *Incendies* circumvent the dominance of the French language in these works, offering a means of expression that asserts the characters' desire to be elsewhere, or in a different state of mind, rather than the ones in which they find themselves when they perform. This desire for difference plays out in the particularities of the characters' voices as they sing in a language different from those that are dominant in *Incendies* and *Persepolis*. The characters are not simply listening to English-language music in these scenes; they also sing in English. The incongruities, then, play out in the particularities of their voices (the marginalized, subversive content of their performances) rather than in the songs themselves (the dominant form that the singers appropriate as their own). That Anglophone music is an expected feature of these works' soundtracks contributes to my reading of the hooks of the characters' performances as specifically citational, but also, and importantly, incongruous.

To elaborate further on the importance of incongruity to the citational hook, I build upon Roland Barthes's concept of the grain of the voice, or the way the particular body of a singer's voice in tandem with a singer's physical body communicates with the bodies of listeners. In the essay 'Le Grain de la voix' (1977), Barthes delineates his conception as a complex of elements that can make a voice distinct, ranging from tone quality and color to particular vocal tics and so-called 'imperfections.' Barthes qualifies the relationship between singer's and listener's bodies

---

1   If, however, I were to address the heteroglossia of theater and cinema in French, I would argue that the use of Anglophone rock music in works like *Persepolis*; *Incendies*; *Littoral* (1998), the first play (and 2004 film) in Mouawad's *Sang des promesses* tetralogy; Claire Denis's *Beau Travail* (1999) and *J'ai pas sommeil* (1995); Olivier Nakache's *Intouchables* (2011); and Céline Sciamma's *Bande de filles* (2014) comprise a global cultural corpus that challenges social anxieties about English-language hegemony in France and French-speaking countries.

as specifically erotic: the voice of the singer, emitted from within the body, is drawn into the body of the listener. The singer's voice will have a sensual effect, Barthes argues, if it beckons with its own particularities.

In developing the concept of the citational hook with the grain of the voice, I am concerned not with erotics, but with the ways in which these performances open up possibilities for new ways of listening within the context of the respective works themselves. So although the hook is parallel to Barthes' grain, the hook is satirical and physically comedic rather than erotic. In the case of Marjane, the hook is comprised of her vocally rhythmic precision, out of step with the erratic pitch and tone of her singing, as well as the particular heavily accented words as she sings in English, complemented by her waxing, dancing, and strutting. Nihad's hook includes his use of broken English and the discrepancy between the image of the gun with the self-reflective lyrics to 'The Logical Song.' The hooks represent the social incongruities of their performances: Marjane, a Persian woman, alternately veiled and wearing aerobics gear, sings with gusto to the Survivor song that served as the theme for the films *Rocky III* and *IV*; Nihad, an Arab sniper wielding a rifle sings to Supertramp's elegy to socially unmolded childhood, singing 'please tell me who I am,' with his rifle as the instrument accompanying his self-reflective song. It's out of place, and that is precisely the point.

This is where the veil and rifle come into play as symbolic representations of identity. In the case of *Incendies*, Nihad's performance complicates cultural representations of Arab men as inherently and intrinsically violent. It resonates throughout the play's dénouement to suggest that his violent image is not grounded in his identity as an Arab man from the Middle East—rather, it arises from the context of his experience. For Nihad, identity is an ongoing process. In *Persepolis*, meanwhile, the 'Eye of the Tiger' montage can be read as a sort of training scene in which Marjane self-consciously constructs a feminine image to try to fit in with her friends under the veil—a constructed image that ultimately fails as the narrative progresses. In both cases, it is upon these interrogations and complications of the character that the narratives turn to their dénouements.

In conceptualizing how a citational hook functions within a larger narrative, then, I turn to film theorist Michel Chion's principle of *synchresis*, 'qui permet de nouer une relation immédiate et nécessaire entre quelque chose que l'on voit et quelque chose que l'on entend' (9) ['the forging of an immediate and necessary relationship between something one sees and something one hears' (5)]. Sound does not simply duplicate meaning: sound in fact allows meaning to arise from film, whether independently of image or in discrepancies between sound and image. The synchreses of sound and image that comprise the citational hooks in *Incendies* and *Persepolis* could be said to function in both ways: sometimes, the sound works independently of the images; other times, there are discrepancies between sound and image. Furthermore, there are moments in both scenes when sound and image complement one another. Sound is crucial for understanding how the citational hooks in these performances function within the broader narratives.

These performances deftly weave together not only the sound of rock music in English, but the particular accents and vocal inflections of characters who perform for their own pleasure in a way that can be read as a kind of musicophilia. As Oliver Sacks writes, 'listening to music is not just auditory and emotional, it is motoric as well [...] we keep time to music, involuntarily, even if we are not consciously attending to it, and our faces and postures mirror the 'narrative' of the melody, and the thoughts and feelings it provokes' (ix, xi). As the characters onstage or onscreen make the narrative of both the melody and lyrics their own, they also engage in listening for pleasure, weaving into the larger narratives of war, loss, and exile the deeply rooted human experience of enjoying music.

The Voice Beneath the Veil:
Marjane Satrapi's 'Eye of the Tiger' in *Persepolis* (2007)

> Rising up, back on the street
> Did my time, took my chances
> Went the distance, now I'm back on my feet
> Just a man and his will to survive
> —Marjane, *Persepolis* (2007)

If the above quotation strikes you as uncannily familiar, yet you cannot quite place it, that is the epigraph at work in a performance mode I call the 'citational hook.' The quotation is from the lyrics to 'Eye of the Tiger' (1982) by Survivor, which Marjane, the main character from Marjane Satrapi's autobiographical animated film *Persepolis* (2007), sings as part of a montage that portrays her re-entry into life in Iran following her teenage years in exile in Vienna.

Through Marjane's 'Eye of the Tiger' performance, I consider how stereotypes of Middle Eastern femininity are questioned and subverted through the citational hook. In my analysis of the 'Eye of the Tiger' performance in *Persepolis*, I first demonstrate how the citational hook functions within cinematic narrative. The first person 'I/eye' in Marjane's performance imbues this song with the hook, a subjectivity that subverts and transgresses the sociocultural construction of Middle Eastern femininity, both within the local context as constructed in *Persepolis*, and for French audiences. Second, I argue that when the 'Eye of the Tiger' performance is read in tandem with the frame narrative of *Persepolis*, set in and around Charles de Gaulle airport outside Paris, Marjane's citational hook challenges French representations of Middle Eastern women wearing veils as necessarily and always oppressed.

The 'Eye of the Tiger' performance takes place shortly after Marjane has returned from Vienna, where she had spent her adolescent and teenage years because of her parents' concern for their outspoken daughter during the Iran-Iraq war. The audience has watched Marjane grow from a fearless and outspoken girl who brazenly negotiates the politics and culture of Iran during the Islamic Revolution, into a sullen yet inquisitive and open-minded teenager in exile in Vienna, into a young woman back in Iran and unsure what to make of her changed home town or how to situate herself within it. Although the war between Iran and Iraq has ended by the time Marjane returns from Vienna, the restrictions on women's freedom (symbolized throughout the film and embodied by the female characters through the mandatory veil) have intensified. Marjane falls into a depression because of both the traumas she escaped and the shift in social norms that seem contradictory to her Western feminism. But when the opening guitar riff of 'Eye of the Tiger' kicks in, it is clear that she aims to get herself back in the game. She springs into action with a series of karate kicks and howls. The musical montage that ensues depicts Marjane 'getting herself into shape,' one could say, to assume this new identity, through waxing her legs, wearing the veil to university, and singing and doing aerobics (a gendered form of exercise that is part of the parody on the original meaning of 'Eye of the Tiger' in the *Rocky* films). As she sings and works out, she wears no veil, and its absence reveals her newly styled hair and spaghetti-strap leotard, in sharp contrast to her usual loose t-shirts and stringy hair.

While *Persepolis* certainly does not come down in favor of the veil, the film can also be understood to question French society's appraisal of the veil as always and necessarily a symbol of the Islamic religion that oppresses women. Veiling in *Persepolis*—and the choices Marjane makes regarding what she wears throughout the film—can be read as cinematic discourse in addition to a mandated religious practice. Marnia Lazreg points out that:

> Veiling is both a discourse—a manner of thinking and talking about it, perceiving it as well as taking it for granted—and a practice. As a discourse it lies at the interface of political ideology, culture, and agency. As a practice, veiling cannot be detached from history. And it is as history—the history of women in relation to men—that it is lived and experienced by women in various parts of the world. (11)

Certainly, the veil serves as a symbol of women's oppression in Iran throughout *Persepolis*. Yet, when we take into account the synchresis of Marjane's voice and her image both within and without the veil, the veil is put into visual dialogue with the normative beauty standards that Marjane embraces as part of her re-entry into Iranian life. In the film's concluding scene, the synchresis of Marjane's voice and her punk feminist guise undermines assumptions that to unveil is the act *sine qua non* of both women's liberation and immigrant assimilation into the French universalist public sphere.

Marjane sings the first verse and chorus of 'Eye of the Tiger':

> Rising up, back on the street
> Did my time, took my chances
> Went the distance, now I'm back on my feet
> Just a man and his will to survive
>
> So many times, it happens too fast
> You change your passion for glory
> Don't lose your grip on the dreams of the past
> You must fight just to keep them alive
>
> It's the eye of the tiger, it's the thrill of the fight
> Rising up to the challenge of our rival
> And the last known survivor stalks his prey in the night
> And he's watching us all in the eye of the tiger.

'Eye of the Tiger' is a first-person narrative, but 'I' is only sparingly evoked. The lyrics are primarily comprised of platitudes evoking redemption ('Did my time, took my chances') and the pursuit of triumph over adversity ('It's the eye of the tiger, it's the thrill of the fight'). The boilerplate nature of the lyrics makes the song ripe for citation.

The training montages in the films *Rocky III* and *IV*, both of which feature the song of 'Eye of the Tiger,' provide the source material for Marjane's performance. Survivor wrote 'Eye of the Tiger' as the theme song for the film *Rocky III*, and it was nominated for the Academy Award for Best Original Song in 1982. The song was subsequently used in *Rocky IV*, and has since been parodied and referenced in dozens of films, television shows, and performances around the world. It is thus familiar to a global audience, but it is mostly through the visual accompaniment of training montages (whether in one of the *Rocky* films or in any of the numerous sendups and parodies) that the song is recognizable.

Citation, as Judith Butler conceptualizes it in *Bodies that Matter* (1992), can be described as a subversive act of embodiment, in which a dominant form is filled with marginalized content. As I conceptualize the citational hook, gender marginalization intersects with ethnic and national marginalization as well. In the *Persepolis* 'Eye of the Tiger' performance, the image of Marjane, a twenty-year-old Iranian woman wearing a veil, proves comically incongruous with her gleefully raucous, heavily accented, off-key—and yet rhythmically precise—rendition of the Survivor song, which is importantly and decidedly both an American and a masculine narrative. The performance registers as something familiar with audiences (for how many readers can say that they have never enjoyed their own private performances of this kind?), yet the specific voice of Marjane as a singer also insistently registers both sociocultural and geopolitical difference.

The incongruity of Marjane's sing-along performance is what renders the citation a *hook*, like a catchy melody in a pop song that draws a listener into the citation at play. It evokes, further, the narrative turn— the shift in a narrative through changes in tone and theme that signals the narrative conclusion. The hook in her performance is the imitation of rock-star posturing to a song familiar to a global audience, unapologetically playing up vocal difference in order to create a humorous misfit. This incongruity is what allows the audience to feel a familiarity with the character, for such private performances are familiar to viewers as something they themselves have done.

While Butler's conception of citation concerns the construction of the feminine, Marjane's citation is more specifically intersectional. In Elizabeth Spelman's conceptualization of the term, intersectionality advocates thinking about 'gender, race and class in ways that don't obscure or underplay their effects on one another' as well as 'the intertwining of sexism with other forms of oppression' (115, 58). Marjane's performance could be understood to engage with the veil debate in France that was ongoing in 2007, as it hinges on the interpretation of visual symbols that 'speak' for women of Middle Eastern extraction. The concept of intersectionality helps demonstrate how the citational hook undermines sociocultural assumptions about Middle Eastern gender roles and tendencies. Marjane's citational hook challenges the notion that veils are always and necessarily a symbol of women's oppression. The temptation for French audiences to interpret Marjane as 'just like me' is thwarted by the intentionally awkward vocal performance that pushes the character's linguistic, ethnic, social, and cultural differences from French audiences to the fore.[2]

The song's original points of reference—the films *Rocky III* and *IV*—give visual form to the lyrics that can in turn be embodied in performance. In *Rocky III*, the character Apollo Creed specifically defines the 'eye of the tiger': he brings Rocky and Adrienne to a training ring in a gym filled with strapping African-American men wearing little more than boxing shorts, Jheri curl, and glistening sweat. The men all stop mid-workout and stare at the three newcomers (they clearly know who they've stopped to observe). Apollo explains: 'See that look in their eyes, Rock? When we fought, I trained hard, Rock, but I didn't have that look in my eyes. You had it, and you won. Gotta get that look back, Rock. Eye of the tiger, man. Eye of the tiger' (*Rocky III*).

Both the graphic novel and film *Persepolis* follow a surprisingly similar structure to the four *Rocky* films taken as an ensemble: the graphic novel is comprised of four volumes, and the film follows this four-part structure. In each of the four periods depicted in Marjane's life, she is confronted with a range of challenges, and has to negotiate the shifting social, political, and cultural landscape in order to triumph over adversity. The *Rocky* films follow not only the same structure and more or less the same story in each incarnation (a loss in the boxing ring leads to a negotiation of the self and a renewed dedication to the sport, and the dénouement comes with triumph in the ring). Following this structural similarity, the 'Eye of the Tiger' performance functions in a similar way to the use of the song as the theme of *Rocky III*. As Apollo Creed's explanation of the 'eye of the tiger' suggests, 'Rock' has lost his drive, and he needs to recover it in order to win the match against the film's antagonist, Clubber Lang. The song thus serves as an anthem for Rocky to recover his drive to win.

In *Persepolis*, the 'Eye of the Tiger' performance acts as a narrative segue from Marjane's depression following her return from Vienna to her renewed negotiation of life in Tehran. Similar to Rocky, who must

---

2 See Spelman 12.

reclaim his 'eye of the tiger,' Marjane's sing-along depicts her 'in training' for her comeback. Before she was sent to Vienna, the adolescent Marjane embraced all kinds of Anglophone rock postures and slogans: she scrawled 'Punk is not ded' [*sic*] on the back of the denim jacket that she wore with her headscarf, and in one scene, Marjane's mother is depicted sighing at her daughter's bedroom door as she plays frenzied air guitar with a tennis racket as Iron Maiden blasts from a boom box. The 'Eye of the Tiger' sing-along, then, can be understood as Marjane's fight for her voice, her individual mode of expression as she attempts to reclaim a space in a society where women are forced into public invisibility. The 'Eye of the Tiger' performance mimics the structure of the training scene in *Rocky III* throughout which the song plays. Just as Rocky prepares for the climactic fight, Marjane readies herself to re-enter Iranian society, using her old girlfriends who stayed in Iran throughout the war as a model: she waxes her legs, washes her hair, and works out in preparation for the racy outfits she will wear under her veil.

Marjane's off-key singing and heavy accent are comedic in their incongruity and imbued with social and political meaning through the visual images of her both with and without the veil. Beginning with her pitch, it is important to note that Marjane is off-key for the entire performance. This was intentional, Chiara Mastroianni explains in the special features on the *Persepolis* DVD. Marjane Satrapi told her she wanted 'Eye of the Tiger' sung with gusto but completely off-key, and sang it for Mastroianni to demonstrate before they recorded the track in the studio. And it is clear in the film that it was intentional: Mastroianni's vocal awkwardness and phonetic instability are part of the artistry of this performance, and what keys the scene as comedic. And Marjane's vocal rhythmic precision represents her confidence as she moves toward her new destiny. It is this confidence that keys the performance as intentionally comedic. The audience laughs with Marjane, not at her.

The 'Eye of the Tiger' performance in *Persepolis* portrays moments that are as incongruous to the training scene in *Rocky III* as Marjane's heavy accent and off-key singing are to the instrumental tracks of the song. Before she begins singing the first verse, Marjane issues a throaty scream following a karate kick that forces her to come face-to-face with the hair on her legs. She screams again when she pulls wax from her leg to rid herself of said hair—and this time, the scream is higher pitched, with a clearer tone. These performative gestures and sounds strip her of the intellectual feminist punk identity she had cultivated during her time in Vienna. In the next frame, Marjane struts through the streets of Iran as she sings in time with both the instrumental track and her walking pace. She wears the mandatory veil that covers all of her hair, head, and shoulders, save the oval of her face. In the first line, 'Rising up / back on the street,' she hits a sharp note on the second syllable of 'rising,' and descends a half-step with the word 'up,' only to fall flat for the rest of this line and into the next, 'Did my time / took my chances.'

Her pronunciation of the word 'chances' is crucial to understanding this performance of 'Eye of the Tiger' as citation: the vowel sound is much closer to the French nasal vowel [ã] than the English [æ]. As Marjane sings the word, she is clad in the obligatory veil as she struts to the swinging university doors and pushes them open. The accompanying visual images suggest that Marjane sings this word with the English definition of 'chances' in mind: she is taking a risk. But Marjane's pronunciation also implies that, following the lyric narrative, she is offering a summary of the last several years of her life through the French word 'chance,' or luck. In other words, this line begins with what seems to be her perspective on her time in Vienna ('did my time') but she then acquiesces to her good fortune to have been able to both leave and return to Iran, the first time in the film that she has admitted just how lucky she was. It is with this line that Marjane appropriates 'Eye of the Tiger' in order to imbue it with her own content.

Marjane's intractable melody as she sings the next line ('went the distance now I'm back on my feet') allows her to assume her own particular subject position within the song. As she sings 'went the distance,' she pronounces 'distance' as something close to [diːtʃnt]. The note she hits on the first syllable is the sharpest of the entire line, which is overall a wild incantation of sharps and flats. The word 'distance' is marked by Marjane's particularly sharp note and mispronunciation for a reason: 'went the distance' in the Survivor song acts as a metaphor to pushing oneself to succeed, rather than a reference to literal distance, which is indeed the case for Marjane. So by the time she sings 'now I'm back on my feet,' the only use of the subject pronoun in the first verse and chorus that renders 'Eye of the Tiger' a first-person narrative, the parodic nature of this marked performance has disappeared, for Marjane has fully assumed the first-person subject position within the song and imbued the lyrics with autobiographical meaning.

This in turn informs the edit during the next line ('just a man and his will to survive'). From the words 'went the distance' through 'just a man,' Marjane is sitting in an all-girl classroom taking a test. It is a check-in-the-box format test, thus she is herself writing, a metaphor, perhaps, for her individual identity being written over by the social strictures imposed by the Islamic regime. Marjane sings, her eyes trained on the viewer as she sits at her desk hunched over the test, surrounded by other female students in the same veil and same hunched position. They all bob their heads in time to the song.

Between the words 'man' and 'and,' there is a cut from the classroom to Marjane in the foreground with a nondescript background, her parents standing slightly behind her. Marjane sings directly to the audience in this shot, still wearing her veil, while her parents, notably, are missing the symbolic gender markers of Islamic oppression. Her mother is not wearing a veil, and—as is the case throughout *Persepolis*—her father has a mustache but no beard. They flank Marjane like backup singers, rocking their heads in time to the song as well. A further noteworthy detail is the bags under and lines around Marjane's parents' eyes: while Marjane and the other women at the university are full of youthful enthusiasm for the self-conscious feminine guises they have assumed under their veils, the signs of worry and exhaustion inscribed on her parents' faces suggest that they, too, embody the struggle that Marjane describes through her citation of 'Eye of the Tiger.'

So while the multiple-choice test represents social strictures, Marjane is also surrounded by sympathetic figures, indicated by the rhythmic precision of the performance extended from Marjane's singing into the movements and dancing of all figures onscreen. This simpatico rhythmic movement thus represents the 'man and his will to survive' in Marjane's rendition, rather than an individual struggle for survival. Her singing along with the others bobbing and rocking their heads in time offers a means of subversion through creative personal expression within the restrictions placed on their bodies and actions by the Islamic regime.

A screen wipe cuts to a bare-headed Marjane clad in a sleeveless leotard, revealing her clavicles and shoulders in addition to her curled hair and bare neck. Following the next edit, Marjane leads an aerobics class in time to the song as it reaches its anthemic chorus, looking into the camera's eye the entire time, and in a jubilant conclusion, she jumps into a holler-inducing split on the word 'eye' before she sings the last few words of the chorus ('of the tiger') and concludes with her vocal rendition of the guitar riff in a final humorous turn that also references her bedroom play as an adolescent air guitarist before she went to Vienna.

The lyrics to the chorus are flanked by the line 'eye of the tiger': keeping in mind Apollo Creed's definition of the phrase in *Rocky III*, it takes on a somewhat different meaning as Marjane sings. The screen wipe from Marjane wearing her veil flanked by her parents to Marjane in leotard leading the aerobics class is synchronized with the song's transition from verse to chorus. Marjane's aerobics class is not, of course, the same kind of exercise regime that Rocky undertakes in every film preceding the climatic fight. In *Persepolis*, 'getting into shape' is more than overcoming her depression following her return from Vienna. It is related, however: part of what seems to leave Marjane at a loose end is that the world she knew in Tehran before she left for Vienna has evolved into something different without her. The streets have all been renamed for martyrs of the Iran-Iraq war. Women's oppression has become even more severe, a key example of which can be found in Azar Nafisi's memoir *Reading Lolita in Tehran* (2003). Nafisi points out that in Iran during the 1990s, 'women were banned from singing, because a woman's voice, like her hair, was sexually provocative and should be kept hidden' (108). So, although it goes unstated in the film, Marjane's singing in and of itself serves as an outspoken act.

It is easy to imagine how, upon her return to the extreme social situation in Iran, Marjane might have been willing to give up her punk feminist style and construct a self-consciously feminine persona, following the lead of her girlfriends. Marjane had gone through puberty and her teenage years without wearing the veil. Where her girlfriends may have adapted to wearing the veil in public, it seems clear that part of what fueled Marjane's depression was that her sense of public self had not evolved under the veil, thus she experienced her return as a sudden erasure from public space. Feminist punk culture requires a society that supports freedom of expression, for it can mark feminist punks as those who choose to inhabit cultural margins, eschewing social norms of dress, hair, makeup, and body art as embodied dissent against mainstream society and culture. While this self-styled marginal social construction can function in private, it needs to be viewed publicly to be fully expressed. If freedom of individual expression is forbidden, then a fundamental element of the punk identity construction collapses. And while Marjane's narration of her time in Vienna indicates that she felt to some extent like she was going through the motions as a participant in the Vienna punk scene, she returns to a similar style of feminist punk dress once she is in France, as portrayed in the scenes that frame the narrative. Even in the conclusion of *Persepolis*, Marjane has yet to lay claim to any social identity beyond that of an exile.

This might explain why Marjane returned to the more mainstream pop music of her pre-Vienna youth to give voice to her return in Iran.

Although as a preteen she wore a denim jacket emblazoned with the words 'Punk is not ded' on the back, her taste in music at the time ranged from Iron Maiden to Kim Wilde to the Bee Gees, not, for example, punk contemporaries of these acts like the Sex Pistols and the Dead Kennedys. Marjane didn't actually start listening to punk music until she got to Vienna. So the 'Eye of the Tiger' represents another sort of return to Iran's cultural landscape around the time of the Iraqi invasion, before Marjane was sent away. Importantly, 'Eye of the Tiger' is in fact part of the narrative. Unlike the *Rocky* films, 'Eye of the Tiger' is sung by the main character in *Persepolis*, rather than played over a training montage as extranarrative music. Marjane sings the chorus relatively in key, save the first time she sings 'eye of the tiger,' during which her voice cracks into a sharp note on the first syllable of 'tiger,' as well as the last line, when her throat constricts and her voice seizes up as she prepares to sing the high note on the word 'eye.' The more consistent melody on the chorus can be understood as Marjane already having embodied the narrative and imbued it with her own meaning. But this performance is not without its complications. Although the song and Marjane's performance represent a sort of return to her pre-Vienna life, her attempts to carve out a space for herself under the Islamic regime result in a self-consciously feminine identity construction that seems estranged from the character the audience has come to know. This estrangement sets up the gendered identity struggle that propels the narrative from Marjane's ill-conceived marriage to her move to France.

It could be argued, on one hand, that the rival in Marjane's rendition is the Islamic regime. If that is case, like the word 'distance,' the word 'our' is literal in Marjane's appropriation of the 'Eye of the Tiger' lyrics, referring to Marjane, her friends, parents, and community. Marjane breaks the frame throughout the montage whenever she is shown in a front-on head shot, staring straight at the viewer. As she sings the last few lyrics of the chorus following her wild crescendo on the word 'eye,' the camera pans in to focus on her eyes alone: they are narrowed in concentration, quite unlike the playful, smiling expression on her face as she danced and sang. The *Rocky III* explanation of the 'eye of the tiger' is elucidated in the next line of the song ('Rising up to the challenge of our rival') through the subject position of a boxer with another boxer as his rival.

On the other hand, in Marjane's rendition of 'Eye of the Tiger,' the 'eye' becomes 'I,' for the performance also depicts Marjane assuming a self-conscious feminine guise. She does aerobics for exercise, not martial arts (which might seem logical given her penchant for Bruce Lee films), and her workout shoes are dance slippers, quite unlike the Nike high-tops that got her in trouble with the Guardians of the Revolution when she was younger. Marjane also assumes the role of lead singer in this montage. She is no longer air shredding on a tennis racket, as she did to Iron Maiden as a preteen. Although women musicians have become more common in twenty-first-century rock culture, guitar, bass, and drums remain a predominantly masculine bailiwick. But even during the early 1980s, when 'Eye of the Tiger' was first released, the role of lead singer was seen as an appropriate one for women in rock bands. So this montage represents a major shift in the construction of Marjane's feminine identity: the 'Eye of the Tiger' montage could be interpreted as Marjane working herself into self-consciously feminine shape.

So although Marjane's appropriation of the lyrics of 'Eye of the Tiger' imbue them with different content, the meaning of the phrase 'eye of the tiger' in the *Persepolis* montage could be understood to parallel Apollo Creed's explanation: the 'eye of the tiger' is that which needs to be looked in the eye, or confronted, in order to overcome it. The lyric subject *I* is not only a female other, but an Iranian female other who lived in exile from Iran during the Iran-Iraq war and returned to find herself dislocated from her social identity abroad, her political and cultural sensibilities, and her familial and social roots in Tehran. And so, the 'eye of the tiger' is not overcoming adversity that is embodied in an opponent. The adversary is Marjane's construction of the exiled Iranian self.

Persepolis offers no overt alternative reading of what the veil might represent for women in Iran. As a contrasting example, Nafisi notes in *Reading Lolita in Tehran* that before it was banned by Reza Shah in the 1940s and was in turn mandated by the Islamic regime in the early 1980s, the veil served for some women as a highly personal religious and/or cultural choice. Marjane's singing as she gives herself a feminine make-over asserts space for oppositional expression under the veil. Through the dance performance of a self-consciously masculine song, Marjane claims a space for herself to experiment with a self-consciously feminine social identity, following the lead of her Iranian girlfriends who had never left home. The effects of this are immediately clear: in the scene that follows the 'Eye of the Tiger' montage, Marjane is on the street with two girlfriends. She is wearing heavy makeup. One of her friends bemoans how hungry she is—she skipped breakfast because she was dieting—as Marjane is eyed by a passing male student, her soon-to-be-husband Reza. The space she has carved out in the 'Eye of the Tiger' montage thus adapts feminine beauty as a means of claiming space for women's lives despite oppression—symbolized by the veil—in Iran.

However, embedded into the dénouement of *Persepolis*, there is a subtle critique of the interpretation that the veil always and necessarily symbolizes the oppression of women. To summarize the film's conclusion following the 'Eye of the Tiger' montage, Marjane's new image as a va-va-voom beauty under the veil wins her the affections of Reza. They soon marry, a decision spurred on when the guardians arrest and interrogate Marjane about their relationship. Her father has to pay a fine so that Marjane won't be punished by whipping. Marjane laments to Reza, 'C'est pas une vie, ça' ['What kind of life is this?']. Reza proposes marriage as a solution, a proposition to which twenty-one-year-old Marjane acquiesces more than accepts. This is the logical conclusion of the 'Eye of the Tiger' misstep: the negation of her feminist identity through self-conscious feminization and matrimony. It is through marriage to Reza that Marjane's feminizing attempts at reassimilation into Iran falters. The scene following the marriage celebration takes place one year later: the couple glowers at one another as Marjane hunts for her car keys and Reza sulks on the couch watching *The Terminator*, represented by a bare-chested Arnold Schwarzenegger wielding a machine gun on a motorcycle. A few scenes later, Marjane weeps as she tells her grandmother that she thinks she needs to leave her husband. Her grandmother lovingly scoffs at her tears, telling her that a first marriage is always practice for the second.[3]

As funny as the 'Eye of the Tiger' performance is, Marjane's adoption of a self-consciously feminine identity represents a remarkable incongruity within the broader narrative of *Persepolis*. It is altogether contrary to the character who has been established thus far. The incongruity of

---

3   As is the case throughout *Persepolis*, the grandmother's dialogue attests to how liberated Iranian women can be, representing, along with Marjane and her mother, the multiplicity of women's voices in Iran. It could be argued that the strength and multiplicity of women's voices in Iran was underscored for the French public in the casting choices: Marjane and her mother are voiced by mother and daughter pair Mastroianni and Catherine Deneuve, and the grandmother by Danielle Darrieux. How this casting nod to strong women's voices was received by *Persepolis*'s French audiences would surely prove productive in an analysis considering the interplay of gender, voice, familiarity, and incongruity throughout the film.

this shift is fully realized when she marries Reza in a further attempt to assimilate to the country where she very much wants to remain now that she has returned. But once her divorce is finalized, the return-to-Iran experiment ends fairly abruptly: Marjane's mother comments that Iran is no place for Marjane.

In the film's penultimate scene, she leaves again, this time for France and for good. As the audience already knows through the scenes that frame *Persepolis* as an autobiography told in flashback, in France she takes up her *intello*-punk-feminist identity once more. In the opening scene, for example, there is a pan from Marjane's combat boots to her bust and face. She is smoking, much to the disgust of the woman sitting near her, who points to a no smoking sign. Marjane extinguishes her cigarette with a sigh. This scene in Charles de Gaulle airport outside Paris, taken in tandem with the 'Eye of the Tiger' performance, speaks directly to the French debate over the veil.

Marjane in France; or, the Veil that Punk Broke

The debate over banning veils in France lasted from the late 1980s until the ban was approved into law in 2010 and went into effect in 2011. Once the law forbidding the wearing of headscarves in public institutions was passed in 2004, a proposed ban on full-body veils in all public spaces throughout France garnered widespread support and the rhetoric in favor of the ban worked from the assumption of polarizing extremes.[4] On one side stood both feminist and extreme right-wing interpretations of French universalism. On the other stood fundamentalist Islam. And at their nexus stood the image of a woman in a veil (whether headscarf, *niqab*, or *burqa*). The woman in the veil did not speak. The veil spoke for her as a symbol of fundamentalist Islam, and understood to be, first, necessarily and without exception hostile to French universalism, and second, necessarily and without exception a symbol of women's oppression. In the years before the veil ban passed into French law, in

---

4   The full name of the 2004 law is Loi n° 2004-228 du 15 mars 2004 encadrant, en application du principe de laïcité, le port de signes ou de tenues manifestant une appartenance religieuse dans les écoles, collèges et lycées publics [Law #2004-228 of March 15, 2004 concerning, as an application of the principle of the separation of church and state, the wearing of symbols or garb which show religious affiliation in public primary and secondary schools].

most universalist interpretations and depictions, a veil always symbolized both women's oppression and fundamentalist Islam. The rhetoric on the veil debate from the feminist organization Ni putes, ni soumises [Neither Whores nor Doormats] (NPNS) proves a valuable source for the contextualization of *Persepolis* in France. The organization was founded in 2002 on the principle of feminist action against fundamentalist Islam. In 2007, NPNS founder Fadela Amara became a secretary of state under the conservative government of François Fillon. NPNS was founded in reaction to the terrorizing and gang rapes of girls in Arab communities in France who refused to wear *hijab* and/or walk accompanied by a male family member. The group is recognized by the National Assembly and a strong voice in the French press on issues related to the rights of minority and immigrant women in France. The rhetoric of NPNS on the veil ban in France is thus at the forefront of the debate but also offers a recognized political voice that explicitly links French universalism to minority and immigrant women's liberation.

Of particular interest to the analysis of *Persepolis* and the 'Eye of the Tiger' citational hook are two particular events that generated Facebook activity by NPNS. The first was a demonstration at place de la République on March 6, 2010, to celebrate the hundredth Journée des Femmes in France. The demonstration had a separate Facebook page that was promoted through the NPNS page. The title given for the rally on Facebook was 'A Paris: Marianne vous donne rendez-vous pour la Laïcité et la mixité!' ['To Paris: Marianne invites you to organize for *laïcité* and *mixité*!'].[5] NPNS encouraged rally participants to don Phrygian caps for the event, and to promote the rally they posted a photo album on Facebook and invited all of NPNS's 6,000 followers to contribute photos of themselves in their red caps.

---

5   I have chosen to leave the terms *laïcité* and *mixité* untranslated because of their specificity in the French context. *Laïcité* can be briefly defined as secularism as a core value of the French state. *Mixité* refers to the goal of anonymous sameness for all citizens in the public sphere, first conceived during the revolutionary period as a response to monarchy and class, and as time progressed, extended to gender and ethnic/national origins. In order to be included in French society, one must assimilate based on a set of criteria that delineates 'Frenchness.' Put another way, in an article called '23 mots pour dire les 1001 maux des exils' ['23 words for talking about the 1,001 ills of exiles'] published in the fall/winter 2008 issue of *Actualités & culture berbères* [*Berber News and Culture*], 'melting pot' was defined as assimilationism and an American English synonym for *mixité*.

At the NPNS rally—which was composed of sixty or so participants, of these, ten or so men—the main spectacle was a giant *burqa* that was thrown over the statue of Marianne in the center of place de la République. The *burqa* was quickly removed, but their point was made in stark visual terms. The gigantic *burqa* stood hulking in the center of the square, surrounded by a small army of protesters in red Phrygian Marianne caps. A rendezvous for *laïcité* and *mixité*? Apparently, that being the case, there was no need to explicitly mention the *burqa* in updates promoting the rally: its centrality in this event was manifest. These images and the NPNS status updates demonstrate that the *burqa* symbolizes two interrelated things in France: the encroachment of the Islamic religion upon French Republicanism, and the oppression of women.[6]

NPNS organized a rally expressly to garner support for the veil ban on May 18, 2010, which was announced on Facebook both through a separate page for the rally itself (called 'Grande soirée à Montreuil contre la burqa!') ['Big night in Montreuil against the *burqa*!'], and with a status update on May 14, 2010 which was cut and pasted from the information section of the separate rally page: 'Parce qu'il est urgent de réaffirmer les valeurs républicaines d'égalité, de mixité et de laïcité, le Mouvement Ni Putes Ni Soumises organise une grande soirée contre la burqa, le mardi 18 mai à Montreuil' ['Because it is urgent to reaffirm the Republican values of equality, *mixité* and *laïcité*, the Ni Putes Ni Soumises movement is organizing a night against the *burqa*, Tuesday, 18 May, in Montreuil']. In its first Facebook status update following the rally, on May 19, 2010, NPNS thanked the rally participants and further asserted that: 'Bien évidemment, nous continuons ces débats, et ces agissements des fondamentalistes ne font que nous conforter dans notre position: Il faut une loi pour dire STOP à l'instrumentalisation de la religion musulmane qui réduit les femmes au silence' ['These debates will continue, and the actions of fundamentalists only serve to reaffirm our stance: we need a law to say STOP to the exploitation of the Islamic religion, which reduces women to silence']. In the organization's next status update, posted ten hours

---

6 As Joan Scott has noted, the interrelated nature of the oppression of women and the threat to French Republicanism symbolized by veils and headscarves points to a constitutive contradiction in French universalist values and *mixité*: gender difference remains a thorn in the side of a system designed with the goal of social parity for all citizens in the public sphere.

later, the veil was decried as a 'symbole d'oppression de la femme' ['symbol of women's oppression']. NPNS status updates pertaining to this rally, thus, ably show how intersectional interpretations of the veil in France roll one into the next.

The claim that the veil, as a visual symbol of the religion of Islam, necessarily and always serves to silence women's voices was in keeping with another popular line of argument in France on the headscarf ban in public schools: that what is being banned is the symbol, not the girls (Caron 2010). With such rhetorical moves, activists and politicians work with the assumption that the veil is a symbol of the Islamic religion, which is hostile to *both* women and the French state (as represented through state and public spaces), and all one needs to do is remove the veil in order to eradicate the oppressive effect of the symbol.

Yet legal moves made in the name of protecting the universalist values of the state have, in fact, privileged the rhetorical force of the veil as a symbol of the religion of Islam over individual women's voices. John Bowen and Joan Wallach Scott have pointed out several examples of this in their respective works on the headscarf ban in public schools. Then there is the June 2008 incident in which French citizenship was denied to Faiza Silmi, a thirty-two-year-old Moroccan woman married to a French national of Moroccan descent, with whom she had four children who were all born and raised in France. Citizenship was denied to Silmi because she wore a *niqab*, a choice for which legal proceedings deemed her to be insufficiently assimilated to French society. Silmi, however, was fluent in French, historically one of the primary criteria for judging assimilation in France. This ruling was eventually reversed, but the privileging of the visual symbol of the veil over the linguistic fluency of the woman wearing the veil seemed to lend a maddening tautology to the debate: we cannot hear her voice in French because the symbol of the veil speaks too loudly. Therefore, women wearing the veil are necessarily silent, regardless of what they say when they speak.

The French media further complicated the terms of the debate in summer 2009, when a swimsuit that both covered the body and veiled the head, called a *burquini*, was introduced on the market. While some French media outlets tried to differentiate between the *niqab* and the *burqa*, this led to another confusion, as witnessed in a chart that explains the differences between these two veils and the *hijab*: they are all grouped under the rubric of 'voiles islamiques,' leaving no room for the possibility that these forms of dress might be evocative of, for example, cultural expression or political leanings.[7]

To bring the veil debate in France back into focus alongside *Persepolis*, it's worth noting that images of Iranian women in *chador*s were used to defend the proposed ban on headscarves in public spaces in France. Joan Scott notes that the complexities of the Iranian situation 'were lost on television viewers, for whom chanting men and women clad in black chadors came to embody a difference that was not only cultural and religious but political' (70). In other words, in borrowing these images, the Iranian people were cast as undifferentiated from the Islamic Revolution to which they were subject. This was done by extracting their images from their local context, erasing individual voices, and appropriating these mute images to demonstrate that if women and girls are allowed to wear headscarves in public spaces in France, the downfall of the secular state will inevitably follow.

Given Marjane's estrangement from her feminist identity upon her return to Iran, it is certainly interesting that she adopts another self-consciously marginalizing uniform once she moves to France: she returns to her punk leanings. Unlike the veil, the punk guise flies under the radar of French universalism as a conscious refusal to adhere to *mixité* as a national principle. Nonetheless, her heavy combat boots and loose-fitting black clothing do not mark Marjane as particularly assimilated into French society—the punk ethos included protest against class inequality from the earliest days of the movement in England and the United States. Notably, Marjane is never shown in Paris: the character who recalls her childhood and adolescence during the Islamic regime and revolution, her time in exile in Vienna, and the impossibility of a permanent return to Iran, does so while smoking in Charles de Gaulle airport, which is both a transitional and a transnational space. In the final scene of *Persepolis*, she gets into a taxi and says, 'Paris,' only to be asked immediately by the taxi driver where she is from, to which she replies, 'Iran.' Here, the incongruity of her accent is poignant rather than comedic, for it belies the possibility of her ever fully assimilating to her adopted home country. The incongruity of her accent as she speaks in educated French will always mark her as a woman in exile from the Middle East.

7 'Les différents voiles islamiques,' *Le Point* 19 June 2009, 11 October 2009, <http://www.lepoint.fr/actualites-societe/2009-06-19/les-differents-voiles-islamiques/920/0/354180>.

The 'Eye of the Tiger' performance is the zenith of the arc of this narrative about self-conscious attempts to construct some feminine version of the self in the face of both exile and oppression. Yet *Persepolis* critiques French rhetoric that condemns the veil as well. If we look only at the visual imagery of the training montage—'training' meant to prepare her for public life under the veil—the narrative about Marjane's self-conscious gender construction clearly calls into question the idea that wearing a veil can liberate its wearer from Western beauty standards. However, when we consider how sound impacts image, we hear Marjane's accents and inflections, whether she is under the veil, in aerobics gear, or in punk garb. Thus, the vocal incongruities in *Persepolis* also contest the idea that the veil is always and necessarily a symbol of women's oppression that, once cast off, will necessarily liberate the women who wear them. Marjane's 'Eye of the Tiger' performance and the final scenes at Charles de Gaulle remind the film's French audience of the particularities of women's voices under the veil. Perhaps most importantly, *Persepolis* asserts that there is no single narrative that encapsulates veiled experiences.

'Please Tell Me Who I Am': Identity as Process in Wajdi Mouawad's *Incendies* (2003)

At a talk in October 2008 at the Institut du Monde Arabe in Paris, playwright Wajdi Mouawad suggested that each of the plays from his *Le Sang des promesses* [*The Blood of Promises*] tetralogy comes at its exploration of origins in a way that can be compared to seeing the Notre-Dame Cathedral from each of its different sides. The first play, *Littoral* (1999), focuses on the aftermath of the Lebanese Civil War, while the second, *Incendies* [*Scorched*] (2003), looks at the legacy of violent origins in Lebanon without explicitly naming the country, from the Palestinian refugee crisis through the Lebanese Civil War. Two scenes from *Incendies*, 'L'Homme qui joue' ['The Man Who Plays'] and 'Les principes d'un franc-tireur' ['The Principles of an Outsider'] might be said to introduce one of the tetralogy's more prominent gargoyles: Nihad, a sniper who, it can later be deduced, is half-Lebanese and half-Palestinian by birth.

In 'L'Homme qui joue,' Nihad prowls to center stage, a masked man who stands wielding a rifle. He is wearing a 1980 model Walkman, and he is singing along at the top of his lungs to Supertramp's 'The Logical

Song' in broken English. Something offstage makes him stop singing, and he shoots in the direction he is looking. He then hustles offstage, and comes back dragging a wounded photographer with him. In the ensuing dialogue in French, Nihad cajoles and threatens the photographer, and becomes indignant when the photographer refers to him as a 'franc-tireur,' a word that most commonly means outsider or social outcast, as well as being an outmoded term for 'sniper.' Nihad shows the photographer pictures he has taken of people he has killed, then rifles through the photographer's bag until he finds a Polaroid camera. He tapes the camera to the end of his rifle. The photographer asks him what he is doing, and he replies, 'J'améliore mes conditions de travail' (74) [I'm improving my working conditions (my trans.)]. The photographer begs him, 'Ne me tuez pas! Je pourrais être votre père, j'ai l'âge de votre mère' (75) ['Don't kill me! I could be your father, I'm the same age as your mother' (67)], and Nihad retorts, 'Ça tombe mal. Je ne connais ni l'un ni l'autre' [Bad news. I don't know either one of them (my trans.)]. He shoots the photographer to death as he snaps a picture of him with the camera. The Polaroid photo falls to the ground with the other images Nihad has cast about. He then interviews himself as a rock star, using the dead photographer's arm as a microphone. As the interview ends, the Police song 'Roxanne' begins, and Nihad continues his performance, this time using his rifle as a microphone. 'L'Homme qui joue' takes place a little more than halfway through the second of two acts, and opens the dénouement of *Incendies*.

To situate Nihad's performance in the broader narrative of the play (which was the basis for a 2010 film by the French-Canadian director Denis Villeneuve), in addition to a plot summary there are two important issues of note: first, aside from the two scenes that are the foci of this analysis and the recitation of the alphabet in Arabic in an earlier scene, *Incendies* is entirely in French. Secondly, the play depicts, but never directly names, the Lebanese Civil War (1975–90). Mouawad has explained that he left Lebanon unnamed because of the vague ways he has always heard immigrants of the Lebanese diaspora from his parents' generation talk about the war. They neither explain nor lay blame. Thus, pinpointing the war's origins becomes impossible, and it is this impossibility that sets the narrative stakes for the exploration of identity and origins in *Incendies*.

Here I explore the ways in which the photojournalist silences Nihad in his photos of him, and how Nihad rejects this act of silencing through singing, dramatization of his autobiography, and violence.

Mouawad's play does not sanction the violence; on the contrary, Nihad's character stands silent in the play's conclusion, not as a result of his social identity but rather because of his violent actions. But his role in the play serves to remind spectators of the call to listen to the stories of marginalized people, and in the case of *Incendies*, Nihad represents both Palestinians and the Lebanese people—as well as the impossibility of pinpointing exact origins, both of people and in the crisis—in the fallout from the Israeli-Palestinian crisis and the Lebanese Civil War.

Mouawad is one of the leading voices in early twenty-first-century Francophone theater. He was awarded the Prix Molière in 2005, which he refused, stating that he did not want to be in competition with other worthy artists. As an associated artist at the Festival d'Avignon in 2009, Mouawad directed a nine-hour performance cycle featuring the four plays that comprise *Le Sang des promesses* tetralogy, *Littoral*, *Incendies*, *Forêts*, and *Ciels*. While his public and dramatic stances tend to address contemporary working conditions for artists, his *œuvre* speaks to history and contemporary politics. At the October 2008 Institut du Monde Arabe discussion, Mouawad responded to an audience member's brusque critique of how unrealistic he found 'The Logical Song' scene by explaining that, before his family left Lebanon, he remembered how older cousins who had been forced into military or militia service often assumed a rock-star like posture. He also mentioned that his memories of the spectacle of nighttime bombings are bound up in the music of Pink Floyd: teenagers treated nighttime bombings as a macabre form of entertainment, he explained, and rock music served as the soundtrack. These sorts of experiences of violence as entertainment in the Middle East are not readily apparent to those who live outside of the situation. It is due to representations of characters such as Nihad that we come to see how the pervasiveness of violence might render it a performance mode—terrifyingly so, and with appalling consequences.

In particular, Nihad's Supertramp performance and interview might suggest a critique of cultural and media representations of Arab men as inherently violent. The scene complicates the already complex theme in *Incendies* of the impossibility of tracing origins and identities in war, exile, and diaspora, and might lead to further questions, such as: What role does the media play in the construction of Arab masculinity as both menacing and outcast? What are the social responsibilities of journalists in portraying violent acts in the Middle East?

Incendies tells the story of twins Simon and Jeanne, whose mother, Nawal, has just died following five years of self-imposed silence. It is revealed in her last will and testament that their father, who the twins thought had died during the civil war in their mother's home country, is still alive, and that they have a brother, of whose existence they had known nothing. In Nawal's will, she stipulates that the twins cannot mark her tomb with an inscribed headstone until they find their brother and father, and deliver letters to them from Nawal, at which time her self-imposed silence will be broken. *Incendies* traces their narratively intertwined yet respective quests to find their brother (Simon's charge) and father (Jeanne's bequest).

Jeanne's and Simon's journeys interlace and overlap with a third narrative thread that depicts Nawal's own journey through her home country in the years leading up to and during the civil war. Her story is structured and heavily influenced by both *Oedipus Rex* and events from Lebanese history from the 1950s through the 1980s. As Simon and Jeanne begin to investigate their mother's life, Nawal's teenage years play out before the spectators' eyes: we bear witness to her love affair with a refugee named Wahab from somewhere south of Nawal's home country, her ensuing pregnancy, and Nawal's mother hiding the pregnant girl in the house until a baby boy is born and taken from her. This leads to a three-decade journey that zigzags through Nawal's home country, as she learns to read and write, then embarks on a journey to find her son with a sister-in-arms named Sawda. Civil war breaks out, Nawal assassinates a militia leader, and Sawda is killed. Nawal is then imprisoned for ten years, during which time she becomes known as 'The Woman Who Sings' because she would sing while she was raped and tortured by a guard named Abou Tarek.[8] At the end of the scene just prior to 'L'Homme qui joue,' Simon tells his sixty-year-old mother how scared he is of what he might find out about her past (in *Incendies* the characters often pace the stage or interact in temporal liminality). As Simon speaks, Nihad takes the stage with his rifle and Walkman.

In this scene, Nihad is situated in historical time only through the scripted prop of the 1980 model Walkman and the scripted choices

---

8 With 'The Woman Who Sings,' Mouawad is perhaps evoking Ovid's Philomela in the *Metamorphoses*, although he has stated that there was an actual 'Femme qui chante' in a Lebanese prison during the civil war, who would sing ABBA to drown out the sound of a woman screaming during regular torture sessions in a neighboring cell (2008).

of 'The Logical Song,' which was released and garnered worldwide success in the summer of 1979, and 'Roxanne,' first released in 1978 and re-released in April 1979, at which point it charted around the world.

The rifle is key to the incongruity of Nihad's performance of 'The Logical Song.' Although it's not a plastic bomb or a box-cutter, it has already been explained in the play that Nihad is a rogue sniper, neither part of a militia nor the government army. His rifle thus carries the same symbolic weight as a terrorist bomb, since any act of violence Nihad commits with this rifle is completely unsanctioned. With Nihad's gun as a symbol of rogue violence in mind, media, social, and political representations of Arab men as inherently violent is part and parcel to the tension in this scene.[9] Through his incongruous, humorous performance Nihad reveals a vulnerable chink in his menacing facade.

It has been argued that in French political, social, and media discourses, Arab men who have taken to rogue violence are not necessarily represented as products of their experiences—rather, the violent acts define their identity as Arab men. This is not to say, of course, that there have not been acts of extreme violence in marginalized ethnic and immigrant communities in France. As sociologist Riva Kastoryano pointed out after the 2005 riots, violence can be seen as a mode of expression in the *banlieue*:

> Rage has settled in those spaces. It is expressed through violence. Verbal violence, political violence, and physical violence guide interpersonal relations in public [...] Violence gives the neighborhood a territorial and ethnic collective expression, a means of ruling by provocation. (non. pag.)

As such, works like Fadela Amara's autobiographical critique of violence against women in the *banlieue* lead to a 'totalizing, causal narrative of new forms of *banlieue* violence and sexism' perpetrated by Muslim men (Dornhof 112). We can look further, to cultural works such as Jean-Paul Lilienfeld's *téléfilm La Journée de la jupe* [*The Day of the Skirt*] (2008), to see representations of teenage boys from the *banlieue* whose characters are defined by violent acts and who are treated as a

---

9 Such as Nicolas Sarkozy's 2005 comment about 'thugs and scum,' which has reasonably been interpreted by some as referring to young men of French suburbs, given the backgrounds of Zyed Benna and Bouna Traore, the young men electrocuted to death in a police chase that is said to be the triggering event of the 2005 riots, as well as the predominant minority population of the *banlieue*, to refer to young men of Arab or other North African, sub-Saharan African, and Middle Eastern ethnicities.

unified front and a symptom of social ills from the margins. From the onset of the hostage crisis in *Journée*, it is assumed by those outside that the perpetrator is one of these young men, and the negotiators and Minister of the Interior are speechless when they realize that it is the teacher (played by Isabel Adjani) who is holding her class hostage. These representations in memoir and film are no accident. They fulfill a social narrative that suggests that ethnic minorities in France will always be marginalized and thus prone to violence. As Kastoryano further argues, 'the term "immigrant" in France has become synonymous with North African, and little distinction is made between North Africans, Arabs and Muslims' (non. pag.), although, as Scott notes, 'not all North Africans are Arabs, not all Arabs are Muslims, and not all Muslims in France come from North Africa' (17).[10]

In terms of the way that gender is deployed in media, social, and political representations, it is important to consider the role of French universalism (or Republicanism) in these discourses. As addressed in the reading of *Persepolis*, in *The Politics of the Veil*, Scott argues convincingly that the objectification of women's sexuality in France serves to veil a constitutive contradiction in French universalism, or the notion that all French citizens embody an anonymous sameness in public that guarantees equality. Extended to former French colonies and protectorates, universalism (or Republicanism, as opposed to the *ancien régime* monarchy) cannot fully account for difference through gender, ethnic, or familial-national identity, nor for power differentials through ethnic or immigrant status. Just as socialization keeps women's voices tied to their bodies, voices are often bound through other social identities as well. As I analyze Nihad's performance, I argue that the way we listen to others is shaped by the speaker's national, ethnic, and gender identities as well as the ways in which the intersections of these categories inform and deflect one another.

To see Nihad sing of unsettled feelings about his identity belies the representation of violent impulses as inherent to his Arab masculinity. The singing performance of this newly introduced character is constituted through a complex of rock star bravado, the brutish awkwardness of both his bearing and voice, and the very presence of the gun. The hook

10 All of these examples predate the Paris attacks in 2015 and the Brussels attack in 2016—and, interestingly, in the aftermath of those attacks there has been increased recognition of the role played by French society in the marginalization and radicalization of young men of minority backgrounds.

provides specificity for this new character, who uses his bravado, bearing, voice, and gun to imbue his incongruous, sing-along performance with a paradoxical humor. His performance serves as a turn in the narrative, and the rest of *Incendies* plays upon this tension.

Nihad's performance does not fit neatly within either of the two central narrative threads. In addition to the fact that these scenes are the only ones in which the dialogue is a mix of French and English, they also stand outside Nawal's story and the twins' investigations of her life—neither Nawal, Simon, nor Jeanne know about this performance. The spectacle is for the audience's eyes alone. Thus, the photographer calling Nihad a 'franc-tireur' might strike a particular narrative chord. There is a turn that takes place in the midst of the two sing-alongs when Nihad drags the photographer onstage: he shifts, ostensibly, from a comedic (and menacing) cipher to a dangerously antagonistic one, although the comedic incongruity of Nihad's broken English as he sings and then postures as a rock star endures throughout these two scenes.

It is also important to point out the significance of this character's introduction to the play. *Incendies* follows much of the narrative logic of *Oedipus Rex*, although, as Jenn Stephenson argues, 'whereas Oedipus himself is the searcher, Nawal already knows the answer at the beginning of *Scorched* when she sets Simon and Jeanne on the two paths that are destined to intersect' (166). The scene in which Nihad sings Supertramp not only introduces him as a character, it is also the closest Mouawad comes to providing motivation for his heinous crimes. Perverse motivation, to be sure, but this scene shows us not only Nihad's capacity for cool performance of horrific violence, but also gives us more of his back story, thus resisting both stereotypes and totalization as an Arab (for, as we will learn, Simon shares Nihad's ethnic heritage, and yet the characterization of Simon suggests that his capacity for violence is limited to his promising career as a boxer).

Nihad's posturing as a rock star is crucial to the reading of this scene. To illustrate this point, consider a counterexample: ethnomusicologist Gabriel Solis writes that the rock performance of Bruce Springsteen can be said 'to refer to the performance of some *thing* that ultimately has some kind of prior essence ([the] performance of an already constituted identity [...])' (Solis 31). In the case of Springsteen, this *thing* with a prior essence is masculine, American, and working class. But Nihad's fictionalized and staged performance of singing along to a recording and fantasizing while doing so renders this sort of performance a *state of doing* rather than a *state of being*, and offers hints of how his past has shaped his identity. In choosing 'The Logical Song' as his star vehicle, Nihad performs an exploration of identity as a process rather than a fixed state of being that hinges around the lyrics to the first verse and chorus of the song, a first-person narrative, which allows Nihad to cite the lyrics. He embodies his own particular 'I' through the song: Nihad's particular 'I' moves in and through it, singing of youth from an older vantage point, lamenting the loss of its magic through images of nature before he describes being sent away to be taught how to be sensible, logical, responsible, and practical, and the world is transformed into a place he knows how to be a part of, yet is detached from: he can be dependable, yet also clinical, intellectual, and cynical. And 'when all the world's asleep,' this constructed world means nothing to Nihad— his identity as a rogue sniper falls away with the line 'please tell me who I am.' Bringing together this particular song with Nihad's image on the stage, then, becomes an embodied performance of questioning one's identity. Nihad's sing-along performance can be understood as an ambivalent posture, an incongruous, performative state of doing. The rifle assumes the guise of an electric guitar, with Nihad awkwardly mimicking a range of guitar heroes. In Stanislas Nordey's 2008 staging of *Incendies* in Paris at the Théâtre de la Colline, the play between social identity and the gun as guitar reached an incongruous, comedic climax when Nihad touched the tip of the gun to the crown of his head as he sang the word 'intellectual.'

In turn, this irony, black humor, and fantasy give way to a particular vulnerability in the armor of his rogue identity. Nihad's swagger is belied by his physical awkwardness, and he belts it out with an untrained voice and in broken language. The effect, again, is incongruity: a gun-wielding sniper takes time out to consider how he got to where he is.

How, then, does Nihad's performance of 'The Logical Song' set the stage for a narrative turn? Consider how Nihad uses the hand and arm of the dead photographer as a mock microphone to give biographical background to his performing career, as he stages an interview of Nihad the rock star by a certain 'Kirk' from 'Star T.V. Show.' That hand, which moments before was used to capture Nihad's image as a sniper, has been transformed into an instrument of Nihad's future fantasy, flopping weakly back and forth as 'Kirk' interviews Nihad in a soliloquy that reveals only slivers of detail about his past, but highlights the vocal imperfection of his broken English. Keeping in mind that the following passage is in the original rather than in translation, the seemingly inadvertent mixing of verb tenses in this passage is telling:

Kirk, I am very habby to be here at « Star T.V. Show » …
Thank you to you, Nihad. So Nihad, wath is your nesxt song?
My nesxt song will be a love song.
A love song!
Yes, a love song, Kirk.
It is new on you carrière, Nihad,
You know, well, I wrote this song when it was war. War on my country. Yes, one day a woman that I love die. Yes.
Shouting by a sniper. I feel a big crash in my hart. My hart colasp. Yes.
I crie. And I wrote this song.
It will be a plaisir to heare you love song, Nihad.
No problème, Kirk. (Mouawad 75)

Nihad-as-interviewer inquires, 'Wath is your nesxt song?' in the present, perfectly in keeping with form. Then, a conjugation error blurs the past and present a few lines later with, 'A woman that I love die.' Nihad-as-interviewee continues to relate his story in the present tense with 'I feel a big crash in my hart,' then shifts into the past with 'and I wrote this song.' Finally, the use of the simple future with 'It will be a plaisir to heare you love song,' suggests that this interview takes place in some future time, removed from the present: he wrote the song when it *was* war, and then he slips into a present-tense retelling of the death of the woman he loves, in so doing relating the immediacy of this death. And he in turn moves into the future through a grammatical shift to the past when he says, 'and I wrote this song.' So in addition to the spatial disconnect offered by Nihad's private performance with Walkman and rifle through his citation of a popular Anglophone rock song, there is temporal shifting at play as well. These spatial and temporal instabilities act as a microcosm of the two broader fragmented and oscillating narratives of *Incendies*. As a microcosm of the two narratives, it shows further how Nihad's anticipation of the future affects his sense of self in the present. The *franc-tireur* stands outside the social and political world of *Incendies* in these scenes, despite the violent behavior he exhibits, which foreshadows what is to come for this character as Simon and Jeanne's research progresses.

As the scene concludes, the gun is used in turn as a means of 'broadcasting' this fantasy Nihad—the stage directions indicate that the scene ends with the beginning of the Police song 'Roxanne,' for which the barrel of the gun serves as Nihad's microphone. A song sung entirely in the present tense in which the singer pleads with a prostitute to quit the world's oldest profession, Nihad has turned his state of *doing* through the interrogation of the self that constitutes the lyrics of 'The Logical Song' into a fantasy state of *being*—Nihad *is* the rock star, in some future time and other place, who sings the song he wrote during the time of war.

There is further evolution of the uses of Nihad's weapon, the object that marks his citation as particular to his own history and identity. His rifle serves as the locus of his subjectivity within the hook: the gun doubles as a guitar, an instrument discrete from the body, for a performance of the self, by the self, in which he questions his culpability through the lyrics to 'The Logical Song.' In sharp contrast to his violent actions in the scene, Nihad's performance suggests that the anonymous 'they' whom he cites in the lyrics made him who he is. The 'guitar' serves as the nexus of this self-fashioned delusion and the reality of Nihad's behavior: it abruptly becomes a gun once more when he shoots the photographer who silences Nihad's performance for the self, by the self, in order to try to capture his identity as a sniper in frozen images. The dead photographer's hand and arm, those body parts that had manipulated the technology that visually fixed Nihad's identity as a sniper, are manipulated by Nihad to become a microphone through which he can dissociate himself from the present, which leads him to his fantasy social identity as a rock star. The rifle, in turn, resumes its evolution, picking up where the photographer's arm left off. But instead of continuing to interrogate his past, the gun becomes a microphone that allows Nihad to close the door to past events and fully assume his self-conscious rock star identity through his performance of 'Roxanne.' The potential for sexual violence to be imbricated with rock stardom is manifold: in the 2008 Nordey production, the actor improvised on the lyrics to the chorus of 'Roxanne,' transforming 'put on the red light' into '*pute* [whore] on the red light,' which he sang in an uncomfortable, halting refrain that exceeded the length of the chorus in the original version of the song.

So what role has Nihad played in Nawal's life? He is, as is anticipated in 'L'Homme qui joue,' Nawal's long-lost son. Keeping in mind that *Incendies* is not specifically linked to Lebanon by name, when he is revealed to be her son, he is also revealed to be, by birth, partially of Nawal's national origins (ostensibly Lebanese) and partially of her teenage refugee lover's national origins (ostensibly Palestinian). These origins are effaced when he is taken from Nawal as an infant. This effacement of his origins reverberates painfully through the play's conclusion. Nihad's performance of the self, for the self marks his

Supertramp performance—the introduction of Nihad as a character—as pivotal. His full identity becomes clear in the next few scenes, which continue to oscillate between the twins' investigations in 2002, and a discovery by an aged Nawal: at a 1997 truth and reconciliation commission and through the scripted use of a clown nose pulled out during his testimony, Nawal sees for the first time her long-lost son, Nihad—who, as Nawal already knows, is also known as Abou Tarek, the identity of her rapist and torturer—and so Nihad is also Simon and Jeanne's father. Following this revelation, Nawal took her vow of silence, which endured beyond her death until Jeanne and Simon delivered the letters to their brother and father.

Two scenes after Nihad's performances of 'The Logical Song' and 'Roxanne,' he continues his interview with Kirk, and says that: 'Every balle que je mets dans le fusil, Is like a poème. And I shoot a poème to the people and it is the précision of my poème qui tue les gens et c'est pour ça que my photos is fantastic' (78) ['Every bullet that I put in the gun is like a poetry. And I shoot a poetry to the people, and it is the precision of my poetry that kill people, and that's why my photos is fantastic' (71)]. This artist's statement on bullets as poems suggests that there are aesthetic and performative—and in Nihad's case, self-fashioning—dimensions to murder: they constitute performances of a rock star caliber in Nihad's moral and artistic universe.[11]

Thus, Nihad's performance can be understood as a siren song that shipwrecks narrative expectations of his character. Although Simon tells his mother in the scene just before 'L'Homme qui joue' that he is afraid of what he will find, there is a paradoxical comedic relief of Nihad's performance, rendering this newly introduced character as possibly sympathetic despite the gun. The scene quite literally comes together only to fall apart: the much-needed comic relief is violently undermined when he wounds, verbally tortures, and then shoots the photographer to death. Yet, through the comedic incongruity of his sing-along performance of 'The Logical Song,' the complexities of Nihad's character and the details of his past are never fully revealed. The lingering questions about his past are left unanswered, save that

---

11   There is a similar moral universe in operation for the central character in Y.B.'s French-language novel *Allah Superstar* (2003) and the narrator's love interest Hanan Shaykh's Arabic-language novel *The Story of Zahra* (1986): both of these characters espouse the aesthetic merits and/or celebrity potential of spectacular killings.

at the time of the 'The Logical Song' performance (which pre-dates his transformation into the prison guard Abou Tarek), he never had met his mother. So no resolution is possible. The siren myth is turned on its head once more in a reversal of the role of the female sirens in the *Odyssey*: part of what the Odyssean sirens threaten is to cut Odysseus's journey short by enchanting him with songs that reveal hidden truths about the fall of Troy. The siren song in *Incendies* entices with the promise of telling Nihad's story, but as the siren is pursued, the audience does not learn the story of his past from the temporal vantage point of 'The Logical Song' performance. Rather, it is Nihad's future—which comes *after* this scene—that the narrative reveals retrospectively. The quest to understand the origins of his identity is thwarted.

The siren song lingers long after the play's conclusion, for Nihad's past is bound inextricably to Nawal's. 'The Logical Song' performance doesn't serve to complicate Nihad's character *per se*, for there is no redemption to be found in *Incendies*, and in the final scene of the play he literally recedes into the background. Rather, Nihad's performance embodies the complexities of the Lebanese Civil War, indicating Mouawad's decision to leave the conflict unnamed in the play. No one wants to point to the root of the problem, and perhaps no one can. But Nihad's embodied citation of Supertramp, 'please tell me who I am' first signals his otherness as both a torturer and an orphan, and in turn becomes 'please tell me what happened' in the larger narrative. It is the gap between lyricist and singer, as well as historical time and cultural spaces, in which the answers silently circulate. So, much as 'please tell me who I am' is answered only by a brash sax solo at the end of 'The Logical Song,' the revelation of Nihad's identity in the play's conclusion puts out narrative fires only to raise further incendiary questions.

I conclude with a brief reading of the scene 'L'homme qui joue' as speaking specifically to the Palestinian refugee crisis: as Nihad sang along to a song imbued with personal meaning, suddenly a photographer appeared, and without permission began to fix his image while rendering it mute. Gone with his movement and voice was the significance of 'The Logical Song'—all that would remain is the image of a young, unhinged man of uncertain national and ethnic background, wielding a rifle while listening to music on a Walkman. His questions about who he is, about how he got to where he is, and his lament for the past and fantasy-focused hope for a better future, are all silenced when he is captured in a still, photographic image. Therein lies the call: in the broader narrative of *Incendies*, Nihad's story offers a horrifying cautionary tale of what can happen when the world looks, but does not listen.

Incendies explores the Palestinian refugee crisis and Lebanese Civil War in equally oblique terms. Yet 'L'Homme qui joue' and 'Les principes d'un franc-tireur' offer a point of departure for considering the roots of violent acts rather than simply denouncing violence as part and parcel of a particular ethnic identity. To make this connection any more explicit in the play might be read as pedantic or polemic and, indeed, this very analysis runs that risk. My point, however, is not that Mouawad is denouncing French media and culture for the portrayal of young Arab men as violent. Rather, Nihad's performance opens up possibilities for new ways of interpreting individual acts of violence within the political crises in Palestine, Lebanon, and the resulting diaspora: it suggests how we might consider origins as a process rather than a fixed and static fact.

PART III

The Performance of Listening in Music

Covering French Universalism

Alter-Globalism in Kabyle Music in France

A Sunday afternoon, spring 2009. I am at the Zenith, a concert hall in Paris's Parc de la Villette. The venue is packed with people of all ages who have come to see Lounis Aït Menguellet, a Kabyle singer-songwriter celebrated in both France and Algeria. The amphitheater-style seating is sold out, and one of my friends comments that the dance floor is an 'animation de dingue,' a space teeming with people dancing and singing.

Many elderly and middle-aged women, as well as teenaged and young girls, wear a traditional Kabyle outfit: a mid-calf-length dress, embroidered across the bodice with loose sleeves gathered above the elbow; a headscarf, twisted back to form a knot with the hair at the nape of the neck; a *futha*, which is an intricately embroidered length of fabric tied at the waist and worn over the skirt; and finally, a separate, beaded scarf, tied at the waist. The last of these is worn only while dancing.

Many have come to the concert in tailored pants, jeans, skirts, blouses, t-shirts, sneakers, heels, but as they make their way to an open spot on the dance floor, they pull their beaded and sequined scarves from their purses and tie them around their hips, and by the time they find their spot to dance the scarves are already undulating, the beads and sequins shaking in double time to the music. It was a typical scene for a Kabyle concert in Paris or the *banlieue*.

But there was one major difference between this Aït Menguellet concert and other Kabyle concerts I had attended: Menguellet spoke to the audience entirely in Kabyle. Kabyle music in France is often sung in several languages (most commonly Kabyle, French, Arabic, Spanish, and English), but the stage banter is almost always spoken in French. Not so in the case of Aït Menguellet: when the audience had a particularly strong reaction, I would lean over to one of the friends with whom I had come to the concert—all of them bilingual in French and Kabyle—and ask them to translate for me. I tried to limit the number of times I asked, however, because I felt, both for myself and my friends, that my requests for translations were disruptive to the experience of the concert. Perhaps that was part of the point. Aït Menguellet was not addressing the general public. He was speaking to the Kabyle audience. Through this indirect address to the minority of the audience who understood French but not Kabyle, then, he established the Zenith as a space in which Kabyle was not only heard but listened to, not only tolerated but understood and honored. In other words, the performance was not for me as a linguistic participant, although I was welcome to observe and listen.

Aït Menguellet's use of Kabyle at the concert was an overt subversion of French linguistic dominance—but it did far more than that. I addressed the Barthesian 'grain of the voice' in the previous chapter, and it's worth considering how critic Peter Dayan further expands upon the grained singing voice in the context of non-literary versus literary or musical language:

> There is nothing essential about the material presence of non-literary language. What matters is its sense; and sense can survive a translation which entirely abolishes the matter of language. (Thus, if I translate 'rain' as 'pluie,' the word is completely changed, but the non-literary sense, which is a signified, remains the same.) But music is nothing without the physical presence of its signs [...]. In song, we hear that physicality as rooted in the materiality of the human body. Barthes has a term for the quality of a sound heard as giving voice, not to a sense, but to that physicality and materiality: he calls it 'le grain'.
>
> Barthes systematically opposes this grained voice to the discourse of the sciences. Science (including what has come to be known, quite properly, as the human sciences), like the languages of paradise and of the bourgeois positivist, names its object, and considers itself adequate, to that object as to its naming; thus it sees through its own language. The grained singing voice does not. But how can we speak of a grained voice without betraying it? For to speak of it as a nameable object would be to reduce it precisely to that which it is not: a scientifically or positively analysable thing. (99)

That is why speaking about the grained voice in the context of film or theater includes the context of body, gesture, and props, in addition to linguistic analysis of the singer's pronunciation and accent. In this chapter, I turn attention to the question of how music—and singing in multiple languages—is framed.

Let's return to the Aït Menguellet concert. The concert hall was full of the ethnic minority in France for whom he was a major cultural figure and spokesperson. I was part of the subverted minority in this case, a French speaker who could not understand the common parlance here in this concert hall on the periphery of Paris, less than ten kilometers from the Académie Française, housed in the Institut de France on the left bank of the Seine and on the very edge of St-Germain-des-Prés, which had, for centuries, been working to impose a codified national language within the boundaries of France and beyond into the colonies and protectorates.

One snippet of stage banter about halfway through the concert elicited a huge response from the audience:

Ay arrac negh, El Dzayer tamurt negh!

I capitulated to curiosity once more and asked what he had said. A friend leaned over to me, and as she smiled and cupped her hand around her mouth, she said in a projected stage whisper, 'Les enfants, n'oubliez pas votre pays!' [Children, don't forget your country!].

In addition to the lyrics and stage banter, a range of elements at the Aït Menguellet concert seemed to assert the imperative not to forget Kabylia. Dramatic stage lighting inflected both the music and stage banter in ways that underscored the dynamic shifts in atmosphere in the concert hall, at turns joyful, mournful, resolute, or contemplative. Throughout the concert, films and photographs of the Kabylia landscape filled the enormous screens that flanked the stage. As is typical at Kabyle concerts, during the encore Aït Menguellet invited onstage some of the local political leaders in attendance, as well as major cultural figures like Djura, the Kabyle singer and feminist activist, and Idir, the singer-songwriter known as the godfather of Kabyle world music, to join in a sing-along. Every element of the concert addressed a primarily Kabyle audience, and urged them not to forget. To keep looking back to Kabylia from France. And, above all, to keep their heritage alive and well—*in* France.

For some of the audience under forty was not only of Kabyle origin, but also *Beur*. As second-generation immigrants to France, they had been educated in French. They may have learned Kabyle at home, but many Kabyle *Beurs* take additional grammar and conversation classes as adolescents at local Berber cultural associations in order to become fluent. They may have been to Algeria several times, or only once or twice; some of them have not yet gone; some will never go.

The nostalgia and anxiety that surrounds *Beur* identity is embodied in the comic figure of the *zémigré*, the *Beur* who does not understand Algerian culture or mores. The *zémigré* (who is most often depicted as male) dresses to suggest a misunderstanding of cultural norms, such as bellbottom slacks, a plaid blazer, a bow tie, and a baseball cap. If the *zémigré* is visiting Algeria, he comports himself in Kabylia like a bull in a china shop, unaware to the point of caricature of how his social identity clashes with his surroundings. In one political cartoon by the Algerian artist Dilem, the *zémigrés* have voted to re-elect Abdelaziz Bouteflika, the president of Algeria since 1999 who has long been criticized for allowing Islamic fundamentalists to terrorize minority groups and journalists. 'It's because of him [Bouteflika] that we are *here* [in Paris]!' cry the *zémigrés*.[1] While the *zémigré* might sound like a minstrel, *zémigrés* are primarily represented in comics for which the intended audience is Kabyle, whether in France or Algeria. The *zémigré* is a self-reflexive figure that allows for the contemplation of what it means to live in one place and have your identity rooted in another, and it advocates the same message at Aït Menguellet's stage banter and video screen images: do not forget from whence you came.

Aït Menguellet's concert exceeded both the spatial and temporal dimensions of the event itself. It promoted cultural heritage and preservation, a call to protective arms, a means of mythologizing what had been left behind in the *bled*, as well as an insistence that the exclusively French-speaking portion of the audience bear marginalized witness to the celebration of it all. In these ways, Kabyle world music transgresses any simplistic nostalgia about *le bled*, akin to what Isabella van Elferen describes of Goth music, in that it 'engenders overlaps between pasts, presents, and futures' (169). While all world music can be typified as an amalgam of musical traditions, instrumentation, and languages, Kabyle music in France—and performances such as Aït Menguellet's—implore Kabyle 'children' not to forget Algeria, while exhorting social and political engagement to forge

1   Many figures in the Dilem cartoon wear t-shirts and carry banners reading *harraga*. In Arabic, *harraga* means 'those who burn,' and the term is used in both Algeria and France to refer to illegal immigrants who attempt to gain access to Europe by taking makeshift boats across the Mediterranean. The plight of the *harraga*s has been addressed in cultural works such as Algerian novelist Boualem Sansal's *Harraga* (2007) and Algerian filmmaker Merzak Allouache's *Harragas* (2009), and received increasing media attention with the Arab Spring and Syrian Civil War.

a new Kabyle identity and lifestyle in France that combines Kabyle cultural pride with French identity.

I have a similar sense about the nostalgic transgression of Menguellet's work as I consider the cover and read the first several pages of the thick volume *Aït Menguellet chante ...* [*Aït Menguellet sings ...*] (1989, 2008). The book is a compendium of Menguellet's lyrics in Kabyle with translations in French, along with a few introductory essays per section. The collection is edited by Tassadit Yacine, a well-known anthropologist with the Centre national de la recherche scientifique, who co-founded the *Cahiers d'études berbères* with the ethnomusicologist Mouloud Mammeri. The epigraphs—one from Jean Amrouche (1906–62) who, along with his sister Taos, is still revered as the defining scholar and archivist of Berber poetry and music, the other from Søren Kierkegaard—offer dual reflections on exile and melancholy. Yacine opens the foreword with the statement: 'Il est aussi difficile que passionnant de travailler avec et sur un poète comme Lounis Aït Menguellet. Car il est poète, au vrai sens du terme' [It is as difficult as it is engrossing to work with and on a poet like Lounis Aït Menguellet. For he is a poet, in the true sense of the term].[2] The preface is an essay about Menguellet written by Kateb Yacine, entitled 'Les ancêtres redoublent de férocité' [The ancestors intensify their ferocity]. This title is shared with one of Kateb's plays, published in the collection *La Cercle des représailles* [*The Circle of Reprisals*] (1959). While self-referential, this title also assumes Menguellet's *œuvre* to be part of the canon of significant postwar Algerian cultural works. Taken in tandem, these prefaces indicate that Menguellet's work is larger than the man himself. His work suggests a mythologization and lionization of not only Kabyle culture, but *Beur* culture as well.

Kabyle music in France requires split frames to address a range of listening publics. With the term 'frame,' I refer to the elements that help organize one's experience of a phenomenon. In the case of Kabyle music in France, the frames include stage banter, CD liner notes, a memoir, and visual accompaniments to the music. These frames are necessarily split when Kabyle music is released in France because of the particularities of the Kabyle community and culture as both a part of and marginalized within French society and culture. Kabyle culture is a minority culture in Algeria, and thus a minority culture of Algerian origins in France as well. Kabyle music in France addresses a range of audiences (French, Algerian, Kabyle) within the perpetually universalizing French society.

---

2 Translations from *Aït Menguellet chante ...* are mine.

What I mean by this is the following: universalism is a political value that privileges social homogeneity in order to level gender, ethnic, and religious difference in pursuit of a unified national identity. However, because, first, it is impossible to completely eradicate all social difference and, second, new differences will always emerge as a society moves through time, the way that Kabyle music is framed in France for different audiences speaks to the notion that universalism as a core French political value is a social process, rather than static reality.

The musics broadly referred to in France as *la world music, la musique mondiale,* or *les musiques du monde* are framed for the following audiences, defined here in three broad categories: 1) French peoples of French and other European origins; 2) French peoples from a range of other ethnic and national origins, predominantly African and Middle Eastern; and 3) both documented and undocumented immigrants in France. Within the second and third categories is an audience subset celebrated through Kabyle music in France, like at Aït Menguellet's concert: these are French people of Kabyle origin and Kabyle people living in France. In a broad sweep across all three identity categories, there are many in France who support French society as a universalist society, this is to say, a society that promotes the sociocultural assimilation of immigrants, the aim of which is an inclusive, universal identity for all citizens (regardless of gender, ethnicity, or religion) in the public sphere. This universal identity is never entirely achievable, since universalism cannot entirely account for gender, ethnic, and class differences. Yet universalism as a national value is regularly accounted for in the framing of world music in France. Sometimes, the frames question and complicate universalism. Other times, the frames accede to it.

Taken in tandem with a music performer's own sociocultural identity, his or her music is framed in particular ways for each marked subset of the listening public in France. When political intent related to the ethnic and national identity of origin is part and parcel of addressing listening publics, the framing of the music is complicated further by the market demand for a range of audiences to be addressed. As such, when we address framing devices such as images, CD liner notes, or stage banter, there is always a 'split consciousness,' as Paul Gilroy might call it, to these iterations. The split nature of the frames, then, articulates different issues in a range of ways, depending on who is reading and how the artist as a political spokesperson is heard in turn.

But it is also important to note that the split frames of Kabyle music released in France overlap. How one audience is privileged over another varies from artist to artist, depending on their cultural and at times political aims which, as is clear from the case of Aït Menguellet, can be both implicit and explicit. But Menguellet's political gestures in framing and lyrics most overtly confront Islamic fundamentalism in Algeria—and, as noted, his message from the stage is less about politics than about preserving Kabyle cultural heritage within France's borders. This is where *dédoublement* comes into Aït Menguellet's music and frames: within Menguellet's fight against Islamic fundamentalism, there is simultaneously a call to preserve Kabyle heritage, and a call for French society to recognize Kabyle difference.

Dédoublement offers one possible framing mode for Kabyle artists. In this chapter, I explore a different kind of framing: the *cover*. In using this term, I build upon two uses of the word.[3] First, there is the music cover, or a cover version of a song. Among the music and frame texts of Idir, I will explore his own 1999 cover of his most famous song, 'A vava inouva' (1973), which radically reinterpreted the song for a new generation and new sets of political circumstances in both Algeria and France. As part of this cover, the liner notes to the CD on which 'A vava inouva 2' is featured offer Idir's narrative about his identity in France as an artist who has fled oppression in Algeria. Second, the term 'cover' refers to covering territory, in this case, claiming France at home while simultaneously acknowledging the political problems that Kabyles, women, artists, and other marginalized and politically stigmatized figures face in Algeria, yet acknowledging also the nostalgia one feels for the *bled*.

One finds this critical nostalgia in the work of the feminist singer-songwriter Djura as well, which I explore primarily through her memoir, *Le voile du silence* [*The Veil of Silence*] (1991). Far from fragmenting her identity in her moves from Algeria to France, from France to Algeria, and back again, Djura's experiences in both countries and her decision to establish her life and career in France gave her a sense of wholeness where before there was a definitive sense of lack, due to the misogyny of her family, presented in her memoir as innate to the Kabyle community whence she came. For Djura, *covering* is a feminist reclamation of her

---

3   The French word for a cover version of a song can do the same critical work as the word *cover* in English. *La reprise* describes a new interpretation of a song; the word also means, among other definitions, 'a return,' 'a taking back,' 'mend,' and 'repossession.' All of these meanings come into play at different moments when I describe covering in the works of Idir and Djura.

Kabyle identity that has taken root in France, and flourished in the terrain of French society and culture.

In framing their music, Djura and Idir offer their own particular versions—or covers—of French universalism. This is to say that each artist works with the notion of French universalism, but they offer their own interpretations of what universalism means. Neither artist offers a prescriptive or utopist vision. As people of Kabyle origin, both Idir and Djura use their own experiences of migration from Algeria to France and back, then settling permanently in France, to create a particular textual weave between music, voices, and written words. With the frame of world music established, their work maintains French universalist values. Yet, in using the world music frame as an entry point, they also present a range of exceptions and expectations within French universalism borne of their experiences as Kabyles. What emerges in both cases is not only the possibility of their own versions—or covers—of French universalism, but also a new textual weave that covers, uncovers, and recovers different aspects of their respectively masculine and feminine Kabyle experiences.

Idir's and Djura's work demonstrates a call to listen that harmonizes with France as a perpetually universalizing society. The framing of Idir's and Djura's music offers a means of indicating to the listening publics in France how their music fits into the universalist picture, while asserting the right to retain Kabyle culture as part and parcel of French universalism. Accordingly, in *The Practices of Everyday Life*, Michel de Certeau offers a productive metaphor of transnational culture in response to this question: 'Là où la carte découpe, le récit traverse' (189) ['What the map cuts up, the story cuts across' (129)]. In other words, where geographic and national boundaries (such as the Mediterranean Sea between France and Algeria) seem to establish strict lines of distinction between two cultures, narrative transgresses those boundary lines and demonstrates the false dichotomies that such distinctions suggest. Following Certeau's assertion, if we take gender and ethnicity into account in the analysis of how Kabyle music is framed in Paris, it becomes clear that once the story cuts across the cut-up map, it proves a productive social challenge to represent a community in ways that do not simultaneously *cover* the voices of vulnerable community members. As we will see in the case of Idir, Kabyle women's voices are covered in the shuffle of multiple ethnic identities. In Djura's work, there are overt condemnations of both Kabyle men and the Kabyle community as a whole as endemically violent toward women, a cover version of stereotypes of Algeria and its men as oppressive to women. Yet, as I demonstrate through the conclusion of my reading of Djura, and the conclusion of the chapter as a whole, these acts of covering actually serve to *uncover* the terms of exclusions that accompany world music in a continuously universalizing France.

These analyses focus on one keyword per artist, each of which is featured in the titles of their work and prominently throughout the frames of the work. For Idir, who advocates a multicultural universalism both in the framing and lyrics of his songs, I consider his use of the word *identités*. My reading of Idir's work considers the way that we can understand his most famous song, 'A vava inouva' (1973), which he rerecorded as 'A vava inouva 2' (1999), through the essay in the liner notes of the CD on which the second recording appeared, *Identités* (1999). I focus attention on how the frames of the second recording, 'A vava inouva 2,' function, and reflect on the nature of this cover for an artist whose redefinition of universalism privileges ethnic difference over gender difference. To contextualize this reading, I also consider Idir's multiethnic protest anthem 'La France des couleurs,' which was released six weeks after Nicolas Sarkozy was elected president of France in 2007.

In the case of Djura, I analyze the way that she defines the word *silence*, as well as the term that serves as the title of her memoir, *Le voile du silence*. With her band Djurdjura and in her 1991 memoir, Djura confronts questions of Kabyle women's rights both in France and in Algeria. So the title of her memoir may seem obvious. Yet, there is the curious fact that Kabyle women do not wear veils—and her memoir does not concern Islamic fundamentalism. So in my analysis of Djura's memoir, one question I seek to answer is, what, exactly, is the veil of silence and, when it is pulled away, what can be seen and heard?

I read the frames of Idir's and Djura's music alongside the ways in which their musical *œuvres* take shape as distinctly masculine and feminine, respectively, *within* the cutting edge of Kabyle social and political negotiation of France. The burden to represent *Beur* culture in ways that will be embraced by the full range of dominant and minority audiences in France (and sub-audiences within both of these larger groups) proves a fruitful cultural and aesthetic challenge that is, nonetheless, never entirely surmountable. Yet, in the act of covering French universalism, these two artists manage nonetheless to overcome the burden of representation in a way that creates new cultural and textual weaves. In so doing, they issue another call to French society—in this case, to always listen for the silences that result from the terms of social exclusions.

Identités: Playing with the Plural(ism)

Idir is a world music star and a spokesperson for immigrant rights in France. He came of age during the Algerian War, and his music often reflects upon this fact. Idir (Kabyle for *Il vivra*, 'he will live') is the stage name of a farmer's son, Hamid Cheriet, who studied geology at university. Idir achieved worldwide recognition in 1973 with the song 'A vava inouva' ['Mon petit père']. The release of 'A vava inouva' predates the late 1980s conceptualization of 'world music,' and Idir is often referred to as the godfather of world music in France. The song 'A vava inouva,' as ethnomusicologist Jane Goodman describes,

> literally stopped Algerians in their tracks. A friend from the capital city of Algiers reported seeing people walk backward down a department store escalator to hear it playing over the ground-floor speakers. Nor did the song's allure stop at the Algerian borders. *A vava inouva* was the first Algerian hit in Europe and the first to be played on French national radio [...] More than twenty years after its release, the opening notes could still produce a roar. When I heard Idir play at the Zenith Hall in Paris in November 1996, he turned this song over to the immigrant crowd, strumming his trademark accompaniment as 7,500 spectators sang the refrain by heart. (49)

I witnessed an audience reaction similar to the one Goodman describes when I saw Idir play a solo acoustic version of 'A vava inouva' in concert at Théâtre Jean Vilar in Vitry-sur-Seine in December 2008. It seemed that the entire audience knew the lyrics by heart. They sang along softly and with reverence. When the song ended, the audience burst into boisterous applause, loud cheers, and ululation.

'A vava inouva' has endured in popularity for over forty years, and is still considered a foregrounding model for world music as a movement and genre. As Goodman has noted, many elements of the song can account for this. First, the scene it portrays features a Kabyle grandmother sitting by a hearth on a snowy night, telling a well-known Kabyle folktale that is similar in theme and story to 'Little Red Riding Hood.' Idir's vocals imitate a female style of vocal ornamentation in the refrain, although the lyrics narrate the cultural memory of storytelling rather than relating the grandmother's story verbatim, a point to which I will return shortly. Second, there is the harmonization of 'the story's familiar refrain on an acoustic guitar, using an arpeggiated chord style associated with popular Western folk stars such as Joan Baez or Bob Dylan' (Goodman 49). The song offered a new formulation of Algeria's

Arab, Berber, and French histories 'so as to produce a dynamic and potentially subversive new synthesis' (Goodman 55).

Idir's dynamic new synthesis—in other words, his cover—of universalism offers a multicultural, or *mondialiste*, vision. The title of Idir's 1999 CD *Identités* offers up some clever rhetorical play. This word shifts in meaning when it moves from oral to written language. With no article preceding the plural noun, there is no way to identify it as plural when spoken, because the final *s* is silent. If one were to say, 'J'aime *Identités* d'Idir,' or 'On écoute *Identités* d'Idir,' there is no way of knowing if the title of the CD is singular or plural. These statements reveal the possibility for further conceptual play: are we listening to the CD by Idir, *Identités*, or to Idir's identity, or Idir's identities? A listener must *read* the title in order to grasp the central theme of the CD, thus demanding listener engagement that plays on the presumed superiority of the written form. This is notable because Kabyle was an oral language until the early twentieth century. Furthermore, this shift from the oral to the written insists upon *identities*, a plurality, rather than a singular, unified (and in France, one could say more specifically, a perpetually universalizing) *identity*. In reading the CD's title, if we move from speaking to reading, the presumed dominance of the culture that privileges both assimilation and textual discourse is subverted, because the written meaning asserts identity plurality rather than a singular, universal identity.

Idir's *mondialisme* has become both a thematic and formal thread through his later work, and over the past fifteen years, more overtly subversive. Take, for example, his CD *La France des Couleurs ...*, which was released in late June 2007, a month and a half after Nicolas Sarkozy was elected president. The album features several world music stars representing a range of ethnic minorities in France, who came to fame two generations after Idir, including Kenza Farah, Disiz la Peste, Nâdiya, and Féfé of the Saïan Supa Crew. The title track—sung in French and Kabyle and with responses to each line of the refrain in English—offers a celebratory refrain that registers the need for political action among minorities in France: 'La France des couleurs / défendra les couleurs de la France / La France des couleurs / Bouge, bouge et mélange' [The France of color / will defend the colors of France / France of color / Move, move, and melange]. This refrain encapsulates the subversive *mondialisme* of Idir's *œuvre*: he advocates a universalism that embraces difference rather than effacing it. The use of the word *mélange* in particular is crucial here: while *mélanger* is a synonym for *mixer* (both mean, broadly, to mix, in a range of contexts), Idir's use of the verb *mélanger* rather than *mixer* registers a protest against *mixité*.[4]

This is the context in which Idir chose to use the verb *mélanger* rather than *mixer* in the song 'La France des couleurs.' To underscore the significance of this choice, it is worth noting that several DJs are featured on this song (along with the coterie of world music artists) and the verb *mixer* is used in sound production in the same way that the verb 'to mix' is used in Anglophone sound production: it means both to level the sounds on a recording and to bring together disparate tracks to create a new unified work, like DJs do. Thus Idir's choice of the word *mélange* could be understood as registering further protest to the deployment of *mixité* that serves to silence and oppress minorities rather than level social difference. Consider the double address of 'La France des couleurs' in the following lines: 'On veut notre identité / [...] On mérite mieux que ces cités / [...] On veut juste être écoutés' [We want our identity / (...) We are worth more than this public housing / (...) We want only to be listened to]. Idir asserts the right to a social identity that includes one's ethnic and national origins within the borders of France as a nation-state. Note particularly that he uses the verb 'want,' rather than 'have,' to describe the conditions for ethnic minority identities in France. In using the verb 'want,' he asserts that these ethnic and social identities have yet to be—yet must be—recognized and accepted by France as parts of both the nation-state and the people. He covers these two terrains here by melding two different political positions, the universalist and the *mondialiste*. Within these lines, then, the double address in fact weaves together both a political assertion and a lived reality.

A forerunner of *La France des couleurs* ..., the *Identités* CD showcases an ensemble of world music stars from across Western Europe who represent a range of ethnic minority identities and rose to fame in the 1980s and 1990s, including Manu Chao, Zebda, and l'Orchestre National de Barbès. The first two pages of the liner notes to *Identités* offer an essay by Idir that illuminates his choice of the

---

4   Accordingly, my translation of the line 'bouge, bouge et mélange' shifts the grammatical structure of the lyric in order to preserve the word 'mélange,' a verb in the original French and a noun in the translation. This translation is less than satisfactory since it suggests that a melange is the result of the 'move, move,' but I wanted to resist using the verb 'mix' in the translation, for obvious reasons. Using 'mélange' also preserves the rhythm and meter of the French original. (I note, too, that in French, the line could be read as either the imperative or the indicative, while my translation can only be taken as the imperative.)

CD's title. The essay is set in quotation marks as if to suggest that it is a transcript of an oral narrative or interview. It is structured through a set of questions and issues surrounding the identity politics of living as an Algerian Kabyle in France. Idir begins with 'un dilemme de taille: comment être algérien à part entière et vivre mon identité berbère entièrement à part?' [a sizable problem: how to be entirely Algerian and live my Berber identity entirely apart?]. The chiastic phrasing of the question in the original French bears on the difficult issues of separation and wholeness in the particular case of Kabyle immigrant identity in France, which parlays into the Kabyle identity debate in light of Algeria's colonial and postcolonial histories.

Idir follows this question with a brief summary of the Algerian War, and the Islamic insurgencies of the 1990s:

> Fier d'appartenir à un pays qui a retrouvé son indépendance au prix de sept années de lutte, baignées de larmes et de sang, je me suis senti frustré de ne pas être reconnu dans ma culture maternelle, les pouvoirs en place ayant installé une identité de substitution de nature idéologique.

> [Proud to belong to a country that had regained its independence at the cost of seven years' struggle, bathed in tears and blood, I was frustrated to not be recognized within my maternal culture, the powers that be having imposed a substitute identity of an ideological nature.][5]

Idir's frustration speaks to a series of historical ruptures: French colonization, the Algerian War, and the rise of Islamic fundamentalism in Algeria which started in the early 1990s and precipitated the civil war. His threefold frustration parallels these ruptures. First, there is the impossibility of public recognition as an artist in his home country. Second, there is the erasure of Kabyle identity in France through the imperative to assimilate. Third, the erasure of Kabyle identity paradoxically echoes the cultural religious identity forced upon the Kabyle people in Algeria through Islamic culture: from the seventh and eighth centuries with the Damascus-based Umayyad dynasty's campaign to convert Berbers throughout North Africa to the rise of Islamic fundamentalism in Algeria in the 1990s that continues to the present day, the Kabyle have in turn embraced and resisted participating in Muslim culture. It is from the erasures of Kabyle identity that Idir works to reconstitute a notion of *identités*: to truly represent Kabyle experience, it must be recognized first as multiple. So, *identité* for Idir is

---

5   All translations mine.

identités: the plural is a homonym of the singular, but in written French we can distinguish one from the other.

Idir's notion of *identités* differs from the Khatibian concept of *dédoublement* in that it ultimately uses multiple identities as a template for *mondialiste* culture: rather than looking at the doubling and redoubling of identity as a shortcoming or a handicap, Idir embraces multiplicity as a vital cultural element to weave into his music. Idir's music, thus, effectively *covers* multiple facets of his identity, and extends beyond his personal identity into the multiple ethnic and national identities represented not only in France, but in Western Europe as well.

Continuing with the liner notes of *Identités*, Idir elaborates on his divided loyalties between Algeria and France: 'L'un m'a enfanté et m'a donné une origine, une histoire et une identité. L'autre m'a adopté et m'a offert un parcours dans lequel je m'exprime totalement' [One gave birth to me and gave an origin, a history, and an identity. The other adopted me and gave me a career through which I can fully express myself]. This is just one of several examples from the essay in which Idir describes the conundrum of his 'identities quest,' one could say. This quest is realized through the recording of *Identités*, as the last phrases of the liner notes suggest. Idir describes what the musicians from many different cultures featured on the CD have done for him: 'ils m'ont permis de montrer que ma culture, aussi minoritaire soit-elle, peut s'inscrire dans l'universel' [They have allowed me to demonstrate that my culture, a minority group though it may be, can inscribe itself in the universal]. Thus Idir sets the terms for listening, as well as giving a definition for what constitutes universalism: his identity, named *Identités*, has been realized with his claim of a multicultural universalism. In other words, this essay implicitly insists upon identification with ethnic minority cultures as an inherent part of the shape of universalist social identity in France.

Let's turn, then, to the remake of 'A vava inouva,' the opening track on *Identités*, entitled 'A vava inouva 2.' In this cover of his own song, Idir is accompanied by Scottish singer Karen Matheson. It is a powerful track: in the song's opening refrain, Matheson sings the traditionally female vocal ornamentation that Idir sang on the original version. Matheson sings this vocal ornamentation in Gaelic style, using primarily chest voice (in contrast to the Berber style, which uses a range of nasal tones). Idir's famous guitar riff that opens the song is joined by a bagpiper. The bagpipes retreat until the coda, and weave in and out of Idir's and Matheson's harmonies. The results are captivating, haunting.

The most reactionary proponents of French universalism might stop in their tracks to listen.

Since 'A vava inouva 2' is the opening track to the CD, the first voice we hear on *Identités* is Matheson's, not Idir's. She sings a nonverbal rendition of the refrain melody in 'A vava inouva' in the opening, during the chorus, and in harmony with Idir through the coda. Idir sings the lyrics (in both versions, entirely in Kabyle) throughout the song until he picks up the harmony to Matheson's melody in the coda. So the first voice we hear in 'A vava inouva 2' is the voice of a Scottish woman, who brings to the song not only the particularities of Gaelic singing style but a different history of Western European domination and oppression.

It is worth noting Goodman's reading of the lyrics to 'A vava inouva,' which makes explicit a nostalgic utopian vision and the prescriptive gender roles embedded in the cultural memory of the Kabyle household relayed by the song. In the refrain to 'A vava inouva,' the covered story of women's experience plays out within Idir's narrative of cultural memory that serves as an allegory for French and Arab colonialism: a father and daughter exchange the words, 'I beseech you, open the door for me, father. / Jingle your bracelets, o my daughter Ghriba. / I'm afraid of the monster in the forest, father. / I, too, am afraid, o my daughter Ghriba' (Idir, qtd. and trans. in Goodman 62). In the longer, untold version of this well-known Kabyle folktale (entitled 'L'Ogre de chêne,' 'The Oak Ogre'), Ghriba and her father try to fool the ogre in the woods by jingling a secret code on her bracelets.

The scene portrayed by the lyrics to 'A vava inouva' would be familiar to anyone who grew up in Kabylia as a family storytelling ritual. The grandmother sits at the hearth, surrounded by eagerly listening grandchildren. The daughter-in-law weaves at the loom. The grandfather sits in the corner, smoking a pipe and dressed in winter wraps. The son worries about how to feed the family. While this scene describes 'a set of complementary gender and generational roles' (Goodman 63), the story told within this setting is represented by only a slim excerpt. Furthermore, in the verses, the daughter and father are 'rendered inert [... making] it clear that storytelling is to be evoked as cultural memory' (Goodman 62). However, given the frames which Idir has established for 'A vava inouva,' the grandmother is unable to transmit cultural meaning to the song's world audience:

> When listeners hear the song, they are not suspended in the story, raptly attentive to the grandmother's next words. Rather, they are simulta-neously looking back at the process of storytelling and across at the

other listeners, who are not the family members sitting around the grandmother but all of Kabylia, Algeria, the international community—especially France, the former colonial power. (Goodman 63–64)

So the lyrics here suggest a few possible understandings of the split frames of 'A vava inouva 2.' There are two gestures of looking in the song: one gestures back to history, in time, and the other reaches across, in space, to an international community, in the midst of narrating the cultural memory of Kabyle storytelling. On one side of the Mediterranean, there is the Algerian audience, for whom the folktale would be immediately recognizable, along with the cultural meanings it relays. On the other side of the sea, because the grandmother's telling of the tale is only excerpted, the listener hears a story of a Kabyle man looking back at his Algerian childhood and Kabyle tradition, while the musical fusion form bridges this memory into his present location, France, and underscores the modern gesture of looking back, which relegates history to the past.

In covering a range of ethnic minority voices in the *Identités* project, Idir powerfully and elegantly asserts a cultural manifestation of multicultural universalism. His songs retain an essential form and style that mark them with a distinctly Kabyle influence, yet show how bringing in other voices can in fact bring together cultural movements that seem distinct into a harmonious whole. As a songwriter and musician, I cannot help but marvel at both the aesthetic and political accomplishments of *Identités*. But as a critic, I wonder: what is hidden—covered up—in 'A vava inouva 2.' While *Identités* asserts a multicultural universalism, it is also a masculine vision. Matheson is the only woman featured on *Identités*, and, somewhat surprisingly, no space was established within the project for a Kabyle woman's voice such as Djura's. This would not have been inconceivable: it has been typical to see Idir and Djura onstage together at encores of concerts such as Aït Menguellet's, and both artists have a long history with the Berber Cultural Association in Paris.

As a cover of an original song (for that is precisely what it is: Idir imbues with new meaning an updated rendition of his classic song with the addition of Matheson's Gaelic sound and the bagpipes as part of the arrangement), the voice of Kabyle women are doubly covered. It is Idir who sings the female voice on the original, and on the cover version, the female vocal ornamentation is performed by a woman of different ethnic origins. What are we to call this double rendering of Kabyle women's voices, then: a cover? A mask? A veil?

In light of the push to assimilate into French society, 'A vava inouva 2' and *Identités* can certainly be interpreted as a rallying cry to a continued fight against presumed French cultural dominance within the boundaries of France. The curiosity is that within this multicultural universalist interpretation of a hallmark song in Kabyle culture, Kabyle women's voices have, in multiple senses of the word, been covered. Furthermore, Kabyle communities both in France and Algeria take great pride in the fact that Kabyle women do not wear veils like their Muslim Algerian counterparts, although Kabyle culture subscribed to many social mores that insist upon women's subservience to men. What are we to make of the covering of a Kabyle woman's voice in 'A vava inouva 2'? Is it necessary to cover some voices in order to establish a collective identity for a group? Must gender be set aside in using *identités* as a frame? In seeking answers to these questions, I turn to feminist Kabyle singer-songwriter Djura—a vocal ally of Idir's distinctly Kabyle voice for *mondialisme*—to present the ways in which women's voices are recovered in Kabyle culture in France.

Djura's Cover of Silence

I am looking at the cover of Djura's memoir. The author's name and title are set in black type on a white background, just under the Livre de Poche logo: 'Djura,' the first line reads, followed by 'Le Voile du silence' in a slightly smaller font. It follows the standard design of all Livre de Poche books. Most of the cover is comprised of a color headshot of Djura. She wears a simplified version of the traditional Kabyle dress in which she performs her concerts. Her dangling earrings are hands of Fatima, a symbol of safety that protects one from the evil eye throughout Islamic and Islamic-influenced cultures.[6] Djura wears heavy black and blue eye makeup and red lipstick. Her hair is long and loose, and she is smiling. Her hand is balled under her chin, and from one finger flashes a Kabyle ring of silver and coral.

---

6   The hand of Fatima is a pan-Mediterranean symbol. In Greece, Turkey, and the Americas it is represented by a blue bead. When worn by Israeli and Palestinian women, the hand of Fatima, or *hamsa* (derived from *khamsa*, which means 'five,' as in five fingers, in both Arabic and Hebrew), represents the wearer's desire for peace between the two communities. In France, it functions for Muslims like a cross for Christians and the Star of David for Jews, but the hand of Fatima has not met the same political resistance in France as the headscarf and veil.

Since I found a new copy of Djura's memoir by chance in a foreign-language bookstore in London, I have puzzled over this cover. The title and image seem completely at odds. The woman on the cover is not marked as veiled in any obvious way, nor do her parted, smiling lips readily suggest silence. So what does this image tell the reader about who this woman is? And what, then, is the veil of silence? And what, here, is the cover covering? I use the term 'cover' here in the sense of what knowledge the cover conveys; in other words, the content it covers, rather than coverage in the sense of veiling.

It could be deduced that the seemingly disparate elements on the cover of Djura's memoir frame the text effectively because it is assumed that the reader will come to it with some foregrounding knowledge of both the author and her subject. Djura and her band, Djurdjura, had nearly two decades of success behind them by the time her memoir was published in 1990. And if a reader were to happen upon this memoir unawares, she need only turn to the back cover:

> Une jeune Kabyle se voit condamnée à mort par sa famille, parce qu'elle a pris un Français pour compagnon et conçu un enfant avec lui.
> Cela se passe à Paris en 1987 et la victime de cette « expédition punitive » n'est autre que l'auteur de ce livre, fondatrice du groupe musical bien connu *Djurdjura*.
> Autour de ce témoignage hallucinant, Djura nous entraîne des montagnes de Kabylie aux cités d'urgence pour immigrés, dans un monde où le déracinement culturel va de pair avec un incroyable archaïsme de la condition féminine.
> Un document saisissant, qui recoupe des thèmes d'une brûlante actualité dans la France et l'Europe contemporaines.
>
> [A young Kabyle woman finds herself condemned to death by her family because she took a French man as her partner and conceived a child with him.
> This event takes place in France in 1987, and the victim of this 'punitive quest' is none other than the author of this book, founder of the well-known musical group *Djurdjura*.
> Through this incredible testimony, Djura leads us from the mountains of Kabylia to emergency public housing for immigrants, in a world where cultural uprootedness goes hand in hand with unbelievably archaic conditions for women.
> A gripping documentary that brings together the themes of a hotly debated reality in contemporary France and Europe.][7]

---

7   Translation mine.

Taken in tandem with the photograph of the cover, all signs point to Djura's memoir as a story of triumph over adversity. But the question remains: what exactly is the 'veil of silence'?

Djura's autobiography could be classified in French literary culture as an ethno-memoir, to appropriate the French term for a specific genre of detective thriller, the *ethnopolar* [ethno-thriller], which situates familiar detective narratives in contemporary postcolonial settings, particularly Algeria. As part of the ethnographic component of the genre, the main characters of *ethnopolars* often bear the weight of historical trauma that results from war or other sorts of political strife, as in Yasmina Khadra's Commandant Llob trilogy.

Djura makes the stakes of representation clear on the dedication page to *Le Voile du silence*, which serves further as a preface of sorts. To contextualize her thoroughly French *dédicace*, let's return for a moment the image of the *zémigré*, the comic *Beur* figure who is almost always portrayed as male. One reason for this particularly gendered depiction is that the typical story of *Beur* women who were perhaps born and certainly raised in France returning to Algeria would not be considered fodder for comedy by most. For the stories of these women, Djura relates, are covered by a socially mandated yet self-imposed silence:

> un voile de pudeur masquait délicatement les peines et les souffrances qui m'avaient été infligées [...] mon sort—si exceptionnel puisse-t-il paraître—était aussi, en partie, celui de milliers de filles, de sœurs ou d'épouses muettes de peur, en quête du bien-être et cependant interdites d'existence. (non. pag.)

> [a veil of modesty discreetly masked the pain and suffering inflicted upon me (...) my fate—exceptional as it may appear—was also, in part, that of thousands of girls, sisters, or wives, who keep silent out of fear, who seek a decent life while they are forbidden even to exist. (non. pag.)]

Le Voile du silence was published by the imprint Michel Lafon in conjunction with Livres de Poche, which is one of the largest paperback publishing houses in France. The book was in print for over twenty years and went through multiple prints runs. By contrast, several of Djurdjura's most successful CDs are no longer available from their original distributors. One exception is a release on Warner Brothers/Luaka Bop Records, volume two of the Adventures in Afropea series, titled—in English, whether distributed in France, the U.K. or the U.S.—*The Best of Djurdjura: Voice of Silence*. The success of these two works suggests that framing Djura's work through the word *silence* beckons readers and listeners in a particularly compelling way. Her uses of the word seem obvious on first blush: metaphors of silence that evoke the oppression of women serve as apt frames for Djura's memoir and music, since she is a well-known feminist singer and spokesperson for the rights of Kabyle women both in France and Algeria.

But silence, in this case, serves as no simple metaphor, for Djura's memoir articulates silence through both visual and textual assertions. Djura's conception of silence gives political and cultural contours to the gap between 1970s feminist rhetorics and twenty-first-century universalist ones. That Djura's metaphor for silence covers this gap is clear only in historical retrospect, of course, but it is canny to say the least, considering that the memoir was published in 1990. This publication date bisects exactingly the period between the political activist heights of the Mouvement de libération des femmes in France in the 1970s, and the country's ban on the veil in all public places in 2010. Here is Djura's first use of the word 'silence' in the memoir:

> En acceptant de me raconter, j'ai voulu lever ce voile du silence pour que cesse un jour cette mascarade qui se réclame des coutumes ancestrales mais qui n'a plus—au sens humain du terme—aucune légitimité. (non. pag.)

> [In agreeing to tell my story, I wished to lift this veil of silence, so that a day might come when we see the end of this masquerade which justifies itself on the grounds of ancestral customs but which has no longer any legitimacy—in the human sense of the word. (non. pag.)]

The veil of silence is Djura's motivation for writing: to lift the veil is an act of self-empowerment, attained by inscribing into the text her right to be explicit and transparent about her experiences as a woman. In asserting this right, Djura smiles, sings, and celebrates her way through the stories of what she has lived and what other women who find themselves covered by the assimilationist gap have lived. Herein lies Djura's own cover of a perpetually universalizing France: she has managed to construct a voice that is recognized and accepted in universalist French culture, although she maintains her Kabyle ethnic heritage in spite of the near-blanket excoriation of Kabyle masculinity in the Kabyle community (there are a few important exceptions to this excoriation, one of which I take particular note in the readings to come). This excoriation, however, effectively *un*covers the exclusion of Kabyle women's voices read through Idir's cover of 'A vava inouva.' In Idir's case, he presents a multicultural universalism that seems indifferent to gender, which, as already noted, follows the limitations of French universalism. In Djura's case, she generalizes Kabyle misogyny in order to reject it, and to demonstrate her allegiance to a feminism compatible with universalist values, while still retaining her ethnic identity as part of her life and work.

Djura makes it clear in the early pages of her memoir that, for her, the political stakes are altogether personal. Consider her variation on the traditional launching-off point for an autobiography, a description of her birth and origins:

> Ma mère se désolait: elle avait espéré un garçon. Toutes les femmes enceintes espéraient un garçon. Et les pères, et les tantes, et le village! Les gens attendaient les youyous, ces cris de joie qui saluent la venue au monde de l'enfant mâle. En cas de youyous, on célébrait cet heureux événement le soir même avec les tambours et les reïtas—des instruments à hanche [sic] dont le son ressemble à celui de la bombarde [...] L'absence de youyous, au contraire, signifiait qu'une fille était née. (24)

> [My mother was devastated: she'd hoped for a boy. All pregnant women hoped for boys. And the fathers, and the aunts, and the whole village! People waited for the yuyus, the cries of joy which greeted the arrival into this world of a male child. When yuyus were in order, the happy event was celebrated the same evening with drums and *reitas*—instruments carried on the hip and which sound like mortars (...) The absence of yuyus, on the contrary, meant that a girl had been born. (11–12)][8]

The event of Djura's birth is constituted not only in silence but through absence. First, her mother is disappointed that she is not a boy, and this disappointment circles and fans outward through the family and the village. The birth of a girl is signaled through silence, and people hope for ululation until their suspicions are confirmed through silence (in other words, the absence of ululation) that the child is a girl. By contrast, when a boy is born, Djura describes, the air is filled with the sounds of ululation accompanied by percussion. Interestingly, she compares the sound of *reitas* to the sound of bombs, which seems to

---

8 'Reïtas' should be described as *instruments à anche*, or wind instruments played with a reed in the mouthpiece, rather than played *à hanche* (on the hip). Because this error was in the original and not a mistake in translation, I have left it rather than modifying both texts. Meanwhile, *la bombarde*, a Breton instrument, is most often translated as 'a bombard' rather than 'mortar' (which is *un mortier* in French)—but it's not clear if the translator interpreted 'la bombarde' to mean the sound of bombs falling—thus I have left the translation as 'mortars.'

foreshadow the disastrous consequences of the birth of boys for most of the women surrounding them: Djura's memoir is full of descriptions of both younger and older brothers subjugating and humiliating their sisters and mothers. In the opening passage of the memoir, it is her brother—along with Djura's niece—who tries to kill Djura and Hervé, her French partner, when she is several months pregnant.

Yet Djura also covers the potential for Kabyle men to be kind to Kabyle women. In fact, in one such passage, the very sound of the Kabyle language resonates through the text. Djura is at the opening of the first film she co-wrote, co-directed, and scored with Hervé. Her father has threatened to assassinate her at the film premiere. An enormous, hirsute Kabyle man who is working at the premiere sees that Djura is scared. To calm her, he 'me dit assez haut, en roulant les r: "Tu n'as rrrien à crrraindrrre!"' (128) ['said quite loudly, rolling his Rs, "You've nothing to be afrrraid of!"' (102)]. The multiple Rs signify the Kabyle /r/, which is pronounced in the front of the mouth (as in Italian or Spanish) rather than at the back of the throat, as in French. In this way, a benevolent, masculine, Kabyle voice resonates through *Le Voile du silence*. Further, this dialogue allows the *sound* of a Kabyle voice speaking in French to weave its way into the text. It is, finally, the voice of Djura's bodyguard, as she calls him ('mon "garde du corps" me présenta au public' [128], 'my "bodyguard" introduced me to the audience' [102]). While this could be read along similar lines to the fresh-off-the-boat Martiniquais who lets his naïveté slip by rolling his Rs in Franz Fanon's *Peau noire, masques blancs*, I argue that Djura's memoir opens aural space for a Kabyle man to assert Kabyle men's potential for kindness to Kabyle women as well. It would be wrong to compare this moment with Idir's nostalgic, covered representation of Kabyle women's voices, for this masculine Kabyle voice rings through the French-language text, opening up space to demonstrate another version of Kabyle difference: rather than entirely relying on social and political representations of Algerian men as threatening to Algerian women, here we see an Algerian man protecting an Algerian woman from a misogynistic facet of their shared community. This passage thus complicates the traditional narrative that some postcolonial scholars refer to as 'white man saves dark woman from dark man.'

Yet it is Hervé who emerges as the feminist hero of Djura's narrative. In a flashback that takes place after the passage at the premiere, Djura recalls how she was encouraged to sing by Hervé, and that moment serves as a touchstone event of Djura's feminist awareness:

Hervé me démontra, à l'époque, que vu les obstacles prévisibles d'une réalisation cinématographique de ce style [un document « provocateur »], la chanson serait un bon moyen d'exprimer ce que j'avais à dire, et de le faire entendre plus vite, et plus facilement.

Ce fut le déclic: j'acceptai de chanter [...] En quête de mélodies pour *Ali au Pays des Merveilles*, je m'étais rendue la première fois chez Hervé pour chercher une voix: je venais de trouver la mienne. [...]

Une voix, et une voie ...

Eh bien j'élargirais le débat! Je chercherais à entraîner dans ma lutte toutes les filles algériennes, maghrébines, africains, arabes d'autres pays, et mêmes quelques occidentales encore sous le boiseau. Je ferais comme Kahina: je soulèverais par mes chants une véritable armée, fidèle aux richesses culturelles de nos pays et cependant rebelle au pouvoir tout-puissant d'un patriarcat suranné. (137–138)

[Hervé pointed out to me that, in view of the predictable obstacles to making a film of this sort, singing would be a good way of expressing what I had to say, and letting it be heard quicker and more easily.

That was the trigger factor: I agreed to sing [...] The first time I had gone to Hervé's looking for music for *Ali in Wonderland*, I had been in search of voices: now I had just found my own. [...]

A voice, and a way forward ...

Well, I'd broaden the debate! I'd attempt to drag all Algerian girls into my struggle, and those from all North Africa, the whole of Africa, girls and women from other Arab countries, and even some from the West whose light was still hidden under a bushel. I would be like Kahina: with my songs I would raise a veritable army, loyal to the cultural wealth of our countries and yet rebelling against the omnipotence of an outdated patriarchy. (111)]

The translation of *entraîner* as 'to drag' colors this passage in a specific way. Let us assume for a moment that this was the meaning that Djura intended: following her description of the ways that the benevolent Hervé led her to sing, how does her desire to *drag* third world and oppressed Western women into the debate change our understanding of Djura's own feminism? And then, to assemble an army of these women?

The Kahina whom Djura envisions herself emulating is one of the most famous figures of Kabyle history and the stuff of legend. A seventh-century religious and military leader, Kahina makes regular appearances throughout Kabyle literature and history in French, most famously, perhaps, in Tahar Djaout's *L'Invention du désert* (1987) and Assia Djebar's *Loin de Médine* (1991). Although very little is known about her life besides the approximate dates she lived and died, in legend Kahina rallies troops against invading tribes, and has three sons, two of whom were adopted captives from other tribes. She is at times mythologized as having committed suicide rather than be taken captive herself by an opposing tribe. These well-known captivity narratives in the legends about Kahina justify Dorothy Blair's translation of the verb *entraîner* as 'to drag.'

But is Djura actually portraying herself as hell-bent on building an army of feminists, regardless of these various women's own inclinations on the issue? For *entraînant*, in the musical sense, refers to a musical hook: *un refrain entraînant* is a refrain that one might want to hear or repeat again and again. *Entraîner* can also refer to sports training or an apprenticeship. Given that, in this passage, Djura herself is feeling the first moments of excitement in her newfound feminist aims, it seems likely that all of these senses of the term *entraîner* are folded into her enthusiasm for recruiting young women from the third world to the cause. And Djura, of course, would be in a particularly privileged position to offer them guidance, since her life experience covers two very different social realities.

So Djura covers both Algeria and France in order to show the multiplicity, rather than duality, of her experience—she writes with a refusal to establish a strict binary between her experiences of French and Algerian cultures. She aims to bring the two together rather than to erase Algerian Kabyle culture in favor of the French.

This assertion is embodied in the memoir's dénouement, which begins with the forging of her partnership with the Breton Hervé. The penultimate lines portray the birth and naming of the son she conceived with him, named Riwan: 'En Berbérie, cela veut dire "enfant de la musique." Dans la Bretagne d'Arthur et de la Table Ronde, cela signifie "le roi qui avance"' (189) ['In the Berber language that means "Child of Music." In the Brittany of King Arthur and the Round Table, it means "The King Who Advances"' (158)]. While the name Riwan reflects the duality of his parents, lest this reading be interpreted as a postcolonial utopia, or as 'white man saves dark woman from dark man,' we should keep in mind that Djura's public persona is her own, not one shared with Hervé. When she sings onstage, she is with her band and backup singers. When she appears onstage with figures such as Aït Menguellet and Idir, she stands alone. Thus the son's name reflects Djura and Hervé's duality as a set of parents, rather than a Frenchman of Breton origins as a Kabyle woman's savior.

An assumption about the strict distinction between Western feminism and non-Western cultures (which are generally assumed to be more retrograde than Western cultures when it comes to feminism) might seem, on first blush, to undergird Djura's memoir as both an ethnic and feminist text. Back to the cover of the memoir: recall the traditional Kabyle ornament of Djura's dress and jewelry. What this image inscribes is the *absence* of a veil, whether a literal or figurative one. The visual absence of an actual veil tips the reader off to the lifting of the figurative veil of silence, and the recovery of women's voices. If we were working with the false dichotomy of non-Western society as sexist, Western society as feminist, then it would seem that Djura sees the feminist value for immigrants in French social mores. But, again, it is important to consider that Kabyle bodyguard whose voice rings out in the text: he demonstrates this dichotomy as one to be complicated, at the very least. Keep in mind as well that, traditionally, Kabyle women do not wear veils. In fact, Djura's appearance on the cover of the memoir asserts the multiplicity of the Kabyle situation: a cultural heritage fraught with two waves of colonization, through which women have been oppressed, celebrated, and, in turn, liberated.

This, then, is the veil of silence: the pat French narrative of assimilation that is justified in the name of women's liberation. As we can see through the example of Djura's *Voile du silence* as one Kabyle woman's memoir, women's stories of immigration, oppression, and marginalization are too complex and variegated to fit simply into the mold that the typical French universalist narrative offers. It is true that Djura's autobiographical portrait concludes with a familiar trope. Hervé coaxes Djura to sing, and she in turn bears him a male child whose name in Breton means 'the advancing king.' But an important question remains: had Djura not keyed the conclusion of her memoir through the 'white man saves dark woman' trope, would it have met such success in publication and distribution? Would it still be in print twenty years later? Think back to the book summary on the back cover, which—it becomes clear through my reading of what Djura covers in her memoir—oversimplifies her story. What is fascinating about *Le Voile du silence* is that, while it initially appears to be an open-and-shut case of a Kabyle woman saved by Breton society (marking a unique and disappearing language within France), in the detailed recollection of this personal narrative some important complexities about contemporary Kabyle immigrant culture are covered, rather than lost.

Ornament

So far in this chapter I have used the word 'ornament' to describe the female Kabyle vocal style that Idir adopted in the 1973 version of 'A vava inouva,' and to describe Djura's traditional Kabyle jewelry. Ornaments can do so much more than gussy something up: whether visual or oral, they always signify. Ornaments can be supplements as well, in the Derridean sense of the term: an ornament can be the extra part that in fact supplements the ostensibly central component in meaning. Ornaments can thus cover, uncover, and recover as well.

I flip through the booklet of Idir's CD *Deux rives, un rêve* [*Two Rivers, One Dream*] (2002), upon which 'A vava inouva 2' was rereleased. When I reach the center spread, featuring a collage of photos of Idir and his band throughout the years, my eyes halt upon a specific image. Idir's cheeks and chin are lathered with shaving cream, and he is shaving. Looking at this photograph, I realize that if Djura's Kabyle jewelry signifies the absence of the veil, then this image of Idir shaving signifies the fact that Idir wears no beard. In France, *les barbus* [the bearded] is a common and pejorative term for Islamic fundamentalists. Idir's act of shaving in the photograph thus becomes an ornament of both uncovering (he is not a fundamentalist Muslim) and recovering (he is Kabyle).

The respective absences of a veil and a beard in the photos that frame Idir's and Djura's voices cover at least the following possibilities: 1) the solidarity of the Kabyle immigrant community with French universalist society—what we are not, these images relate, is a fundamentalist or Arabo-centric Muslim minority, even if we are a distinctly Algerian one; and 2) an acute awareness of the assimilation imperative in a perpetually universalizing France. It is as if, in order for the music of an ethnic minority to be recognized, there were a necessary nod to their difference as part of the frame. Image offers a particularly potent supplement to music as a framing device, whether we are discussing videos, film projections during concerts, press photos, or CD covers. And so, with these images that convey Kabyle difference, further political ground is covered through Djura's and Idir's music: in defining the Kabyle community against the Islamic community, this minority group in

France edges ever closer to recognition as an integrated component of French society—with a difference, as Idir's *mondialisme* asserts.

The signification of the absence of the beard and the veil as an implicit recognition of France's assimilation imperative resonates through other Kabyle cultural works in France. In summer 2005, I saw Fellag perform his one-man show *Le Dernier chameau* at the Théâtre des Bouffes du Nord in Paris. In the final skit, he described a surprise encounter between the protagonist, an Algerian man who in the show's dénouement is newly emigrated to France, and a *pied-noir* woman who was a childhood friend in Algeria, during the war for independence: 'Je lui ai parlé avec l'accent. Nous, les Algériens, chaque fois qu'on rencontre un pied-noir, on est obligé d'adopter leur accent sinon ils nous prennent pour des … des Arabes!' (169) [I spoke to her in the accent. We, the Algerians, each time that we meet a *pied-noir*, we are obliged to adopt their accent or else they take us for … for Arabs!].[9] That the narrator, who is newly arrived in France at the time of this encounter, subconsciously changes his accent attests to the fact that the assimilation imperative in France transgresses national boundaries. This detail of the accent attenuation is incidental to the skit: it's taken as an aside, and a given, within the performance. Yet this detail covers further important territory: not only does Kabyle difference require recovery both in France and in Algeria, but French universalist mores release their proponents of the duty to even discern between different minority groups.

Let's turn back to consider the encore at Aït Menguellet's concert as a spectacular event. I have noted that Djura always performs in traditional Kabyle garb. Menguellet, Idir, and other male Kabyle musicians who first released albums in the 1970s, however, tend to dress in dress pants, button-down shirts, and occasionally a blazer or jacket. This was indeed the case at Menguellet's concert: Djura's ensemble was a splash of satiny white and embroidered primary colors alongside the blacks, browns, and grays of men in button-down shirts and blazers. Can we deduce, then, that men's traditional dress represents a protest against modernity or universalism more readily than women's traditional dress does—save, of course, the veil? Are certain forms of women's traditional dress tolerated as a reminder of how French universalism has served women from Algeria? The latter question is supported by Idir's 'A vava inouva': in looking back with a nostalgic gaze at the Kabyle family hearth, might covering a Kabyle woman's voice suggest an *effacement*

9 Translation mine.

of her oppression? If the narrative is constituted through the gaze from Paris through France to Algeria, Matheson's adaptation of the female Kabyle ornamental vocal style could be said to suggest empathy for and solidarity with Algerian women, and an assertion that they have a right to their own voices. Alternately and importantly, Matheson's voice demonstrates a point related to the voice of the Kabyle bodyguard that rings out in *Le Voile du silence*: Her voice insists upon a range of identity narratives, rather than a single, universalist identity story.

The potential interpretations of contextual frames for Kabyle music in France layer and imbricate endlessly, and at times elusively, depending on which way the critical ear is bent and for which sociocultural audience the music is framed. This is one of the central problems for an immigrant cultural spokesperson in a universalist society: is it ever fair to assume that a single cultural figure can speak for a marginalized collective as a whole? After all, it is often a challenge for an immigrant artist just to find a receptive audience within a national cultural landscape. As David Caron, among many other critics, has pointed out, immigrant culture and social practices in France are often upheld in order to have something against which French culture can be defined. This last point leads us to a final and crucial aspect of what the frames of Kabyle music in France demonstrate: in the experience of listening, we must always keep in mind the terms of our exclusions.

CHAPTER SIX

Beirut Calling

The Performance of Listening
in Digital Discourses of Conflict

On the night of July 15–16, 2006, Lebanese avant-jazz trumpeter and visual artist Mazen Kerbaj set up his recording equipment on the balcony of his Beirut apartment. Once the mics were set up and he had checked sound levels, he hit record. He then improvised on his trumpet to the sight and sounds of bombs falling from Israeli fighter jets. Over the thirty-three days of the 2006 Israeli War, Kerbaj recorded over nine hours of improvisation with the bombs.[1] On July 16, 2006 an unedited excerpt from Kerbaj's first night on the balcony appeared in the sidebar of his blog (http://mazenkerblog.blogspot.com/). Entitled 'Starry Night,' this minimalistic improvised piece remains available on the blog's sidebar.

Digital media has upped the ante for sound in culture and, by extension, the possibilities for the performance of listening. The novel was the primary cultural genre through which the French Revolution, the War of 1812, and the many shorter revolutions over the course of the tumultuous nineteenth century was documented, processed, and understood. The novel served as a response to revolution that was literary, aesthetic, and/or philosophical, rather than violent. And if the novel was the genre of nineteenth-century revolution, then digital media is the genre of twenty-first-century conflict. With digital works, however, there is more flexibility in terms of artistic media, as well as higher speed and lower cost of production and distribution. The higher speed and lower cost of digital media transmission are of particular interest in considering how blogs issue a call to listen, and are among the reasons why Kerbaj's 'Starry Night' and related blog posts are the focus of the

[1] Email correspondence with Kerbaj, 28 May 2007.

conclusion for this work. Kerbaj's 2006 performance and posts presaged the use of social media in the Arab Spring and the role of drones, digital media, and leaks of confidential information and correspondence in the Syrian Civil War, Daesh (the Islamic State), and terrorist attacks around the world. Digital discourse has changed so much about our cultures and societies, and the call to listen in postcolonial Francophone culture is no exception: as I will explain, it was digital discourse that led to Kerbaj not only becoming an important figure in French culture, but also becoming an artist who expresses himself in French, by choice—as a non-native speaker of French.

The Kerblog, Kerbaj's blog, served as one of his primary promotional tools for his various projects from 2004 through 2010. Since, he has turned to microblogging via platforms like Flickr, Instagram, and Twitter. But when Israel began bombing Lebanon on July 14, 2006, the Kerblog was his one readily available mouthpiece. The image that Kerbaj posted on his blog the day he posted 'Starry Night' speaks to one of his aims for the musical piece: with no clear and urgent way of expressing his experience through the visual, he turned to the sonic.

'Starry Night' is both avant and minimalist writ large. To listen to the piece is at first disorienting in its quiet, then destabilizing in the abrupt and violent sounds that emerge. The piece offers the listener an aestheticized yet immediate experience of six and a half unedited minutes during one night of bombing, early in the 2006 Israeli War. Much of the piece is quiet, if not silent—although the quiet-to-silent sections of 'Starry Night' might remind us of John Cage's theorization of silence through his 1953 composition '4'33"': there is no such thing as silence; it is a matter of how one listens.[2] In 'Starry Night,' this idea

2   Musicologist Kyle Gann describes the premiere performance of Cage's '4'33"', which took place on August 29, 1952, at the Maverick Concert Hall just south of Woodstock, New York: 'Pianist David Tudor sat down at the piano on the small raised wooden stage, closed the keyboard lid over the keys, and looked at a stopwatch. Twice in the next four minutes he raised the lid up and lowered it again, careful to make no audible sound, although at the same time he was turning pages of the music, which were devoid of notes [...] Years later, Cage described the sounds heard during the 1952 performance, which conveniently fell into three movements, paralleling the intended structure: "What they thought was silence, because they didn't know how to listen, was full of accidental sounds. You could hear the wind blowing outside during the first movement. During the second, raindrops began pattering the roof, and during the third the people themselves made all kinds of interesting sounds as they talked or walked out"' (3–4).

Figure 2: Mazen Kerbaj's 'Beirut: 16 July 06 2.10 AM'

is in evidence through the sounds of the bombs, of course, but also the ambient night noises of banal life that fill the air when there seems to be no musical or military sound.

The dynamics of listening to a musical work such as 'Starry Night,' published on a blog and thus available to anyone with computer access, varies entirely depending on when, where, and by whom the piece is heard. Just as Sophocles's *Antigone* was understood in its time as a meditation upon the folly of tyranny within the particularities of the Greek democracy (many details of which have fallen ephemeral), in this analysis of 'Starry Night,' I focus on the structural elements of the piece as a musical work, treading lightly on the context of the conflict between Israel and Lebanon and allowing Kerbaj's perspective on the conflict as voiced on his blog contemporaneously to filter through this reading as a call to listen.

I divide 'Starry Night' into four movements, with the sound of the bombs hitting the ground marking the end of one movement and the beginning of the next. On first listening, it can be difficult to distinguish between the sounds of conflict and music in the first fifty seconds of the piece, due to Kerbaj's innovative use of the trumpet to imitate the drone of the distant fighter jets.

The first movement comprises a little less than the first third of 'Starry Night,' and as the piece progresses it becomes clear that this improvisation is both calculated and calibrated. There is a musical method at work within this sonic context of violence. There are three structural elements of this section of the piece that I would like to note.

First, the everyday continues as bombs fall: some of the sounds we hear in the piece include dogs barking, cars passing, and a range of car alarms set off by the bombs. We realize, then, that people in Beirut were still setting their car alarms. The alarms burst onto the sonic landscape of 'Starry Night,' triggered by the bombs, yet asserting the continued presence of a mundane and routine sound that can be heard in any contemporary city.

Second, Kerbaj's performance on the trumpet gestures toward two modes of engagement: on both artistic and musical terms, he is engaging directly with the war. Hezbollah kidnapped and held hostage three Israeli soldiers. In retaliation, Israel began bombing the whole of Lebanon, including hospitals, Red Cross buildings, bridges, roads, and airport runways. And then Kerbaj intervened musically with his performance, recording, and posting of 'Starry Night' on his blog.

Third, it becomes clear that he can see the planes before we can hear them: the drone of his trumpet traces the movement of the planes as they approach Beirut. Kerbaj also sees the bombs before they go off: he uses the sight of the bombs being dropped from the planes as his visual cue so that he can lead in a call and response when the first set of bombs are heard in the piece. He intones low, three times, before we hear the first bombs go off. In sum, through innovative avant-jazz practice, Kerbaj asserts refusal to engage with the conflict, while improvising his art within the grand-scale violence of the 2006 Israeli War.

'Starry Night' conveys a visceral sense of what it was like to stand on that balcony in Beirut as the bombs fell. As Michael Allan addresses in '"Reading with One Eye, Speaking with One Tongue": On the Problem of Address in World Literature' (2007), postcolonial writers and artists are faced with the problem of split publics—in other words, the way their texts can be understood through reading by those who share the writer's background and personal experience, or by those on the other side of the postcolonial divide. Kerbaj's 'Starry Night' trumpets through the split-public issue, confronting the Israeli War not only as a first-hand experience, but also through the refusal that living through this experience is beyond artistic representation.

For listeners who didn't experience the 2006 conflict first-hand, then, there is also the emotional experience of the piece to consider. For my part, I have listened to this piece enough that I know when I'll hear the bombs touch the ground, but my entire body still tenses up in anticipation. The piece elicits both physical and emotional reaction in the listener as a reaction to a document of war. And this is an important distinction between the novel and digital media: Kerbaj's work is not a purely aesthetic representation of conflict. What we are hearing *is war*. As such, we can see how Kerbaj's personal statement about 'Starry Night' evolves over the course of the war. Four days after he posted the piece, he posted a reaction called 'fuck interviews':

> i did today another interview with a swedish radio about my music in general and about the 'starry night' piece. it was good to talk about music for a while.

> i am receiving a lot of propositions for other interviews.
> i hate to do that. especially in theses times.
> i feel that the attention my work is given is somehow unjustified [...] in 4 days there was already more than 1000 readers. god knows how much there is now. i hope a lot. and i hope that others are coming.
> the thing is that today i feel a sort of responsibility, and it is like i have to make my voice heard [...] but it put me in the position of a sort of hero

defending the lebanese citizens with my art, while the sad reality is that i can do nothing to even protect myself. people are dying under the bombs and i am giving interviews!!!

But a week later, he seeks to reclaim the piece as pure art—or, as pure as can be mustered under the circumstances:

[…] i was asked twice so far: 'don't you think that your piece of music and bombs is of a bad taste?[']
i answered twice: 'do you think that it is of a good taste to throw a bomb on a bus with civilians escaping their village?'
it is incredible that some people, listening to this piece in their living room in london or in paris, ask themselves if they like it or not. […]

also, for the new comers on this blog, i repeat my now famous sentence (a sort of personal 'to be or not to be' kind of stuff):
[…]
THIS IS BLOG DEDICATED TO ART.
AND AS SUCH, IT VOMITS ON ANYTHING CALLED POLITICS.

Art for art's sake. Or is it? Kerbaj doesn't claim to be *a*political. 'This blog is dedicated to art,' Kerbaj writes, but he nonetheless reacts to politics—and in his reaction, engages with and implicates himself as an artist not only *in* politics, but directly *with* conflict. Kerbaj's improvisation with the sound of Israeli bombs represents a sea change in cultures of conflict: with digital media, we have the possibility of transcending representation and embodiment, as 'Starry Night' attests. The question that 'Starry Night' poses for critics is how to analyze art in which violent acts contribute both form and content to the work of art itself.

As Kerbaj's musical confrontation to military assault, 'Starry Night' also serves as a narrative that subverts representations of Arab men as inherently violent. For Kerbaj's performance stands in sharp contrast to, for example, Nihad's sing-along performance to 'The Logical Song' in Wajdi Mouawad's *Incendies*. Where Nihad's performance might lead audiences to consider the origins of his horrific behavior, Kerbaj's performance insists upon passive resistance. In place of violence, he opens a darkly humorous dialogue between himself as musician and the Israeli military forces. In the image included on the next page of the Kerblog, which Kerbaj drew to depict himself recording 'Starry Night,' his nose is a trumpet, his arms hang limp at his sides, and the look on his face suggests shellshock. The bombs, meanwhile, are represented as stars. This image asserts a counternarrative to the Western and Israeli notion that 1) the Lebanese people represent a united front that supports organizations such as Hezbollah; 2) that Hezbollah can be taken as synonymous with the Lebanese people, which, to listen to Israeli justifications for the violent destruction of Lebanese infrastructure, hospitals, and residences, among many other sites, would seem to be the case.

How, then, does 'Starry Night' enter into postcolonial Francophone culture? To explain, I need to go back to the serendipitous moment when I first encountered Kerbaj's work. In May 2007, when I was doing some preliminary research for this project in Paris, I was at the Gibert Jeune bookstore looking for the new complete edition of Marjane Satrapi's graphic novel *Persepolis*, the film version of which had just been released in France. Sitting on the new releases display shelf right next to *Persepolis* was a thick volume with a cream-colored cover featuring a cartoonish image of a cityscape going up in flames and smoke. The volume was entitled *Beyrouth: juillet–août 2006* [*Beirut: July–August 2006*]. The book is a hard-copy edition of Kerbaj's blog account of the Israeli War. The print volume was entirely translated into French and published by L'Association, a well-known Parisian graphic novel publisher that specializes in works from the Far and Middle East. The translated print edition of Kerbaj's July–August 2006 blog was published in December 2006 in France, less than six months after the war ended. So when I found this work, in addition to the many drawings by Kerbaj that spoke in ways personal, political, and creative to the theoretical questions I was posing, I was struck by the simple fact that a print edition of the blog had been translated into French and published so quickly, and had found its way into my hands in Paris.[3]

While 'Starry Night' reminds us of the fluid, portable, and immediate potential of contemporary cultural works, the translated print edition of the blog speaks directly to the French public on the critical social issues I have thus far raised about 'Starry Night.' What happens when we listen to or read about others listening? What can Kerbaj's politically engaged musical practice reveal about media, social, and political representations of Middle Eastern men as inherently violent? The print edition of the blog, then, serves as another iteration of the call to listen.

Beyrouth: juillet–août 2006 also allows me to point out the fact that the call to listen is never issued by writers and artists as a solo endeavor. Kerbaj did not pull off the call to modern France alone. He did so with a French publisher that concerns itself particularly with representing

---

3   Kerbaj's 2006 blog about the war was published in the United States in 2017 by Fantagraphics under the title *Beirut Won't Cry*.

Figure 3: 'Recording Session: Mazen Kerbaj (Trumpet) vs. The State of Israel (Bombs)'

minority voices in France. Kerbaj has found much success in the decade since the 2006 war—he currently lives in Berlin, and tours and performs regularly as both musician and visual artist. While his journal of the 2006 Israeli War was translated into French, he has since published graphic novels that were written in French, including *Cette histoire se passe* [*This history happens*] (Tamyras, 2011), *Lettre à la mère* [*Letter to the mother*] (L'Apocalypse, 2013), and *Un an: un journal d'une année comme les autres* [*One Year: a journal of a year like the others*] (Tamyras, 2014). He has also collaborated and contributed to several other volumes of graphic novels and visual art. Kerbaj has even gone so far as to criticize Francophone support for artistic works: in a 2013 promotional email he sent for the release of *Lettre à la mère*, he wrote:

> for those who are not in lebanon, the book is available in bookstores in france (and the half-dead francophone world)
> for the rest of the world, it is available online at amazon.fr. (Kerbaj 2013)

I considered contacting Kerbaj to ask him what he meant by 'half-dead francophone world.' But I decided, instead, to let the statement stand for consideration. Whether he means that the people, the society and cultures, or the publishing industry in Francophone countries outside of France are half-dead, the questions can still extend well beyond. My primary reason for narrating Kerbaj's transition to Francophone expression is that it brings out a final point regarding the cultural phenomenon of the call to listen in postcolonial Francophone culture. The call to listen is not simply put forth to protest French notions of exclusion. Although contemporary Republican narratives in France tend toward circumscribing minority identities as they are defined by French society, there is a long-standing tradition in French culture that arises from gendered, linguistic, and/or political difference. The call to listen is already woven into the fabric of French culture and, as a counter-narrative to Republican narratives of assimilation, it allows the process of unweaving these silencing narratives to begin.

Bibliography

Adorno, Theodor W. 'The Curves of the Needle.' *Essays on Music*. Trans. Susan H. Gillespie. Berkeley: University of California Press, 2002. Print.

Aït Menguellet, Lounis, perf. Le Zénith, Paris. 17 May 2009. Performance.

Allan, Michael. '"Reading with One Eye, Speaking with One Tongue": On the Problem of Address in World Literature.' *Comparative Literature Studies* 44.1–2 (2007): 1–19. Print.

Bande des filles. Dir. Céline Sciamma. Perf. Karidja Touré, Assa Sylla, Lindsay Karamoh, Mariétou Touré. Hold-Up Films, 2014. Film.

Bakhtin, M.M. *The Dialogic Imagination: Four Essays*. Ed. Michael Holquist. Trans. Caryl Emerson and Michael Holquist. Austin: University of Texas Press, 1981. Print.

Barthes, Roland. 'Le Grain de la voix.' *L'obvie et l'obtus: essais critiques III*. Paris: Éditions du Seuil, 1982. Print.

Bauman, Richard. *Story, Performance, and Event: Contextual Studies of Oral Narrative*. Cambridge: Cambridge University Press, 1986. Print.

Beau Travail. Dir. Claire Denis. Perf. Denis Lavant, Michel Subor, Grégoire Colin. La Sept-Arte, 1999. Film.

Ben Jelloun, Tahar. *French Hospitality: Racism and North African Immigrants*. Trans. Barbara Bray. New York: Columbia University Press, 1999. Print.

——. *Hospitalité française: racisme et immigrations Maghrébine*. New ed. Paris: Seuil, 1997. Print.

Bowen, John R. *Why the French Don't Like Headscarves: Islam, the State, and Public Space*. Princeton: Princeton University Press, 2007. Print.

Butler, Judith. *Bodies That Matter: On the Discursive Limits of 'Sex'*. London: Routledge, 1993. Print.

Calle-Gruber, Mireille. *Assia Djebar ou la Résistance de l'écriture: regards d'un écrivain d'Algérie*. Paris: Maisonneuve et Larose, 2001. Print.

Caron, David. 'Nearness.' At Home in Diaspora/Diaspora at Home Symposium. Stanford University, Stanford, CA. 26 April 2010. Lecture.

Certeau, Michel de. *L'invention du quotidien: 1. arts de faire*. Paris: Gallimard, 1990. Print.

——. *The Practice of Everyday Life*. Trans. Stephen Rendall. Berkeley: University of California Press, 1984. Print.

Chion, Michel. *L'audio-vision: son et image au cinéma*. 2nd ed. Paris: Nathan/HER 2000. Print.

——. *Audio-Vision: Sound on Screen*. Trans. Claudia Gorbman. New York: Columbia University Press, 1994. Print.

Cité de la Musique. 'Il faut le voir pour l'entendre.' Message to subscribers. 27 February 2009. Email.

Cixous, Hélène. 'The Laugh of the Medusa.' *The Routledge Language and Cultural Theory Reader*. Ed. Lucy Burke et al. London and New York: Routledge, 2000. Print.

——. 'Le rire de la méduse.' *L'Arc* 56–63 (1974–75): 39–54. Print.

Conquergood, Dwight. 'Performance Studies: Interventions and Radical Research.' *The Drama Review* 46.2 (2002): 145–156. Print.

Dayan, Peter. *Music Writing Literature, From San via Debussy to Derrida*. Aldershot: Ashgate, 2006. Print.

Dilem. Cartoon. *Adel Life Blog*. 6 April 2009. Web. 28 November 2014. https://adelife.wordpress.com.

Djaout, Tahar. *L'Invention du désert*. Paris: Seuil, 1987. Print.

Djebar, Assia. *L'Amour, la fantasia*. Paris: Albin Michel, 1985. Print.

——. *Fantasia: An Algerian Cavalcade*. Trans. Dorothy S. Blair. London: Quartet, 1985. Print.

——. *Femmes d'Alger dans leur appartement*. Paris: Albin Michel, 2002. Print.

——. *Loin de Médine*. Paris: Albin Michel, 1991. Print.

——. *Women of Algiers in Their Apartment*. Trans. Marjolijn de Jager. Charlottesville: University of Virginia Press, 1992. Print.

Djura. *Le Voile du silence*. Paris: Michel Lafon, 1990. Print.

——. *The Veil of Silence*. Trans. Dorothy S. Blair. London: Quartet, 1992. Print.

Djurdjura. *The Best of Djurdjura: Voice of Silence*. Luaka Bop/Warner Bros., 1993. CD.

Donadey, Anne. *Recasting Postcolonialism: Women Writing Between Worlds*. Portsmouth: Heinemann, 2001. Print.

Dornhof, Sarah. 'Regimes of Visibility: Representing Violence against Women in the French Banlieue.' *Feminist Review* 98 (Jul. 2011): 110–127.

Elia, Nada. *Trances, Dances, and Vociferations: Agency and Resistance in Africana Women's Narratives*. New York: Garland, 2001. Print.

Fanon, Franz. *A Dying Colonialism*. Trans. Haakon Chevalier. New York: Grove Press, 1965. Print.

——. *Black Skin, White Masks*. Trans. Richard Philcox. New York: Grove Press, 2008. Print.

——. *L'An V de la révolution algérienne*. Paris: La Découverte, 2001. Print.

——. *Peau noire, masques blancs*. Paris: Seuil, 1952. Print.

Fellag. *Le dernier chameau et autres histoires*. Paris: Lattès, 2004. Print.

Forsdick, Charles. 'Between 'French' and 'Francophone': French Studies and the Postcolonial Turn.' *French Studies* 59.4 (2005): 523–530.

Foucault, Michel. *Histoire de la sexualité I: la volonté et le savoir*. Paris: Gallimard, 1976. Print.

——. *The History of Sexuality: An Introduction, Volume I*. New York: Vintage/Random House, 1990. Print.

Gann, Kyle. *No Such Thing as Silence: John Cage's 4'33'*. New Haven: Yale University Press, 2010. Print.

Gilroy, Paul. *The Black Atlantic: Modernity and Double Consciousness*. Cambridge: Harvard University Press, 1993. Print.

Goodman, Jane E. *Berber Culture on the World Stage*. Bloomington: Indiana University Press, 2005. Print.

'La Grande Nouba.' Promotional image. *Cité de la Musique*. Web. 7 July 2010.

Hayes, Jarrod. *Queer Nations: Marginal Sexualities in the Maghreb*. Chicago: University of Chicago Press, 2000. Print.

Homer. *The Odyssey*. Trans. Robert Fagles. New York: Penguin, 1986. Print.

Hutcheon, Linda. *A Theory of Parody: The Teachings of Twentieth-Century Art Forms*. Urbana: University of Illinois Press, 2000. Print.

Idir. *Deux rives, un rêve*. Sony Music France, 2002. CD.

——. *La France des couleurs …* Sony BMG Music, 2007. CD.

——. *Identités*. Sony Music France, 1999. CD.

Incendies. Dir. Wajdi Mouawad. Perf. Annick Bergeron and Eric Bernier. Théâtre de Quat'sous. Théâtre 71—scène nationale Malakoff. Malakoff, France. 18 January 2004. Performance.

——. Dir. Stanislas Nordey. Perf. Claire Ingrid Cottanceau and Laurent Sauvage. Théâtre National de Bretagne—Rennes. Théâtre de la Colline. Paris, France. 21 October 2008. Performance.

Intouchables. Dir. Olivier Nakache. Perf. François Cluzet, Omar Sy, Anne Le Ny. Quad Productions, 2011. Film.

Irigaray, Luce. *Ce sexe qui n'en est pas un*. Paris: Minuit, 1977. Print.

——. *This Sex Which Is Not One*. Trans. Catherine Porter with Carolyn Burke. Ithaca: Cornell University Press, 1985. Print.

J'ai pas sommeil. Dir. Claire Denis. Perf. Yekateria Golubeva, Richard Courcet, Vincent Dupont. Agora Films, 1994. Film.

Johnson, James H. *Listening in Paris: A Cultural History*. Berkeley: University of California Press, 1995. Print.

Journée de la jupe. Dir. Jean-Paul Lilienfeld. Perf. Isabel Adjani, Denis Podalydès, Yann Collette. Arte France, 2008. Film.

Kadari, Louiza. *De l'utopie totalitaire aux œuvres de Yasmina Khadra, approches des violences intégristes*. Paris: L'Harmattan, 2007. Print.

Kastoryano, Riva. 'Territories of Identities in France.' ssrc.org. SSRC, 11 June 2006. Web. 11 November 2013.

Kerbaj, Mazen. *Un an : un journal d'une année comme les autres.* Tamyras, 2014. Print.

——. *Beyrouth: juillet–août 2006.* Trans. Mazen Kerbaj and Fanny Soubiran. Paris: L'Association, 2006. Print.

——. *Cette histoire se passe.* Paris: Broché, 2011. Print.

——. 'fuck interviews.' *www.mazenkerblog.blogspot.com.* 20 July 2006. Web. 11 April 2016.

——. 'i am sorry to decline your proposition.' *www.mazenkerblog.blogspot. com.* 27 July 2006. Web. 11 April 2016.

——. *Lettre à la mère.* Paris, L'Apocalypse, 2013. Print.

——. Perf. *Starry Night. www.mazenkerblog.blogspot.com.* 17 July 2006. Web. 11 April 2016.

Khadra, Yasmina. *L'Attentat.* Paris: Julliard, 2005. Print.

——. *L'Écrivain.* Paris: Juillard, 2001. Print.

——. *Les Hirondelles de Kaboul.* Paris: Julliard, 2002. Print.

——. *Les Sirènes de Bagdad.* Paris: Julliard, 2006. Print.

——. *The Sirens of Baghdad.* Trans. John Cullen. New York: Anchor, 2007. Print.

Khalifa, Wajdi. 'La Diva libanaise Fairouz enflamme Damas malgré la polémique.' *arabesque48fm.blogspot.com.* 2 February 2008. Web. 7 July 2010.

Khatibi, Abdelkebir. *La Mémoire tatouée: autobiographie d'un décolonisé.* Paris: Denoël, 1971. Print.

Lazreg, Marnia. *The Eloquence of Silence: Algerian Women in Question.* New York: Routledge, 1994. Print.

——. *Questioning the Veil: Open Letters to Muslim Women.* Princeton: Princeton University Press, 2009. Print.

Le Clézio, Jean-Marie Gustave. 'Lullaby.' *Mondo et autres histoires.* Paris: Gallimard, 1978. Print.

Lemonde.fr, 'Nicolas Sarkozy continue de vilipender "racailles et voyous,"' *Le Monde* 11 November 2005. Web. 25 May 2011. http://www.lemonde.fr.

Lepoint.com, 'Les différents voiles islamiques,' *Le Point* 19 June 2009. Web. 11 October 2009. http://www.lepoint.com.

Littoral. Dir. Wajdi Mouawad. Perf. Steve LaPlante, Gilles Renaud, Isabelle LeBlanc. EGM Productions, 2004. Film.

Martin, Laure. 'Burqa: légiférer au nom de la laïcité,' *L'Hémicycle* 21 September 2009. Web. 11 October 2009. http://www.lhemicycle.com.

Meriem. Letter. *Le Courrier de l'Atlas: Le Magazine du Maghreb en Europe* 18 (2008): 6. Print.

Merini, Rafika. 'The Subversion of the Culture of Voyeurism in the World of Leïla Sebbar and Assia Djebar.' Diss. SUNY-Binghamton, 1992. Print.

——. *Two Major Francophone Women Writers, Assia Djébar and Leïla Sebbar: A Thematic Study of Their Works*. New York: Lang, 1999. Print.

Miller, Christopher L. *Theories of Africans: Francophone Literature and Anthropology in Africa*. Chicago and London: University of Chicago Press, 1990. Print.

Mouawad, Wadji. *Ciels*. Montreal and Arles: Actes Sud/Leméac, 2009. Print.

——. *Forêts*. Montreal and Arles: Actes Sud/Leméac, 2006. Print.

——. *Incendies*. Arles: Actes Sud/Leméac, 2003. Print.

——. 'Liban, une guerre indicible.' Institute du Monde Arabe, Paris. 30 October 2008. Discussion.

——. *Littoral*. Montreal and Arles: Actes Sud/Leméac, 1999. Print.

——. *Scorched*. Trans. Linda Gaboriau. Toronto: Playwrights Canada, 2005. Print.

Mouvement ni pûtes ni soumises. 'Grande soirée à Montreuil contre la burqa!' Public event. facebook.com. Web. 24 September 2010. <http://www.facebook.com/event.php?eid=1172956249773472>.

——. 'Ma photo en bonnet (phrygien et autre!)' Photo album. facebook.com. Web. 24 September 2010. <http://www.facebook.com/album.php?aid=148565&id=39147024640&ref=mf>.

——. 'RDV à République avec Marianne pour lui rendre son bonnet!' Note. facebook.com. 3 March 2010. Web. 24 September 2010. <http://www.facebook.com/notes/mouvement-ni-putes-ni-soumises/rdv-a-republique-avec-marianne-pour-lui-rendre-son-bonnet/339724659638>.

——. Status update. facebook.com. 14 May 2010. Web. 24 September 2010. <http://www.facebook.com/niputesnisoumises?ref=ts>

——. Status updates. facebook.com. 19 May 2010. Web. 24 September 2010. <http://www.facebook.com/niputesnisoumises?ref=ts>

Murray, Jenny. *Remembering the (Post)Colonial Self: Memory and Identity in the Novels of Assia Djebar*. Bern: Lang, 2008. Print.

Nafisi, Azar. *Reading Lolita in Tehran*. New York: Random House, 2003. Print.

Orlando, Valerie Key. 'Beyond Postcolonial Discourse: New Problematics of Feminine Identity in Contemporary Francophone Literature.' Diss. Brown University. 1996. Print.

Ovid. *Metamorphoses: A New Verse Translation*. Trans. D.A. Raeburn. London: Penguin, 2004. Print.

Persepolis. Dir. Vincent Paronnaud and Marjane Satrapi. Perf. Chiara Mastroianni, Catherine Deneuve, Danielle Darrieux, Simon Abkarian. 2.4.7 Films, 2007. Film.

Ratcliffe, Krista. *Rhetorical Listening: Identification, Gender, Whiteness*. Carbondale: Southern Illinois University Press, 2005. Print.

Reynolds, Simon and Joy Press. *The Sex Revolts: Gender, Rebellion, and Rock 'n' Roll*. Cambridge: Harvard University Press, 1995. Print.

Rice, Alison. *Time Signatures: Contextualizing Contemporary Francophone Autobiographical Writing from the Maghreb*. Lanham: Lexington, 2006. Print.

Rich, Adrienne. 'Cartographies of Silence.' *The Fact of a Doorframe: Poems 1950–2001*. New York: Norton, 2002. *American Poems*. Web. 28 March 2011.

Ringrose, Priscilla. *Assia Djebar: In Dialogue with Feminisms*. Amsterdam: Rodopi, 2006. Print.

Roach, Joseph. *Cities of the Dead: Circum-Atlantic Performance*. New York: Columbia University Press, 1996. Print.

Rocky III. Dir. Sylvester Stallone. Perf. Sylvester Stallone, Talia Shire, Carl Weathers. Chartoff-Winkler Productions, 1982. Film.

Sacks, Oliver. *Musicophilia: Tales of Music and the Brain*. New York: Knopf, 2007. Print.

Satrapi, Marjane. *The Complete Persepolis*. Trans. L'Association and Anjali Singh. New York: Pantheon/Random House, 2004. Print.

——. *Persepolis*. Paris: L'Association, 2007. Print.

Schafer, R. Murray. *The Tuning of the World: Toward a Theory of Soundscape Design*. Philadelphia: University of Pennsylvania Press, 1980. Print.

Scott, Joan Wallach. *The Politics of the Veil*. Princeton: Princeton University Press, 2007. Print.

Sebbar, Leïla. *Les Carnets de Shérazade*. Paris: Stock, 1985. Print.

——. *Le Fou de Shérazade*. Paris: Stock, 1991. Print.

——. *Shérazade: 17 ans, brune, frisée, les yeux verts*. Paris: Stock, 1982. Print.

——. *Sherazade: Missing, Aged 17, Dark Curly Hair, Green Eyes*. Trans. Dorothy S. Blair. London: Quartet, 1991. Print.

Sebbar, Leïla and Nancy Huston. *Lettres parisiennes: histoires d'exil*. Paris: Barrault, 1986. Print.

Shaykh, Hanan. *The Story of Zahra*. Trans. Peter Ford. New York: Anchor, 1994. Print.

Solis, Gabriel. '"Workin' Hard, Hardly Workin' / Hey Man, You Know Me": Tom Waits, Sound, and the Theatrics of Masculinity.' *Journal of Popular Music Studies* 19.1 (2007): 26–58. Print.

Spelman, Elizabeth V. *Inessential Woman: Problems of Exclusion in Feminist Thought*. Boston: Beacon Press, 1988. Print.

Spivak, Gayatri Chakravorty. 'Can the Subaltern Speak?' *Marxism and the Interpretation of Culture*. Ed. Cary Nelson and Lawrence Grossberg. Urbana: University of Illinois Press, 1988. 271–313. Print.

Sterne, Jonathan. *The Audible Past: Cultural Origins of Sound Reproduction*. Durham: Duke University Press, 2003. Print.

Stone, Christopher Reed. *Popular Culture and Nationalism in Lebanon: The Fairouz and Rahbani Nation*. London and New York: Routledge, 2008. Print.

Supertramp. 'The Logical Song.' *Breakfast in America*. A&M, 1979. CD.

Survivor. 'Eye of the Tiger.' *Eye of the Tiger*. Volcano, 1985. CD.

Ticktin, Miriam Iris. 'Between Justice and Compassion: 'Les Sans Papiers' and the Political Economy of Health, Human Rights and Humanitarianism in France.' Diss. Stanford University, 2002. Print.

van Elferen, Isabella. *Gothic Music: The Sounds of the Uncanny*. Cardiff: University of Wales Press, 2012. Print.

Woodhull, Winifred. *Transfigurations of the Maghreb: Feminism, Decolonization, and Literatures*. Minneapolis: University of Minnesota Press, 1993. Print.

Worth, Robert. 'A Lebanese Diva, Performing in Syria, Creates Drama in More Ways than One.' *New York Times*. 4 February 2008. Web. 7 July 2010.

Yacine, Kateb. *Le cercle des représailles*. Paris: Seuil, 1959. Print.

Yacine, Tassadit. *Aït Menguellet chante ...* Algiers: Alpha, 2008. Print.

Y.B. *Allah Superstar*. Paris: Bernard Grasset, 2003. Print.

Zainea, Adelina. '23 mots pour dire les 1001 maux des exils.' *Actualités & culture berbères* 60–61 (2008): 35–55. Print.

Index

'4'33"' 158

'A vava inouva' 135, 137, 138–139, 142
'A vava inouva 2' 135, 137, 142–145,
    154
ABBA 117n
Académie Française, 28, 131
accent 35, 36, 94, 96, 97, 100, 102, 113,
    114, 130, 155
Adjani, Isabel 119
Aéroport Charles de Gaulle 98, 109,
    113, 114
Afghanistan 60
Africa 7, 43
Africans 7
Aït Menguellet, Lounis 129–135, 144,
    152, 155
Algeria 4, 5, 17, 28, 32, 40, 44, 46, 59,
    86, 129, 131, 132, 133, 135,
    136, 137, 138, 141, 142, 144,
    145, 147, 148, 152, 155, 156
    1830 French invasion of 25
Algerian
    peoples 5, 6, 17, 25, 26, 27, 28, 29,
        30, 32, 40, 45, 52, 144, 150,
        151, 155
    Revolution (War) 5, 17, 25, 28, 29,
        30, 32, 40, 48, 49, 50, 52, 53,
        138, 141
Algiers, Algeria 17, 32, 33, 138
Allah Superstar 124n
Allan, Michael 161
Allouache, Merzak 132n

alter-globalist (altermondialiste)
    culture 19, 129–156
Amara, Fadela 110, 118
L'Amour, la fantasia 35
Amrouche, Jean 133
Amrouche, Taos 133
Un an: un journal d'une année comme
    les autres 165
Antigone 160
Arab 28, 47, 56, 60, 62, 63, 64, 65, 96,
    110, 119, 120, 155
    -Andalusian 84
    colonialism 143
    countries 151
    history 139
    masculinity 94, 96, 116, 119
    peoples 19, 59, 96, 116, 118, 126,
        162
Arab Spring 3, 158
Arabic 5, 32, 35, 36, 47, 49, 67, 78,
    129
Arachne 2
assimilation 3, 12, 99, 108, 112, 134,
    139, 148, 153, 154, 155,
    165
    see also intégration
l'Association 163
l'Association de Culture Berbère
    (Paris) xii, 144
Aulnay-sous-Bois 48

Baalbeck Festival 77n
Baez, Joan 138

Baghdad, Iraq 18, 59, 60, 61, 62, 63,
        64, 65, 68, 72, 74, 76, 78,
        79, 80, 81, 82, 83, 84, 86,
        87
Bakhtin, M.M. 60n, 76
Bande de filles 95n
Barberousse prison 32
Barbès (Paris) 40
Barthes, Roland 18, 95, 96, 130
Bauman, Richard 10, 11, 18
    see also performance event
Beau Travail 95n
Bee Gees 106
Beirut, Lebanon (*Beyrouth*) 60, 61,
        62, 64, 65, 71, 74, 76, 78,
        80, 82, 83, 84, 86, 157–163
Beirut Won't Cry 163n
Ben Jelloun, Tahar 8, 23
Benna, Zyed 118n
Berber (*Berbère*) 28, 47, 131, 133, 139,
        141, 142, 152
    see also Kabyle
Berlin, Germany 165
Berry, Chuck 48
*The Best of Djurdjura: Voice of
        Silence* 147
Beur 24, 52, 53, 131, 132, 133, 137,
        147
    identity 40–52, 132
    peoples 52, 53, 147
Beyrouth: juillet-août 2006 163
Bhaduri, Bhuvaneswari, 11–12
Blair, Dorothy S. 42, 47, 152
Bodies that Matter 92, 100
    see also Judith Butler
Bowen, John 3, 112
Britain 9
Brussels, Belgium
    2016 attack 119
burqa 86, 109, 111, 112
Bush, George W. 44n
Butler, Judith 18, 93, 100

Cage, John 158
Cahiers d'études berbères 133

the call to listen (cultural theory)
        1–20, 29, 52, 60, 86, 87,
        116, 136, 157, 158, 160,
        163, 165
Calle-Gruber, Mireille 28
Caron, David xi, 112, 156
Carte de séjour (band) 46, 47, 49
Centre national de la recherche
        scientifique 133
La Cercle des représailles 133
Certeau, Michel de 136
Cette histoire se passe 165
chador 113
Chao, Manu 140
Chateaubriand, François-Rene de 4
Cheriet, Hamid 138
    see also Idir
Chion, Michel xii, 18, 96
Ciels 92, 116
citational hook (critical mode of
        listening) 18, 91–126
Cixous, Hélène xii, 6–8, 42, 52
Cochran, Eddie 48
colonialism 2
    Arab 142
    French 9, 142
covering (critical mode of listening)
        10, 18, 19, 91, 129–156
Crazy Cavan 48
Créteil 47, 48
Crimée 47, 48
cut sound (critical mode of listening)
        18, 23–54

Daesh 3, 158
    see also Islamic State
Damascus, Syria 56, 57, 58, 141
Darrieux, Danielle 108n
Dayan, Peter 130
The Dead Kennedys 106
dédoublement 19, 135, 142
    see also split consciousness
Delacroix, Eugène 25, 26, 27, 44
Deleuze, Gilles 11
Deneuve, Catherine 108n

Denis, Claire 95n
Le Dernier chameau 155
Derrida, Jacques 11, 12
Deux rives, un rêve 154
diaspora 116
    Lebanese 115, 126
    Palestinian 94, 126
Dilem 132
Disiz la Peste 139
Djaout, Tahar 152
Djebar, Assia 1, 16–18, 24, 25–39, 45,
    46, 52, 67, 152
Djura xii, 1, 19, 45, 131, 135, 136, 137,
    144, 145–154, 155
Djurdjura (band) 137, 146, 147
Donadey, Anne 28
Dylan, Bob 138

Einstein, Albert 60n
Elia, Nadia 28, 31
The Eloquence of Silence:
    Algerian Women in
    Question 28
    see also Marnia Lazreg
ethnic(ity) 3, 8, 9, 18, 25, 40, 49, 92,
    93, 100, 101, 118, 119,
    120, 125, 126, 134, 136,
    137, 140, 142, 144, 149,
    153
    Kabyle 148
    Middle Eastern identities 19
    minorities in France 119, 131, 139,
        140, 142, 154
    multi- 137
European 7
    accent 36
    domination 143
    identity 62
    oppression 143
    origins 134
    peoples 17, 30, 31, 39, 47, 82
exile 66, 71, 91, 97, 98, 105, 107, 113,
    114, 116, 133
'Eye of the Tiger' 91, 92, 96, 97–109,
    110, 114

Faïrouz 56–58, 60, 61, 76, 77, 78, 79,
    80, 81, 82, 83, 86, 87
Fanon, Franz 4–6, 53, 150
Farah, Kenza 139
Féfé (Saïan Supa Crew) 139
Fellag 155
femininity 19, 92, 93, 97, 98
feminism 24, 31, 98, 149, 151, 153
    see also Mouvement de libération
        des femmes
feminist xi, 6–7, 17, 19, 24, 28, 29, 31,
    36, 39, 40, 42, 43, 45, 53, 93,
    108, 109, 110, 113, 131, 135,
    145, 148, 150, 152, 153
    punk 99, 102, 105, 109
Femmes d'Alger dans leur
    appartement (book) 18,
    25–29, 31
'Femmes d'Alger dans leur
    appartement' (novella) 16,
    18, 24, 25–39, 40, 45, 52–54,
    67
Fillon, François 110
Flickr 158
Forêts 92, 116
Forsdick, Charles 61n
Foucault, Michel 11
France xi, xii, 1, 3, 5, 10, 16, 19, 28, 40,
    43, 44, 46, 59, 60, 77, 86, 87,
    95, 105, 106, 109, 119, 163,
    165
    immigrants in 8, 9, 19, 23, 47, 118,
        119, 129–156
    2005 riots in 3
    veil debate in 98, 100, 109–114, 148
France Culture 28
La France des couleurs... 19, 137,
    139–140
Francophone 3, 5, 9, 165
    culture(s) xi, 1, 158, 163, 165
    as French-sounding 5
    literature 1
    societies 10
    studies 3, 20, 29
    theater 116

French 3, 17, 19, 24, 25, 28, 29, 31,
          35, 36, 40, 45, 47, 58,
          84, 86, 95, 98, 103, 112,
          113, 114, 115, 120, 129,
          130, 131, 139, 141, 142,
          145, 147, 150, 151, 152,
          158, 165
     1830 invasion of Algeria 25
     broadcasting in Algeria 5–6
     citizens 3, 119
     citizenship 112
     colonialism 9, 141, 143
     colonies 3, 119
     culture xi, 10, 40, 41, 126, 133, 136,
          148, 152, 156, 158, 165
     decolonization 1
     feminist 24
     film in 94
     history 24, 40, 46, 49–51, 139
     identity 40, 133
     literature in xi, 28, 31, 59, 60, 147
     media 92, 93, 110, 112, 118, 126,
          138
     narrative 10, 153
     peoples 5, 9, 29, 32, 33, 44, 45, 98,
          101, 114, 133, 134, 146, 150,
          153, 163
     Republicanism 3, 10, 111, 119
          see also universalism
     Revolution 157
     society 9, 10, 24, 28, 40, 46, 48, 49,
          50, 98, 112, 113, 133, 134,
          135, 136, 137, 145, 153, 154,
          155, 165
     -sounding 5
          see also Francophone
     speaking 6, 19, 131, 132, 158
          see also Francophone
     state 112
     studies xii, 3, 20, 29
     theater in 94
     translation 32, 35, 133, 163, 165
     universalism 9, 10, 19, 99, 109, 110,
          113, 119, 129–156
          see also Republicanism

     veil debate 98, 100, 109–114,
          148
     world music 19
fundamentalism
     Islamic in Algeria 59, 135, 141
     religious 3, 59, 135, 137

Gainsbourg, Serge 84
Gann, Kyle 158n
gender 8, 9, 18, 25, 40, 45, 49, 63,
          91–126, 134, 136, 137, 143,
          145, 147, 149, 165
Gibran, Kahlil 78
Gilroy, Paul 19, 76, 134
     see also split consciousness
globalization 2
Goodman, Jane 138, 139, 143, 144
Goth music 132
'Le Grain de la voix' 95
the grain of the voice 18, 95–96, 130
     see also Roland Barthes
graphic novels 1, 101, 163, 165
Greece 145n

Hamdani, Dorsaf 85
Harraga (novel) 132n
Harragas (film) 132n
Haydn, Joseph 4
Hayes, Jarrod xi, 28, 42, 44
headscarf 3, 102, 109, 112, 129
Hezbollah 160, 163
Hitler, Adolf 47, 48
Holocaust (*le Shoah*) 40, 47, 48, 50,
          52

Identités (CD) 19, 137–145
Idir xii, 1, 19, 131, 135–145, 148, 150,
          152, 154, 155
     see also Hamid Cheriet
immigrant(s)
     in France 3, 8, 9, 19, 23, 40, 41, 45,
          47, 52, 99, 110, 118, 119,
          131, 134, 138, 141, 146,
          153, 154, 156
     of the Lebanese diaspora 115

Incendies (Scorched) 18, 91–97, 114–126, 162
Instagram 158
Institut du Monde Arabe (Paris) 114, 116
intégration 3
  see also assimilation
intersectionalism 93, 100, 101, 112
Intouchables 95n
L'Invention du désert 152
Iran 91, 97, 98, 99, 102, 103, 105, 106, 107, 108, 109, 113
Iran-Iraq War 98, 105, 106, 107
Iraq 60, 63, 74, 77, 98
  see also Second Iraq (Gulf) War
Irigaray, Luce 93
Iron Maiden 102, 106, 107
Islam 59, 98
Islamic
  community 154
  culture 141, 145
  fundamentalism 59, 74, 86, 109, 110, 132, 135, 137, 141, 154
  insurgencies in Algeria 141
  Khadra's fictionalized fundamentalist 59, 60, 74, 109
    see also Louiza Kadari
  oppression 104
  regimes 104, 106, 107, 113
  religion 111, 112
  Revolution 98, 113
  State 3, 158
    see also Daesh
  veils 112
Israel 158, 160
Israeli-Palestinian crisis 116
Israeli War (2006) 157–164

J'ai pas sommeil 95n
Johnson, James H. 4
La Journée de la jupe (film) 118

Kabyle 129, 40–52
  see also Berber
  community in Paris xii, 40–52, 129–156
  music 19, 129–156
  peoples 1, 19, 40–52, 129–156
Kabylia (Algeria) 131, 132, 143, 144, 146
Kadari, Louiza 59, 74
Kahina 151–152
Kastoryano, Riva 3, 118, 119
Kateb, Yacine 133
Kerbaj, Mazen xiii, 1, 157–165
Khadra, Yasmina 1, 18, 59–87, 147
  see also Mohammed Moulessehoul
Khalifa, Wajdi 56, 57
Khatibi, Abdelkebir 19, 142
Kierkegaard, Søren 133
Kulthum, Umm 56

laïcité 3, 110, 111
Lazreg, Marnia 28, 29, 99
Lebanese
  Civil War 92, 94, 114, 115, 116, 125, 126
  diaspora 115
  history 117
  peoples 1, 56, 57, 77, 83, 92, 116, 157–65
  radio 57
Lebanon xi, 44, 56, 57, 77, 114, 115, 116, 123, 126, 158, 160, 165
Le Clézio, J.M.G. 12–16
Le Pen, Marine 3
Lee, Bruce 107
Lettre à la mère 165
Lilienfeld, Jean-Paul 118
lip-synching 58
Little Red Riding Hood 138
Littoral 92, 114, 116
Livres de Poche 147
'The Logical Song' 19, 91, 92, 93, 95, 96, 116, 118, 121, 123, 124, 125, 162
Loin de Médine 152

London, England 61, 80, 82, 146, 162
Louvre, 85
Luaka Bop Records 147
'Lullaby' 12–16

Mammeri, Mouloud 133
La Martinique 5, 43
masculinity 19, 92, 94, 116, 119, 48
Mastroianni, Chiara 102
Matchbox (band) 48
Matheson, Karen 142, 143, 144, 156
Maverick Concert Hall
        (Woodstock, NY) 158n
Medea 75
Mediterranean Sea 59, 86, 136, 144
Metamorphoses 2
Mexico 59
Michel Lafon 147
the Middle East xi, 1, 3, 56, 59, 60,
        74, 86, 95, 96, 113, 116,
        163
Middle Eastern
    ethnic identities 19, 86, 100, 134
    femininity 19, 97, 92, 97, 98
    gender identities 91–126
    Khadra's trilogy 60
    masculinity 19, 92, 97
    modernity 87
    oppression 19
    other 93
    peoples 19, 74, 92, 93, 98, 163
    tradition 62, 87
mission civilisatrice 9
mixité 9, 10, 110, 111, 113, 140
modernity 26, 55, 59, 61, 64, 76, 80,
        83, 87, 155
Montreuil, France 111
Mouawad, Wajdi 1, 18, 91, 92, 95,
        114–126
Moulessehoul, Mohammed 59
    see also Yasmina Khadra
*Mouvement de libération des
        femmes* 148
Munch, Edvard 68, 86
Murray, Jenny 28

Musée de la Musique (Paris) 84, 85
music 1, 4, 10, 18, 19, 20, 25, 34, 40,
        43, 46, 47, 49, 50, 51, 52,
        53, 56, 57, 58, 60, 61, 72,
        76–82, 84, 86, 87, 91, 92,
        94, 95, 97, 98, 105, 106,
        116, 125, 126–156, 158, 160,
        161, 162, 163
musicians 1, 19, 50, 107, 142, 144, 155,
        162, 165
    see also ABBA; Lounès Aït
        Menguellet; Joan Baez;
        Bee Gees; Chuck Berry;
        Carte de séjour; Manu
        Chao; Hamid Cheriet;
        Eddie Cochran; Crazy
        Cavan; The Dead Kennedys;
        Disiz la Peste; Djura;
        Djurdjura; Bob Dylan;
        Faïrouz; Kenza Farah;
        Féfé; Serge Gainsbourg;
        Dorsaf Hamdani; Idir; Iron
        Maiden; Umm Kulthum;
        Chiara Mastroianni;
        Matchbox; Nâdiya;
        Philomel; Pink Floyd; The
        Police; Elvis Presley; Saïan
        Supa Crew; The Sex Pistols;
        singers; Bruce Springsteen;
        The Stray Cats; Supertramp;
        Survivor; Rachid Taha;
        Gene Vincent; Kim Wilde;
        Zebda

Nâdiya 139
Nafisi, Azar 105
narrative 2, 3, 6, 7, 8, 9, 10, 11, 12, 13,
        14, 16, 18, 25, 41, 47, 52, 62,
        91, 92, 93, 94, 96, 97, 99,
        100, 101, 103, 114, 115, 117,
        118, 119, 120, 121, 125, 135,
        136, 141, 147, 150, 152, 153,
        156, 165
    cinematic 92, 97–109
    comic art 162

extra- 95, 106
   literary 18, 21–87, 91
   lyric 103
   musical 143, 162
   theatrical 92, 114–126
national identity 92, 119, 134
nationalism 29, 56
Ni putes, ni soumises 110
niqab 109, 112
Nordey, Stanislas 121, 123
North Africa xi, 1, 3, 85, 86, 119, 141,
   151
   see also Algeria
North African
   see also Algerian
   immigrants in France 19, 119
   peoples 86, 119
novellas 17, 18, 24, 25–39, 52–54
novels 18, 24, 40–54, 59–84, 86, 157,
   161

Odysseus 2, 125
The Odyssey 2, 125
Oedipus Rex 117, 120
'L'Ogre de chêne' 143
l'Orchestre National de Barbès 140
Ovid 2

Pahlavi, Reza Shah 107
Palestinian
   diaspora 94
   origins 114, 123
   peoples 60, 116
   refugee crisis 114, 125, 126
      see also Israeli-Palestinian crisis
Parc de la Villette (Paris) 129
Paris, France xi, xii, 4, 40, 45, 55, 84,
      85, 98, 109, 110, 113, 114,
      121, 129, 131, 132, 136, 138,
      144, 146, 155, 156, 162, 163
   2015 attacks 3
performance 18, 19, 40, 41, 43, 46, 47,
      46, 49, 51, 52, 56, 57, 58,
      91–126, 129–135, 155, 157,
      158, 160, 162

event (critical concept) 10–11, 18,
      62, 63
   see also Richard Bauman
   narrative 16
   studies xi, 3, 18, 20
performative 3, 51, 102, 121, 124
Persepolis (film) 18, 91–113, 114, 119,
      163
Persepolis (graphic novel) 101, 163
Philomel 2
Picasso, Pablo 25
Pink Floyd 116
Place de la République (Paris) 110, 111
Plato 93
The Police 93, 115, 122
The Politics of the Veil 119
   see also Joan Scott
The Practices of Everyday Life 136
   see also Michel de Certeau
Presley, Elvis 48
Prix Molière 116
punk 102, 105, 106, 109, 113, 114
   feminist 99, 102, 105, 109
   music 106
   Nazi 40, 49, 53

race 8, 9, 100
racism 43
Rahbani, Assi 56, 57
Rahbani, Mansour 56, 57
rape 2, 25, 72, 110, 117
Ratcliffe, Krista 9
Reading Lolita in Tehran 105, 107
Red Cross 160
'Regard interdit, son coupé' 25, 29, 36,
      38, 46
Remarque, Erich Maria 4
Republicanism 3, 10, 111, 119
   see also universalism
rhetoric 9, 112, 114, 139, 148
Rice, Alison 9
Ringrose, Priscilla 28
riot grrl 44
riots
   2005 in France, 3, 118

Roach, Joseph 24, 41
    see also surrogation
rock 18, 40, 46, 47, 48, 49, 50, 51, 92,
    94, 95, 97, 100, 102, 107,
    115, 116, 119, 120, 121, 122,
    123, 124
rockabilly 48
Rocky III 96, 98, 99, 100, 101, 102, 104,
    105, 106
Rocky IV 96, 98, 99, 100, 101, 105,
    106
'Roxanne' 93, 95, 115, 118, 122, 123,
    124

rue St-Denis 42, 44
St-Germain-des-Prés 131
Sacks, Oliver 97
Sagan, Françoise 28
Saïan Supa Crew 139
Le Sang des promesses 92, 114, 116
Sansal, Boualem 132n
Sarkozy, Nicolas 118n, 137, 139
Satrapi, Marjane 1, 18, 91, 97–109,
    163
Schafer, R. Murray 4
Schwarzenegger, Arnold 108
Sciamma, Céline 95n
Scott, Joan 112, 113, 119
Sebbar, Leïla 1, 18, 24, 40–54
Second Iraq (Gulf) War 60
The Sex Pistols 106
sexuality 7, 28, 119
Shaykh, Hanan 124n
Shérazade: 17 ans, brune, frisée, les
    yeux verts 18, 24, 40–54
silence 1, 2, 3, 5, 6–12, 13, 16, 18, 19,
    23–54, 58, 66, 67, 68, 69, 77,
    80, 86, 91, 111, 112, 115, 117,
    123, 124, 125, 135, 137, 140,
    145–154, 156, 158
Silmi, Faiza 112
sing-along 18, 19, 91–126, 145, 162
singers 1, 19, 24, 40–52, 53, 54, 56–58,
    85, 91–126, 129–156
    see also musicians

singing 18, 35, 40–52, 54, 77, 80, 81, 86,
    87, 94, 96, 91–109, 114–126,
    130, 143, 151
Sirènes de Bagdad, Les 18, 59–84, 86
sirens 18, 63, 64, 76–84, 85, 86, 87, 124,
    125
the Sirens 2, 63, 80, 125
La Soif 28
Solis, Gabriel 120
Sophocles 160
sound 1, 4, 5, 6, 10, 11, 16, 18, 23, 24,
    25, 26, 27, 30, 34, 37, 51, 57,
    58, 59, 60, 61, 63, 64, 65, 66,
    67, 68, 69, 70, 72, 76, 78,
    79, 80, 82, 83, 84, 85, 86,
    87, 91, 96, 97, 102, 103, 114,
    130, 132, 140, 144, 149, 150,
    157, 158, 160, 162
    see also cut sound
sound production 140, 157
sound studies 3, 4, 20
sound technologies 2, 24
    analog 1, 2
    boom box 102
    cassette (tape) 34, 77
    cassette deck 17
    compact disc (CD) 19, 133, 134, 135,
        137–145, 147, 154
        covers 154
        liner notes 19, 133, 134, 154
    digital 1, 2, 76, 157–165
    headphones 17, 34, 61, 77, 78
    microphone (mic) 49, 51, 53, 92, 93,
        115, 121, 122, 123, 157
    mp3 1
    podcast 28
    radio 1, 2, 4–5, 25, 56, 57, 61, 72,
        76, 80, 81, 138, 161
    speakers 82, 84, 138
    tape recorder 34
    Walkman 61, 76, 77, 91, 114, 117,
        122, 125
sounding 5, 11, 76
    the text (critical methodology)
        10–20, 86

soundscape 4
soundtrack 69, 95, 116
Spelman, Elizabeth 100
Spivak, Gayatri 11–12, 27, 50
split consciousness 19, 134
 see also dédoublement
Springsteen, Bruce 120
'Starry Night' (composition) 157–165
Stephenson, Jenn 120
Stone, Christopher 56–57, 78
The Story of Zahra 124n
The Stray Cats 48
subaltern 11–12, 27, 30
Supertramp 19, 91, 96, 114, 116, 120,
 124, 125
surrogation 40–52
Survivor 91, 96, 97, 99, 100, 103
synchresis 96, 99
 see also Michel Chion
Syrian Civil War 3, 158

Taha, Rachid 47
the Taliban 60
Tel Aviv, Israel 60
The Terminator 108
Théâtre de la Colline (Paris) 121
Théâtre des Bouffes du Nord (Paris)
 155
Théâtre Jean Vilar (Vitry-sur-Seine)
 138
Ticktin, Miriam 45
Timaeus 93
Tlemcen, Algeria 32, 34
torture 17, 30, 31, 32, 36, 92, 117, 124,
 125
tradition 26, 59, 62, 64, 65, 68, 74, 76,
 80, 83, 84, 87
Traore, Bouna 118n
Tudor, David 158n
Tunisia 85
Turkey 145n
Twitter 158

Umayyad dynasty 141
United States 9, 28, 113

universalism 9, 10, 19, 99, 109, 110,
 112, 113, 119, 129–156
 see also Republicanism
University of Baghdad 60, 65

Van Elferen, Isabella 132
veils 19, 25, 26, 27, 92, 93, 96, 97, 98,
 99, 100, 101, 102, 103, 104,
 105, 107, 108, 137, 144, 145,
 146, 153, 154, 155
 debate in France 98, 100, 109–114,
 148
 see also burqa; chador; headscarf;
 niqab
Vichy (government) 53
Vienna, Austria 91, 97, 98, 101, 102,
 103, 104, 105, 106, 113
Villeneuve, Denis 115
Vincent, Gene 48
violence 3, 48, 59, 61, 64, 66, 68, 70,
 72, 73, 74, 75, 78, 80, 83, 94,
 115, 116, 118, 119, 120, 123,
 126, 160, 161, 162
Vitry-sur-Seine, France 138
Le Voile du silence 19, 135, 145–154

War of 1812 157
Warner Brothers 147
*Why the French Don't Like
 Headscarves* 3
 see also John Bowen
Wilde, Kim 106
Woodhull, Winifred 28
world music 10, 19, 129–156
World War I 4
World War II 92
Worth, Robert 57

Y.B. 124n
Yacine, Tassadit 133

Zaqout, Rafed 57
Zebda 140
zémigré 132, 147
Zemmour, Eric 3
Le Zénith (Paris) 129, 130, 138

www.ingramcontent.com/pod-product-compliance
Lightning Source LLC
Chambersburg PA
CBHW071113100726
47908CB00008B/2363